ME AND
DIMAGGIO

ME AND

A BASEBALL FAN GOES IN SEARCH OF HIS GODS

DIMAGGIO

CHRISTOPHER LEHMANN-HAUPT

THE LYONS PRESS

Printed in the United States of America

10   9   8   7   6   5   4   3   2   1

Library of Congress Cataloging-in-Publication Data

Lehmann-Haupt, Christopher.
        Me and DiMaggio: a baseball fan goes in search of his gods /
Christopher Lehmann-Haupt.
                p.   cm.
        Originally published: New York: Simon and Schuster, c1986.
        ISBN 1-55821-623-5
        1. Baseball—United States—History.   2. DiMaggio, Joe, 1914–   .
I. Title.
GV863.A1L39   1998
796.357'0973—dc21   97-30433
                                        CIP

The author is grateful for permission to reprint from *The Complete Poems of
Marianne Moore*, copyright © 1961 by Marianne Moore, originally published
in *The New Yorker*. Reprinted by permission of Viking Penguin.

FOR
NATALIE,
RACHEL,
AND NOAH,
WHO
CHEERED

CONTENTS

Fanaticism? No. Writing is exciting
and baseball is like writing.
You can never tell with either
how it will go
or what you will do;
generating excitement—
a fever in the victim—
pitcher, catcher, fielder, batter.
Victim in what category?
Owlman watching from the pressbox?
To whom does it apply?
Who is excited? Might it be I?

From Baseball and Writing,
Marianne Moore

PREFACE

NOTHING OF WHAT FOLLOWS has been invented, though some of it may have been distorted by perception or memory. All dialogue that appears in the form of a transcript was recorded on a tape machine. All dialogue in quotes was reconstructed from notes and memory as soon as possible after it occurred.

More people than I can name or recall contributed in various ways to what follows, though of course I alone am responsible for whatever errors or misinterpretations there may be. The contributions of those who appear in this adventure are self-evident, so I shall not commit the redundancy of acknowledging most of them here.

I am particularly grateful to my friend Steven M. L. Aronson, who fine-combed the text for stylistic snarls; to my brother Carl, who offered an ear to many a late-night ramble; to my old friends Hugh Nissenson, who suggested the title as well as made me stretch for more than I thought I could reach, and Sidney Zion, who gave me invaluable help every step of the way; and to my editor, Herman Gollob, who pulled it all out in the late innings.

I am also grateful for various forms of help and encouragement to Chuck Adams, Roger Angell, Howard Angione, Martin Appel, Dr. Robert Ascheim, Carole Baron, Richard W. Baron, Susan Bell, Zerina Bhika, June Bingham, Jonathan Bingham, Dr. Philip W. Brickner, Sean Byrnes, Edith Camp, Murray Chass, Paul Cunningham, Robin Cynar, Lou D'Ermilio, Mary Downing, Henry Eckert, Jonathan Fast, Paul K. Feldman, Lewis Finkelman, Robert Fowlow, William D. Fugazy, Hon. Louis Fusco, Richard Gilman, Deborah Gordis, Dan Green, Letitia Grierson, Daniel Harris, Brian Iwama, Jeff Kernan, Nan Lehnemann, William T. Loverd, J. Anthony Lukas, Peter McWilliams, Christopher Meeks, Yvonne Meier, Lester Migdal, Hon. E. Leo Milonas, Victor S. Navasky, Lynn Nesbit, Judy Newman, Marilyn Nissenson, Hon. Benjamin F. Nolan, Christopher Ottaunuck, Charles Pate, Allen H. Peacock, Erik Perkins, Richard Ravitch, Anne Reynolds, Dr. I. Herbert Scheinberg, George Sheanshang, Dina Sheridan, John Sterling, Hon. Anne E. Targum, Mary Frances Veeck, Christina Warner, Robert A. Wirz, and Bill Yates.

The following institutions and organizations also helped in various ways: the office of the baseball commissioner, the Baseball Hall of Fame at Cooperstown, New York, Elias Sports Bureau Inc., the Royal Ontario Museum, the Baltimore Orioles, Boston Red Sox, California Angels, Chicago White Sox, Detroit Tigers, Los Angeles Dodgers, Montreal Expos, New York Mets, New York Yankees, Philadelphia Phillies, Pittsburgh Pirates, San Francisco Giants, Seattle Mariners, Toronto Blue Jays, and my employer, the *New York Times*, without whose support I couldn't even have thought about undertaking this project.

C. L-H.
New York City 1985

CHAPTER

ROOTING

In the autumn of 1978, a young book editor telephoned to say that he had an idea for me. His name was Tom Tracy, he had recently been hired by a small new publishing house called Methuen—actually an old English house that was trying to start a colony in the New World—and he felt his idea was irresistible. Could we meet?

I told him at once that it was out of the question for me to write a book. My job as daily book reviewer for the *New York Times* left me no leisure. What was his idea?

He proposed a book about baseball. Certain reviews I'd written over the years had revealed my special enthusiasm for the game—I had said, for instance, of Macmillan's *Baseball Encyclopedia* that I'd happily be marooned with it.

Yes, but what would this baseball book be about?

Tom Tracy's notion was to team up two unlikely people—one to write a text and the other to take photographs. He was convinced the result would be "synergistic—greater than the sum of its parts." He hadn't settled on a photographer yet—he was thinking of Francesco Scavullo, Richard Avedon, Annie Gottlieb, or someone like that, who would go well with a critic known to have an owlish interest in sports. The plan would be to spend the entire 1979 season exploring the world of baseball. We would go everywhere—to spring training in Florida, to the All-Star game in Seattle, to the World Series wherever it was, to the winter meetings in Toronto—travel, accommodations, press passes, and other logistics to be arranged by the publisher.

"Sounds fantastic. But how can I possibly do such a job?"

"I'll bet you can find a way," Tracy said.

For the next few days, I could think of little else, even when I was supposed to be meeting deadlines. In the middle of an absorbing book, I'd find myself staring out the window, trying somehow to justify a project I knew I lacked the time and experience to take on.

It was true that I was a baseball fan. A deeply addicted baseball fan. There were days that could be brightened by what for me amounted to a stiff drink—the news that the team I rooted for had won. Or if I reached the end of a very good day—even the day I got married, or the days on which my children were born, or the day I got my present job, which I'd always dreamed of having—only to discover from the late sports news that my team had lost, I would fall asleep with a sense that the balloon of my well-being had sprung a small leak.

I'd gotten hooked on a Sunday afternoon in May 1948, when I was thirteen years old, relatively late for a baseball fan. Before that fateful Sunday, I'd tried halfheartedly—and failed—to understand what all the excitement was about. As early as I could remember, I'd sensed that something important was going on around me: in the New York City apartment building where I grew up, when the other children would shout and argue about what must have been the comparative merits of the Yankees, Dodgers, and Giants; or at school, when the tall fathers with pipes or cigars in their mouths would come in the spring to take their sons away to the opening-day game of the season, or in the fall to the World Series. But the shouting and the arguing meant nothing to me; they might just as well have been about the Donkeys, the Nightingales, and the Windjammers. And my father wasn't an admirer of baseball.

A transplanted German intellectual who was curator of rare books at Columbia University's library and the coauthor of a history of American book publishing, he harbored nothing but disdain for the "silly game they play in little boys' knickers, with the man on the hill who acts like a dog at a hydrant." In the privacy of our home, he would often rail against "that great American hero Babe Ruth, a drunken bum in a monkey suit." My father did not take me out of school to attend opening day or the World Series.

Of course, when he did show up at school for such occasions as parents' day, he would muffle his hostility to the game. Now and then, to make conversation with the other fathers, he would tell a story I'd heard several times before—about how, a few summers earlier, one May Lott, a baseball player, had sublet our apartment in the Riverdale section of the Bronx. As a courtesy, this May Lott had pressed a couple of tickets on my father and even provided Mrs. Lott as an escort. It would be years before I made the connection between May Lott and Mel Ott, the New York Giants' great right fielder, with the *e* in his name drawn out a European shade too long.

Perhaps I sensed in my father's ambivalence a concession that however much he might dislike the game, he saw baseball as a passport to American culture. In any case, his son kept trying to become a fan. I dimly felt that there had to be something wrong with an American boy who didn't root for a major-league team. This message was conveyed to me most acutely in 1947 during a year my family spent in Berlin, when my father, who had worked for the Office of War Information in London during World War II, was recalled to government service and assigned to track down works of art that had been confiscated by the Nazis. In the corridors of the school for U.S. military dependents, I was literally backed against the wall and asked for what amounted to my credentials as an American.

"What team you for?"

"What team?"

"Yeah."

"Uh, well . . . New York."

"New *York*! New York what? The Giants or the Yankees?"

"The New York . . . uh. . . ."

"Where you from in New York?"

"Riverdale. The Bronx."

"The Bronx Bombers!"

"The Bombers?"

"The New York Yankees, dumbo."

"Yes, the Yankees. I'm for *them*."

I was for them, yes. But I barely knew what they were.

Then a year later, on a Sunday afternoon in May, just three weeks before I would turn fourteen, I was wandering around my mother's Manhattan apartment with nothing much to do. My parents' marriage had failed to survive their cultural differences—she being a Scottish Protestant and he being a German half-Jew raised as a Lutheran—which were exacerbated by my father's having been sent overseas during the war. They had divorced shortly after the Berlin interlude. My mother now occupied the roomy top floor of a West Side brownstone with two of her three sons, my brother Carl and me, while the third one, Sandy, was living with my father and his second wife in our old apartment in Riverdale. Staying with us in the brownstone was a young Canadian couple to whom my mother had rented a room to supplement her high-school teacher's salary. Eventually that Sunday afternoon, I found myself standing on the threshold of this couple's room.

The door was wide open, but the occupants didn't seem prepared for visitors. Bed linen and assorted items of clothing lay scattered everywhere. The woman sat on the near side of the bed filing down a fingernail, the hem of her negligee drawn up over her crossed knees. The man lay sprawled beside her in white boxer shorts, dangling a cigarette in his fingers and cocking his head toward the radio on the night table beside him. The smell of mingled perfume and sweat vaguely repelled me. I stood there anyway. The two of them looked up.

"You're listening to a baseball game?" I asked, at a loss for anything else to explain my presence on the threshold.

"Sure," the man said. "Want to come in?"

"Who's playing?"

"Yanks and the Indians. In Cleveland. Come on in and listen."

"Who's up?"

The man turned to regard the radio for a moment, then looked back. "DiMaggio's up."

"Who's pitching?"

"Feller."

"Bobby Feller? He's good, isn't he?"

The man smiled and nodded. Silence hung in the room for a moment. Then the radio burst into a staticky roar, above which the announcer's voice seemed to grow hysterical.

"What's happening? It sounds like something important. A home run?"

The man gestured for quiet and leaned closer to the radio. "Hey, you're right! It's a home run!"

"Joe DiMaggio?"

The man smiled and nodded again. The woman looked up and laughed.

"Wow. That's something, isn't it?"

It was the first time I'd ever been moved by a broadcast of baseball. Indeed, it was the first time a mystifying code had broken into the clear for me. In Berlin, when I was told it was World Series time, I dutifully went home and did what all the other American kids seemed to be doing—I listened to the broadcasts on the Armed Forces Radio Network of the games between the Brooklyn Dodgers and the Yankees. Every evening, seven evenings in a row, I listened. Years later I would come to understand that I'd heard one of the more dramatic Series in history. It was the one when Yankee pitcher Floyd Bevens came within one out of pitching a no-hitter, only to lose when Cookie Lavagetto doubled home two runs in the ninth. It was also the one when Al Gionfriddo made his great acrobatic catch to rob Joe DiMaggio of a three-run homer. But at the time, between the radio's static and my own ignorance, I barely understood a word of what I was hearing.

Now Joe DiMaggio had nailed a home run into my head.

Half an hour later, I found myself at the enthralling open door once again. The bed had become a couch. The woman had put on a dress; the man was in a robe. But the radio buzzed on.

"Who's up now?"

"Tommy Henrich. Then comes DiMaggio. Come on in. Sit down."

DiMaggio came to bat again. Feller pitched. Against the noise of the crowd the announcer's voice went metallic—"going, going, gah-own!"

"He did it again!" I yelled.

"I'll say he did. Joe DiMaggio."

"But that's amazing, isn't it?"

"It's really something. Not a record though."

"Could he do it again?"

"I doubt it. But anything can happen. Shhhh, let's listen."

Suddenly, I understood everything the announcer was saying. While I listened, the woman unfolded an ironing board and began sprinkling liquid from a bottle over a rumpled shirt. The man lit a cigarette, leaned back, and inhaled deeply. The radio announcer— Mel Allen—said that Feller was being taken out and a new pitcher brought in, Bob Muncrief. Soon it was DiMaggio's turn at bat again.

"What if. . . ?"

"Shhhhhhhh . . . listen."

It was more than curiosity I was feeling now. I was aware of my heartbeat, and there was pressure in my throat. My mind was racing ahead to the fulfillment of a wish. The extraordinary act, if accomplished, would belong to me alone.

". . . swings and it's going deep! If it stays fair . . . and it's going, it's going, it's GAH-OWN. Another home run! Joe DiMaggio has just hit his third straight home run, folks. Three straight home runs for the Yankee Clipper! How a-bout that!"

"My God, he did it! He did it!" I wanted to embrace the man, who was slapping his knee repeatedly and saying softly, "Hey! Hey!"

"Joe DiMaggio hit three home runs in a row!" I cried out.

"He sure did!"

"Has anyone ever done it before?"

"Lou Gehrig once hit four."

"In one game?"

"Yup, in a row, too."

"Lou Gehrig, the Pride of the Yankees guy? Gary Cooper?"

"That's the one."

"Lou Gehrig's the only one?"

"Far as I know. In nine innings, anyway."

"How 'bout three?"

"Lotta guys did that."

"DiMaggio ever before?"

"Yup. 1937."

"Is twice the most anyone ever did it?"

"Heck, no. Johnny Mize has done it four or five times, I think. Lotta guys twice."

"How many does DiMaggio have for the season?"

"Let's see. Seven as of yesterday. That makes ten."

"Is that the most?"

"No, Kenny Keltner of the Indians has about thirteen."

"Are the Yankees in first place?"

"They're close. A little behind the Indians."

"Who do they play tomorrow?"

"Off-day tomorrow."

"Tuesday?"

"Tuesday, it's the Tigers."

"The Detroit Tigers?"

"That's right."

"You going to listen?"

"Why not? You want to listen?"

The woman looked up from her ironing and smiled.

So I was a fan at last. An authentic baseball fan. A fan despite my mother, too, who, as the daughter of a Scottish academic knighted for his work in seventeenth-century English literature, was also an alien to baseball culture and would soon be biting her lip and worrying aloud that my obsession with baseball would interfere with the serious business of my life. As for my father, even as late as the 1960s, when Mickey Mantle and Roger Maris were the stars of the Yankees, he would continue to taunt me by asking how Babe Ruth was doing. "Dad, he died more than ten years ago," I would groan. "Died?" he would riposte gleefully. "How could he die? He was such a great American hero, that drunken, whoring baseball player in his monkey suit." I was a baseball fan despite my subliminal awareness that the movers and shakers of history would never squander on the game of baseball the time and energy that I was now more than happy to sacrifice to the "silly game."

Every morning for the rest of that summer of 1948, I would turn to the sports pages to see where Joe DiMaggio stood among the batting leaders and to find out what team the Yankees would be playing next. In those days, WINS, the radio station that broadcast Yankee games—with the sponsorship of White Owl cigars, among other products—would run a daily advertisement in the form of a cartoon of a pin-striped player wrestling with a tiger or a senator or a pair of white socks or an Indian chief. So I would look forward to contests between the Yankees and a variety of animated objects. And in the afternoon or evening, I would lie back on my bed and let Mel Allen's voice fill my imagination.

What I would do to hear that voice! The following summer, I was loaned out for a month to a farm family in Vermont, on my mother's well-meaning assumption that milking cows and forking hay would be healthy for a 128-pound city boy who was by now spending most of his time with his ear to the radio or his eyes on the sports pages.

But I outfoxed her. If the corn rows that required daily weeding were many and endless, they also formed a screen against prying eyes. I could duckwalk behind them to the edge of the field, and from there it was just a short run to the bunkhouse, where the innards of an old radio sat on a bench by my bed. The machine had no switch, no volume control, no tuning knob, not even a dial. But by stretching myself prone on my bunk and reaching both arms through the space between the headbar and the mattress, I could make the thing work. With my right hand I would hold a loose wire against a terminal at the back of the chassis to get power, and with my left hand manipulate the variable condenser to tune in different stations.

In the daytime it was impossible to pick up New York City, but it usually took just a few seconds to find a local news broadcast with a roundup of ball scores at the end of it. In an instant I would be back down the stairs and out again among the corn rows pulling up weeds as if *they* were what stood between the Yankees and the pennant. At night, if the atmosphere was clear, it was possible to catch the Yankee broadcasts directly, though it was always a challenge to chase after the signal as it faded in and out of the nearby frequencies. I had to be careful also to hold the loose wire steady, for at the slightest tremor of my fingers the circuit would break and the signal would die. But if I did everything right, Mel Allen's bronze gong of a voice would ring in the darkness around me with a description of a game being played hundreds of miles away. No, not a description really, for the words didn't call up a picture of reality; they *were* reality. The phrase *home run*, the words "it's going, going, *gah-own*"— these didn't summon an image of the ball arcing into the grandstand, but rather the feeling of the event—a surge of ecstasy if it was

18

a score for the Yankees, a pang of despair if the enemy had struck. So I would pass evening after evening in the darkness of the bunkhouse, literally tuning in my fantasies, until my arms would fall asleep from the pressure of the mattress, my fingers grow numb, the wire slip, and a vicious shock would jar my hand as the old radio short-circuited.

But even electrocution couldn't kill the dream. On days when everything else had gone wrong for me, yet my team had won, I would drift off to sleep imagining the next day's victory and the one the day after that, an endless string of winning days winding all the way to October and another championship—a dream of perfection. And on days when my team lost, I would tell myself that my fixation on baseball was pretty silly after all, a personality quirk, a residue of adolescence—I might even go so far as to promise myself to swear off the game. Yet just before nodding off, my mind would slip to a level deeper than discipline. And at the border of sleep and dreaming, I would discover again, as if it were a coin in tall grass, the hope that my team might win tomorrow.

So I cared for the game enough to write a book about it. That wasn't the trouble. Too many other handicaps loomed up whenever I considered accepting the editor's offer. There was the very real problem of time. Turning out five book reviews every two weeks consumed at least eleven full days out of every fourteen. I was no speed-reader, and getting through a long and difficult book could take me as much as thirty hours. True, I took extra time off during the year in compensation, but it was still hard to picture adding the task of researching and writing a book to an already overloaded schedule.

Then, too, there was the highly personal nature of my attachment to the game. I'd turned professional baseball into a figment of my imagination. It was voices over the airwaves that had first brought the game to me, and it was as voices from some unreal kingdom that the game continued to hold me. Baseball was a collection of images I carried around inside my own head. And in many ways, I liked those images better than reality. What a shock it had been to see my first "live" game. It was at Yankee Stadium on a Sunday afternoon in September 1948, a little more than three months after that magic day when Joe DiMaggio had hit his three home runs. The Yanks were playing the Red Sox in a close pennant race that eventually wound up in a tie between the Sox and the Cleveland Indians. After an early lunch in Riverdale, I set out alone on the bus and subway, made the connection to River Avenue and 161st Street, and bought a general-admission ticket for a seat far back in the right-field grandstand. But it wasn't only a baseball game I experienced: it was also a gigantic crowd that gave off powerful smells of tobacco, beer, and mustard, and let loose frequent baffling roars of celebration and disdain. Way off in the distance, beyond a huge gray rivet-studded pillar that blocked out a third of the playing field, tiny figures were moving about. The one in center field must have been my hero, Joe DiMaggio, though I couldn't tell for sure. Late in the game, a player whom the echoing public-address system identified as Ted Williams-*illiams-illiams* lofted the ball in a long, lazy arc that ended somewhere behind the pillar. I could tell by the excited buzz of the crowd and the leisurely way the batter jogged around the bases that a home run had been hit, the first I'd ever actually seen. But it wasn't a home run as I understood that supreme baseball event. It had not seemed to be walloped by the great Ted Williams, "Ted the Thumper," "The Splendid Splinter"; instead it had been nicked by a tiny gray form swinging a slender toothpick. It lacked the voice of Mel Allen to give it substance: "Williams swings and sends a loooooooong drive. It's going, going, gah-own!" Though a home run had been hit in real time and space, it hadn't happened inside my head.

And in real time and space the Yankees lost to the Red Sox that September afternoon. But it didn't happen for me until I read about it in the newspaper over breakfast the next morning and saw that the Yankees had fallen even farther behind in the diagram called "Major-League Standings." For the rest of that season, I would rely on airwaves and newsprint for my nourishment, as the Yankees dropped out of the running and Boston and Cleveland raced to a tie. Then, in the first playoff game in the nearly half-century history of the American League, the Indians beat the Sox, 8–3, behind the hitting of Lou Boudreau and the pitching of Gene Bearden.

It was only on paper and over the airwaves that the ballplayers seemed alive to me. There they weren't tiny figures moving obscurely on miniature lawns. They were "Joltin' Joe" DiMaggio, "the Yankee Clipper"; Joe "Flash" Gordon; "Sad Sam" Zoldak; Vic Raschi, "the Springfield Rifle"; Vern "Junior" Stephens; Lou Boudreau, "the Boy Manager"; Charlie "King Kong" Keller; and Li'l Phil "the Scooter" Rizzuto—fabulous, bigger-than-life beings, not tiny people you had to crane your neck to see. In fact, they weren't people at all. They were baseball players, and that was all I wanted them to be.

Of course all modern fans have suffered the rude discovery that baseball is a business and that the players regard themselves as performers. But luckily, the first stages of my disillusionment were gentle. In 1962, after I had finished graduate school and had started my first job (as an editor in a book publishing company), I happened to read Bill Veeck's *Veeck—As in Wreck*, the autobiography of the man who owned the Cleveland Indian team that won the 1948 championship and that DiMaggio had hit those three home runs against. It was the first book I'd come across that didn't treat baseball as a game played by clean-cut young men devoted to setting an example for the youth of America.

Reading Bill Veeck's book, I was amazed at what sensitive nurturing of human quirkiness it took to put a winning team together. Creating the right combination of people seemed to be what Veeck was particularly good at, especially if it meant exploiting one player's idiosyncrasy or camouflaging another's weakness or tending a few sprigs of advantage until they grew into a forest of invincibility. He was certainly good at describing how it was done. Some of the best stories he told in his book were about how he pieced together that 1948 world champion Indians team—how he made a few phone calls, pulled off a couple of key trades, called in some old debts, had the gumption to hire Larry Doby and Satchel Paige, the first two black men to play in the American League, and even nursed along a player, Russ Christopher, who had been born with a hole in his heart but had lived to pitch in the major leagues. His best story of all was about the pitcher Gene Bearden, whom Veeck had acquired as an afterthought in a 1947 deal that sent pitcher Allie "Superchief" Reynolds from the Indians to the Yankees in exchange for infielder Joe "Flash" Gordon—one of those ideal trades that end up helping both parties. Gene Bearden's money pitch was a sinkerball that dropped actually *before* it reached the strike zone, so that if batters had known to wait him out, all his best pitches would have been balls instead of strikes. But only Bearden's minor-league manager, Casey Stengel, knew the truth about the sinker and Casey didn't tell when he advised Veeck to grab Bearden in the trade with the Yankees. Bearden's weakness remained a secret for the 1948 season, and he won twenty games, including the playoff against the Red Sox that gave the Indians the pennant. He won one game and saved another in the World Series defeat of the Boston Braves. He was even signed by Hollywood to pitch against Jimmy Stewart in a movie about a one-legged pitcher called *The Monte Stratton Story*. Then Casey Stengel was hired to manage the Yankees. When Bearden pitched against the Yanks, Casey made his players wait him out and force him to throw his easily hit curve or fastball. The word spread, and that was just about the end of his career. He bounced around the league for a few years, but never again won more than eight games in a season.

After I read Veeck's autobiography it was impossible to go on thinking of baseball players as mythical creatures. He made the game seem more like show biz. It was disillusioning in a way, but it was also inspiring to discover how a smart baseball operator could work with limited material. Meeting Bill Veeck would be one thing I would have to do if I took the editor up on his offer.

Far more disillusioning events would occur in the years that followed my reading of *Veeck—As in Wreck*. Disenchantment was already in the air at the time the book appeared. Perhaps its publication in 1962—along with the appearance two years earlier of another candid baseball book, Jim Brosnan's diary of a relief pitcher, *The Long Season*—was an omen that baseball was about to undergo a change. But as the 1960s progressed, the players began to act more and more like real people. They wanted more money, as real people tend to do. Certain outstanding players had always demanded higher pay and had sometimes even gone so far as to withhold their heroic services until their demands were met. In a few extreme cases, players had sat out whole seasons. But holdouts had always been part of the colorful ritual of the game, a perquisite of stardom, an objectification of immortality. (Indeed, as I later found out, owners were not above conspiring in salary disputes with their star players, if only for the sake of enhancing the splendor of all concerned.) But deep down, I still believed—or wanted to believe—that all players were like the young Willie Mays, who was said to love the game so much that he spent his off-hours playing stickball with children on the streets of Harlem.

Yet from the mid-1960s on, the players began to act as if baseball wasn't to be played for the pure fun of it. In 1966, they got together and formed that most unplayful of organizations—a labor union! The Major League Baseball Players' Association, they called it. In the years that followed, they threatened various job actions. And eventually they would go on strike—over such issues as the size of their pension fund and their right to seek outside arbitration in salary disputes. They actually thought of themselves as working for a living.

Then in 1970, a veteran outfielder for the St. Louis Cardinals by the name of Curt Flood decided that he didn't want to play for the Philadelphia Phillies baseball club, even though his owner had traded him to it. Flood hired a lawyer to attack the very idea that someone had a right to tell the players where to work. Though he ultimately lost in the Supreme Court, his cause was not abandoned by his fellow players. They won it a few years later when an arbitrator ruled that no contract bound a player to a ballclub for more than a year after that contract had lapsed. Slavery in perpetuity was thereby declared null and void. The players had received their manumission.

But it seemed to me that behind all this ferment lay a highly subversive message. The players were saying that they weren't going to stand for being treated like children any longer. Baseball was a profession, they were insisting, and they were professionals. That was fair enough. But then it made no more sense to root for a baseball game than it did to cheer the outcome of an appendectomy or a stock transaction. If my fantasy figures wanted to be taken so seriously, then why bother with them at all? If they wished to sell their services to one team or another like so many Hessian soldiers, then I could think of them as mercenaries and no longer as Indians, Tigers, Giants, Cubs. I could banish them from my dreams forever and root instead for my doctor and my stockbroker.

Besides, the owners had tampered with the game and in doing so had tainted it. Organized baseball had become disorganized. Various teams had somehow broken loose, drifting all over the North American continent. The old Boston Braves had started it all by moving west to Milwaukee in 1953 and then, when attendance there dropped off because the Braves stopped winning, had marched south to Atlanta.

The resulting void in Milwaukee had been filled by a new team, the Seattle Pilots, which had become the Milwaukee Brewers and eventually been replaced in Seattle by an even newer team, the Mariners. The Brooklyn Dodgers and New York Giants had moved to California and been joined there by two newborn teams, the California Angels and San Diego Padres, as well as by the old Philadelphia Athletics, which had become the Oakland A's by way of Kansas City and a madly innovative owner named Charles O. Finley. The gap in Kansas City had been filled by the freshly minted Royals. The Washington Senators had gotten tired of last place and moved themselves out of the territory and up in the standings, to become the winning Minnesota Twins. A new Washington Senators team had been coined to replace the old one and then almost immediately converted into the Texas Rangers. By the late 1970s, the face of baseball had been punched to pieces and none too artfully rearranged. There were even two teams in Canada.

The owners had also scrambled the format of competition. With so many new teams, they had had to subdivide the two major leagues into two additional sections and then add two playoff rounds to an already expanded season to determine which teams would meet in the World Series. It was all too much. It left one, well, confused. It also left one purged of any illusion that the teams existed for the sake of regional loyalty. The point of it all was money.

And having overexpanded and saturated the market, they had tried to undo the damage with gimmicks—exploding scoreboards, organs that imitated bugle calls, bizarrely colored uniforms as clinging in the thigh as winter underwear, and, in the American League at least, the so-called designated hitter rule, which allowed each team in a game to appoint a batter whose only function was to come off the bench and hit in place of the pitcher. The point of the DH was to strengthen each team's batting order and produce more run-scoring excitement. But since the rule also removed the manager's option to pinch-hit for his pitcher, its effect was coincidentally to eliminate a whole strategic dimension of the game. While obvious excitement had been added to baseball in the form of stronger hitting, a subtle source of drama had been taken away with the loss of the tantalizing crisis that arose in so many close, well-pitched games over whether to pinch-hit for the pitcher and risk trading offense for defense.

Even if I weren't disenchanted with the game I would be the wrong person to go out and write a book about it. Having internalized the game and reduced the players to toys, I had denied myself knowledge of how baseball was really played. I simply didn't know enough—either about the profession or about the people who worked in it. And this, it seemed to me as I contemplated the editor's proposition, was part of my character. It was no coincidence I earned my living by sitting at home reading and writing about books. It was the way I had designed my life—to look at the world from a distance and on my own terms. I would make a lousy reporter. I had no experience observing events as they happened. I had little skill at thinking on my feet. What would I ask a baseball player if I could even get up the courage to interview one? What would *I* see in an actual game that others hadn't, ten thousand times before?

Everything I could think of was an argument against accepting the offer. I would have to say no to Tom Tracy.

Still, actually to attend spring training camp. And the All-Star game. And the World Series. To be able to visit Yankee Stadium any time I wanted and even go into the clubhouse. And to be paid for it! How could anyone turn down such an opportunity? It was a fan's wildest fantasy come true. Maybe just being near the Yankees would inspire me—to do work I doubted I could do, to "play over my head," as the saying went.

Yet there was one other explanation for my disillusionment with baseball. This was the decline and fall of the New York Yankees. It was curious to observe how the cooling of my passion had coincided with the sinking of the Yankees from first place in 1964 to last place in 1966. Last place, for the first time since Harry Wolverton had brought them home fifty-five games behind in 1912! And then the team had barely twitched throughout the remainder of the sixties and the first half of the seventies. No wonder the obituary page had seemed more fun to read than the sports section.

And it was more curious still when the shipbuilder George M. Steinbrenner III had come sailing into town with his holds full of loot and begun rebuilding the team with clever trades and winning bids at the free-agent auctions, how my interest was rekindled. It was astonishing how my perspective changed when the Yankees began to win again. Suddenly, it mattered not in the least that their owner was a felon convicted for making illegal contributions to

Richard Nixon's campaign funds. As one grateful fan put it, "George has restored my childhood and made my kid's a better one."

Suddenly, it didn't matter that some of the best players on the Yankees were men who had demanded and won their freedom and then sold their services to the highest bidder. They might as well have been swaddled in pinstripes, as far as I was concerned. Suddenly, all baseball had seemed bright and beautiful again—the new and colorful teams from all over the continent (more meat for my lions), the tighter uniforms that streamlined the body, the scoreboards that lit up the night skies, the bugle-organ calls that set the blood to tingling, and the sensible designated-hitter rule that prolonged the careers of aging baseball stars.

Why did I root for them, my beloved Yankees? I knew the litany of curses. They were cold and arrogant, contemptuous of human frailty. They were rich—they *bought* their championships. They were invincible—they always won. Rooting for them was like rooting for U.S. Steel, people said. They lacked the honey of human sentiment. They made a habit of trading away their best players while they could still get something of value in exchange—Roger Maris, Vic Raschi, Joe Gordon, even Babe Ruth himself. They were one of the last teams to field a black player.

I knew all this, and still I could defend myself. There was the matter of propinquity: both the team and I were from The Bronx, and that had mattered, at least in those dangerous school corridors in Berlin. And if I hadn't lived in New York I wouldn't have heard DiMaggio's three home runs that afternoon. Had I lived in Pittsburgh, it might have been Ralph Kiner and a whole different story.

And now that I was old enough to understand more about myself, I'd come up with some deeper answers. I was the oldest of three brothers, and the Yankees were a team for oldest brothers. If you were the oldest you were expected to win; you couldn't afford ever not to win, otherwise you'd lose the authority thrust on you by the primacy of your birth. You had to win and go on winning just to stay in place, and the Yanks were as close to a perpetual-motion winning machine as it was possible to identify with. If you were a younger brother, an underdog, you rooted for the Brooklyn Dodgers, who were riffraff and upstarts. I hated the Dodgers for being scrappy, ragtag opportunists, diggers and levelers, the salt of the earth. I was indifferent to the New York Giants—uncles and friends' fathers were for the Giants; so I thought of the Giants as potbellied and sclerotic. As for the New York Mets—I could only see them as a team for *youngest* brothers and for children. The rest of the teams played in the hinterlands. I loved the Yankees. The Yankees were for winners.

Besides—as I liked to bait my many friends who hated the Yankees—it was no picnic rooting for them. You had so much to live down—the winning tradition, the arrogance, the reluctance to bring along black players, the imperious reign of George Steinbrenner. It was easy to root for underdogs and losers. It took character to be a Yankee fan.

If I did decide to write a baseball book, I would start off with the Yankees, of course. I'd head straight for their spring training site in Fort Lauderdale and wander among them as if I were an art student examining old masters. For they were inspired—those twenty-five world champions who the previous season, 1978, had achieved the greatest comeback in baseball history. I imagined that I'd find them all on exhibition as in a great museum. Standing before its entrance I would gaze up at the sculpted figures of the entablature and see scenes from the Yankee past—Babe Ruth pointing his bat at a distant target, reminding us of his called home run in the 1932 World Series against the Chicago Cubs; Lefty Gomez on the mound staring up at an airplane; Tommy Henrich taking off toward first base as Dodger catcher Mickey Owen muffs Hugh Casey's third-strike pitch in the 1941 World Series; Joe DiMaggio at bat in his famous widespread stance; Roger Maris at the plate watching his record sixty-first home run sail into the stands; Casey Stengel trudging toward the pitcher's mound, his head vultured forward and his hands plunged awkwardly into his back pockets.

Stepping inside the entrance hall of this museum of my own imagining, I would find display cases filled with famous Yankee artifacts—the ball that pitcher Jack Chesbro threw wild to lose the 1904 pennant; a yellowing copy of DiMaggio's hundred-thousand-dollar contract, the first ever given a major-leaguer; the clumps of Roger Maris's hair that fell out during his record home run season; a copy of the lawsuit filed by a Bronx delicatessen owner seeking damages for injuries sustained during the 1957 brawl at the Copacabana nightclub, the incident that provoked the Yankees to trade Billy

Martin to Kansas City; an X ray of Tony Kubek's neck, showing the damage done by the bad-hop single that ended up costing the Yanks the 1960 Series against the Pirates, as well as cutting short Kubek's playing career; pitcher Jim Bouton's hat, covered with dirt from the hundreds of times it had fallen off his head as he threw his frantic fastball.

In an exhibition room behind the entrance hall, I'd find life-size dioramas along the walls showing scenes from the previous season—Graig Nettles suspended horizontally, making one of his impossible diving stabs of a smash that would have eluded most other third basemen in baseball history; catcher Thurman Munson rearing up out of his crouch to skewer a would-be base stealer sliding hopelessly into second; Reggie Jackson bunting foul with two strikes on him against the Kansas City Royals, an act of rebellion that ended up costing manager Billy Martin his job in favor of Bob Lemon, whose calm disposition helped the team to come from way back and win the pennant; weak-hitting Bucky Dent popping the three-run homer off Boston pitcher Mike Torrez that put the Yankees ahead of the Red Sox in the one-game playoff for the Eastern Division championship; right fielder Lou Piniella stabbing at and luckily snaring a line drive he had lost in the sun, which kept the tying Boston run from scoring and enabled the Yanks to hold the lead against the Sox in that playoff game; Roy White hitting the home run that beat the Kansas City Royals in the final game of the American League Championship Series; Reggie Jackson shooting out his hip to deflect a throw to first by Dodger shortstop Bill Russell, allowing a key run to score in the fourth game of the World Series, which the Yanks wound up winning, four games to two.

Behind this exhibition room would be the Hall of Yankee Pitching, with a special section roped off for statues of the heroic 1978 staff—Jim "Catfish" Hunter, his left cheek bulging with his tobacco chaw; Ed Figueroa, who that year had become the first Puerto Rican pitcher ever to win twenty games in a major-league season; Rich "Goose" Gossage, rearing back to throw his smoking fastball; and, in a place of honor marked by a spotlit circle, the incomparable Ron Guidry, Ron the nonpareil, who in 1978 not only had put together one of the greatest statistical records ever compiled by a pitcher, but had somehow managed to win every game that really mattered to the Yankees.

And finally, as I imagined it, I'd step through a door at the back of the Hall of Pitching to find, cavorting in the Florida sunshine, the living players themselves. They would gather around and welcome me when they saw what a passionate fan had joined them! I'd return their affection, slapping high fives and patting their hips, offering congratulations and reassurances. I'd drag Reggie Jackson aside and convince him that, despite all his misgivings, New Yorkers really did admire and cherish him. I'd plead with Graig Nettles to give in and sign a new contract, and point out that nowhere else would his spectacular skills be so prominently displayed as in the Big Apple. I'd corner Roy White and persuade him that no matter how shabbily Yankee management might have treated him, his fans would never overlook his quiet but steady performances. I'd commiserate with manager Bob Lemon over his son's death in a car crash only a week or two after the Yankees had won the World Series last October; I'd say how much all of us appreciated his bearing up the way he had. I'd even say hello to owner Steinbrenner and general manager Al Rosen, unless of course they were preoccupied with working on trades to improve the club.

Later, when practice was over, I'd join a few of the more fun-loving among them—Piniella? Nettles?—and repair to a roadside tavern full of moody woodwork and animated beer ads. Together we'd down a few and play some leisurely rounds of shuffleboard. Later still, we would go back to somebody's hotel room—maybe Reggie's—pull together two beds, and deal stud poker into the small hours of the morning. Whether I won or lost, I'd do so with aplomb and grace. For at last I'd be one with the figures of my fantasies.

One week after Tom Tracy had made his book proposal, I called him and told him that he had a deal.

2

TRAINING

EARLY IN THE AFTERNOON of the first day I spent at the New York Yankees' Florida spring training site, I found myself sitting on the slatted bench in the Yankee dugout, vacantly considering the spike marks on the wooden floor. Bob Lemon, the manager who the previous year had guided the team to its miracle finish from fourteen and a half games behind, was seated nearby, staring silently out at the field with a cigarette cupped in his hand. Al Rosen, the president of the team, was standing next to him, natty in summer pastels, his crew-cut white hair blazing. None of us spoke. Lemon had just been approached by three men who introduced themselves as members of Miami's Cuban community. When they asked him if he would speak at a dinner the following week to honor the pitcher Luis Tiant, Lemon did the old Marlene Dietrich routine: "Sure, I'll come. When is it? Oh. Well, I've got to be someplace else that night, and I can't be two places at once, can I?"

Rosen, whom I had met the day before, seemed to be staring at a cloudbank in the distance. I had never exchanged a word with Lemon. Though the two of them were more than professional associates—they'd been teammates on the Cleveland Indians in the their playing days, and it was through Rosen that Lemon had been hired to replace Billy Martin the previous July—Rosen had not bothered to introduce his friend to me. As the three of us stared in our various directions, I puzzled over Rosen's peculiar breach of etiquette. Or maybe it wasn't a breach of etiquette. Maybe it was out of place to introduce people to each other in baseball dugouts or on playing fields. It *felt* as if it would be a little out of place, now that I considered it.

Maybe it was just as well, too. I recalled the promise I had made to myself that the first thing I would do if I were introduced to Lemon would be to say how sorry I felt about his son's death—an insupportable loss to a father under any circumstances, but especially devastating, it seemed to me, coming at one of the high points in Lemon's life. Yet it was a loss that had gone unmentioned all winter in the many articles that had appeared on Lemon and the Yankees. No one had even hinted how Lemon was feeling. I couldn't understand how he had found the strength to go on managing the Yankees. But condolences too seemed out of place in a baseball dugout. If Rosen had introduced Lemon to me, I would probably have said nothing about his son and then disliked myself for the omission afterward. So maybe it was just as well that Rosen was remaining silent. But I still didn't understand why he wasn't introducing us.

My confusion was part of a larger sense of disorientation I was beginning to feel on my first day with the Yankees. A low point of sorts had occurred just half an hour earlier. A young woman from a Miami paper had come up to me and asked if one of her colleagues might do an interview. With whom? I asked, certain that she had mistaken me for a Yankee official. With you, she said. She explained somewhat elaborately how she had learned that I was the *New York Times*'s book reviewer from listening in on a dugout conversation between Tom Tracy and one Edith Camp, a widowed socialite in her seventies who was doing an article on spring training for *Town & Country*.

I succumbed reluctantly as the young woman's colleague, a boyish-looking reporter, approached. What was I doing in Fort Lauderdale? I was supposed to be writing a book about baseball. What sort of book? Well, that hadn't been absolutely determined yet. Well, what kind of interviews was I conducting? Um, I wasn't sure about that, either. Was the photographer Francesco Scavullo here to work on the project? Yes, he was. Was that really the editor of the book who was with us? Why, yes, it was. Wasn't it a little unusual for a book editor to be traveling with his author? Perhaps it was, but he was here to coordinate things between me and Scavullo, since we had never met until this morning. Oh; well, good luck and thanks. You're most welcome.

The interest in my presence only signified how little was happening in camp. Exhibition games weren't due to begin for several days yet; it was even too early for intrasquad play. The day's activities were confined to calisthenics, batting and fielding practice, and a little jogging in the outfield; and so far only a handful of local reporters had shown up to cover the team.

Meanwhile, the Yankees went about their business with supreme indifference to the reporters present, only reacting to them if confronted formally. But since I hadn't worked up the gumption to approach any of the players, let alone thought of any questions to ask them, I was forced to regard them as if they were inside an enormous bell jar, against whose cold exterior I was pressing my nose. And the more I pressed the more uncomfortable and lonely I began to feel. Now I had been reduced to worrying why Al Rosen wasn't introducing me to Bob Lemon.

Actually, I had been forewarned by the man from the baseball commissioner's office. A few days before leaving for Florida, Tracy had set up dinner in a mid-Manhattan restaurant with one of Commissioner Bowie Kuhn's publicity people, who had assured us in well-tested phrases that professional baseball considered it in its best interests to make its players accessible to anyone interested in writing about the game. Yes, I said, I'm sure it does. But what did the players themselves really feel about writers?

The man from the commissioner's office tugged at his collar. Well, he said, you had to understand that despite enormous progress since the days of the ignorant characters described in Ring Lardner's book *You Know Me Al*, baseball players remained essentially middle-American types suspicious of creative people, particularly creative people from New York City. So what did the players really think of writers? Not to put too fine a point on it, they considered them "a bunch of New York fags."

Perhaps to fill the silence that followed, the man from the commissioner's office asked what our book was going to be about. I said it remained to be seen; we would be tracing the progress of the season. Tracy leaned forward and extended his arms dramatically—looking a little like the concert pianist he'd in fact once aspired to become—and picked up the salt and pepper shakers at the center of the table, one in each hand.

"What I'm looking for is synergism, you see? Take a book critic like this man and a fashion photographer like Francesco Scavullo; get them working together; and you have synergism, a total greater than its parts."

As he spoke he slowly brought the salt and pepper together until they touched.

"Like that. Do you understand?"

"No," said the man from the commissioner's office.

The conversation wound down after that. Soon the man from the commissioner's office looked at his watch, announced that he had a train to catch, and saluted us farewell.

The meeting had shaken my confidence in the forthcoming venture. I had gone home and looked in the mirror, trying to see myself through the eyes of someone accustomed to hanging around with specimens of physical grace and power. What I saw there was not entirely discouraging. I was tall, about six feet two, and not yet wholly gone to fat; while I weighed 195 pounds, a hint of the skinny kid I'd once been still remained. But even though I'd played a little baseball in high school and college, there was no suggestion of the athlete in my ectomorphic frame. With my jowls, my wire-rimmed eyeglasses, and my chewed-down pipe I looked exactly like what I was, a person who sat indoors all day, reading books and writing about them for a living.

But as I stood there regarding my image in the mirror, it occurred to me that the best athletes I had ever known or competed against had mostly turned out to be doctors, poets, stockbrokers and teachers. Few of them had ever even contemplated a professional career in sports. In fact, the only professional-to-be I'd ever measured myself against on the playing field was one Dick Hall, with whom I'd overlapped a single semester at Swarthmore College. Having played a few dozen games as an outfielder and third baseman for the Pittsburgh Pirates the previous season, Hall had a semester's worth of work to go toward a B.A. in economics. Naturally, he was no longer eligible to compete intercollegiately. But his exploits were legendary on campus: he had pitched for the baseball team and hit over .450 two consecutive years; in his junior year he had also won a letter in track and still held the college record for the long jump. And I had played pickup games of touch football and half-court basketball with him. He stood six feet six and seemed as quick as a whippet. Competing with him was like contending with a superman. I could still remember catching a football pass fully twenty feet in the clear, yet being tagged by him before I had run three steps. And still for all his physical gifts, he was never able to hit major-league pitching. It was only as a control artist that he'd built a long and successful career as a relief pitcher for the Philadelphia Phillies and Baltimore Orioles, giving up only twenty-three unintentional bases on balls in his last seven seasons. And his style was considered so clumsy that someone had once said of him that he looked like "a giraffe on a skateboard" when he wound up and threw the ball. And because he was smart and a little ungainly by comparison with other players, he won the reputation among his teammates of being an intellectual.

If an athlete as awesome as Dick Hall was judged to be an awkward intellectual, then what was the average baseball player going to be like? It was a world of aliens I was about to enter. It made me nervous.

Still, the adventure had gotten off to an auspicious start. While waiting to get a shoeshine at Kennedy Airport, I'd looked up from my newspaper to see who was next in line and observed a stocky figure with a white burr of hair advancing toward the shoeshine chair. The man was somebody; when another customer tried to slip ahead of him he asserted in a quiet but firm voice that left no doubt of his authority that he was next in line, buddy. But it was not until I had paid for my own shine and left the parlor that it dawned on me exactly who the burr-headed gentleman was. And when Tom Tracy and I located the two first-class seats separated from one another that the airline had apologetically given us—Tracy suffered from fear of flying and had been counting on my support during take-off—mine turned out to be right next to the man I'd seen in the shoeshine parlor. It was Al Rosen, the president of the New York Yankees.

Of course I still had to bridge the remaining foot or two that separated us. This should have been no problem, or no harder than breaching the wall that a tough-minded businessman accustomed to traveling alone normally carries around with him.

But as well as being a portly middle-aged baseball executive, my traveling companion also happened to be an image off a baseball bubble gum card whose type might read: "Rosen, Albert Leonard (Flip); born Feb. 29, 1924, Spartanburg, S.C.; 3B Cleveland Indians, 1947–1956; lifetime batting average, .285; lifetime slugging percentage, .495; in his best year, 1953, led the American League in Home Runs, Slugging Average, Total Bases, Runs Batted In, Runs Scored; 1953 Most Valuable Player, the only player ever to be elected unanimously." There had been dozens of occasions when as a Yankee fan I had quailed to hear that Al Rosen was coming to bat. One did not speak idly to a face from a bubble gum card.

Still, despite my shyness, I knew I had to seize the opportunity that luck had given me and breach that wall.

"Are you flying through from somewhere else, or coming from New York?"

The question was meant to have a little spin on it. Rosen had most likely been in New York, where—I had been told by a neighbor of his with whom I regularly played poker—he kept an apartment on East Sixty-eighth Street. On the other hand, he might be coming from another city, in which case he had probably been there on business (such as maybe completing a trade for the Boston Red Sox's slugging outfielder, Jim Rice?) and I would have an opening to ask him about it. But the question was hardly out of my mouth when I remembered that the Red Sox, like the Yankees, were now in Florida, and besides it was probably out of season for trades. So I was already flushed with embarrassment when Rosen slowly turned his head, stared through the tiny hole I'd poked in his wall, said "I'm coming from New York," and withdrew.

"Uh. How's the weather in Florida?" (This would establish whether he had already been down there with the team and had just flown up to New York for a family visit or an errand.)

"The weather in Florida is beautiful." (Was there a trace of irritation in the cold blue eyes?)

Now I was forced to play a card I happened to be holding—the name of a mutual acquaintance to whom I had mentioned my forthcoming trip to Florida and who had urged me to use his name in case I ran into Rosen.

"I think we know someone in common—Sidney Zion."

Rosen's demeanor thawed at the mention of the lawyer, reporter, and man-about-town who had recently done a piece on the Yankees for *New York* magazine, and whom I had gotten to know years earlier at Yale when I was attending the drama school and he the law school. Rosen's eyes focused on me. His hand reached out and clasped mine. We traded names. We began to exchange small talk. Before too long he asked me what I was planning to do in Florida, and when I told him I would be visiting some of the training camps to research a book on baseball, he asked if I was planning to come to Fort Lauderdale Stadium, where the Yankees trained.

"I'm hoping to be there first thing in the morning."

"Then by all means drop by my office first. It's in the trailer just outside the park."

After I thanked him, we began to run out of small talk. I thought for a while and tried to frame a question that might interest him.

"What's it like dealing with the contemporary player compared with what it was like for management when, say, you were a player?"

"Well, Christopher, I don't begrudge the players their money any more than you would deny wealth to writers like Robert Ludlum"—he tapped a paperback copy of *The Holcroft Covenant* he happened to be holding in his hand—"Mickey Spillane, Ross Macdonald or whomever. But we've got to set some limits. As it is, with Pete Rose signing a nearly four-million-dollar, five-year contract at the age of thirty-eight, we're rushing headlong toward suicide. I can promise you the owners are very serious about the renegotiation of the contract with the players this winter."

Actually, I couldn't have cared less about the upcoming negotiations, so long as the world champion Yankees stayed intact and didn't lose their All-Star third baseman, Graig Nettles, or their doughty shortstop, Bucky Dent, both of whom were threatening to become free agents. But I was reluctant to expose my rooting bias to the businessman sitting next to me, so I groped for a mature approach to the topic of holding on to Nettles and Dent.

"Yankee management isn't having any trouble meeting its payroll, is it?"

"Well, we have our little problem with Nettles."

"Do you think he'll sign?"

"I think he wants to. Of course, we're oceans apart just now. What he doesn't seem to understand is that he's just not the drawing card that a Rice or a Jackson or a Luis Tiant or a Tommy John is."

"Are you having a peaceful training camp?" I was worried about the disruptions that had theatened the Yankees' success in the past.

"Very. Probably more peaceful than it'll be next year."

"You mean . . . you guys are serious about rehiring Billy Martin?"

Rosen looked at me hard and nodded slowly.

This was astonishing. I had purposely refrained from alluding to Billy Martin's future, assuming—perhaps too politely—that in the privacy of airplane travel a person was entitled not to be taxed for his sins by his seatmate. Yet here was Rosen bringing up the subject himself and offering his assurances, in the face of the deepest public cynicism, that the Yankees meant to follow through on their commitment to rehire Martin, even though every fan and his grandmother knew that the promise to rehire Martin had been made the previous July only to get every fan and his grandmother off Yankee management's back.

Rosen had all but confided in me. He had given me a glimpse of the Yankees' inner workings. I felt elated. It was difficult to concentrate on the movie we now stopped our conversation to watch. Ah yes, here I was aboard Eastern Airline's flight to Fort Lauderdale, exchanging shoptalk with the president of the New York Yankees. As Al Rosen was telling me the other day on our flight down to Florida . . .

I had taken my first tiny steps as a reporter. Maybe I could handle this project after all.

My elation continued when Tom Tracy and I presented ourselves to Rosen first thing in the morning and he instructed Mickey Morabito, the Yankees' publicist, to give us passes to the playing field and the locker room of Fort Lauderdale Stadium. Suddenly, in a day of brilliant Florida sunshine, we were standing at a guarded gate to the field. I was there; my dream had come true. No, it was even better than the Yankee museum I had imagined. I was looking out at a perfect baseball field, as green and symmetrical as any I had ever seen, set down in a perfect little toy of a park, complete with grandstands and advertising billboards. Beowulf, read the bright red letters of the one bordering right-center field, lending an incongruous literary note to the atmosphere.

Nervously we showed our passes to the guard at the gate and made our way past a small crowd of people with looks of longing and expectation on their faces. Poor commoners, I caught myself thinking. On the other side of the gate, we found the field empty except for a few groundskeepers. There wasn't a pinstripe in sight. Still half-expecting to be stopped and asked where the hell we thought we were going, we walked through a door that seemed to lead underneath the grandstand, followed a passageway that took several turns, pushed open another door, and found ourselves looking out on a large airy room filled with people and the smell of liniment.

It looked like every locker room I had ever seen, only much larger. It also reminded me of an army barracks without the cots. Men were milling about in various stages of dress—some naked, others in uniform shirts and jockstraps, still others in tights the length of pedal pushers—were they for protection when sliding? Along the waistband of a man in underwear standing right next to me were the Magic-Markered letters J A X. J A X? JAX! The last place I had seen that word was on the center-field scoreboard at Yankee Stadium, flashing JAX JAX JAX JAX SMAX to celebrate an enormous World Series home run that had just been hit by Reggie Jackson. Sure enough, the surprisingly normal-sized though muscular man standing with his back to me *was* Reggie Jackson. He was announcing to anyone within earshot that "Marvin Miller will be here any second to meet with us in the locker room. Please stick around." And the squat figure next to Jackson was Yogi Berra. And coming through the door of what looked like the trainer's room was Ed Figueroa. And inside, reclining on a training table like some burly Roman gladiator resting up for the battle, was Luis Tiant, with a huge black cigar in his mouth, just as the photos on the sports pages had always presented him.

I was so transfixed that I wasn't in the least aware that I was standing with my pipe in my mouth ogling a roomful of half-naked men. It didn't trouble me as yet that no player seemed to take the slightest notice of me. Nor was I bothered when Marvin Miller, executive director of the Major League Baseball Players' Association, who had just walked into the locker room—presumably to brief the Yankees on the progress of the current contract negotiations with the owners—smiled and said softly but firmly, "No," when I asked him, with an uncharacteristic burst of pluck, if I might stay for the meeting. While Tracy went off to look for Scavullo, who was expected any moment, I waited in the Yankee dugout with the handful of other reporters who were attending the day's practice. I still felt as if I were living out a dream.

Soon the meeting with Miller was over, and the players started trickling out of the passageway from the locker room and heading out to right field, where they arranged themselves in ranks and files and began desultorily to do warm-up exercises to the shouted cadence, interspersed with jovial needling, of an older man wearing uniform number sixty-four, one Hopalong Cassady according to the media guide that Mickey Morabito had given me. Standing near the right-field foul pole, I could pick out in the sea of pinstripes such familiar figures as Mickey Rivers, Catfish Hunter, Thurman Munson, and the newly signed free agent Tommy John, who, as he joined the group at a trot, did a little leap into the air and clicked his heels together jauntily. But again I was reminded of the army, or a mockery of the army. Cassady was a parody of a drill instructor, not expecting for a moment to be taken seriously; the ranks and files were without symmetry (Mickey Rivers, obviously feeling lonely in his ten square feet of grass, was wandering about looking for cronies to kibitz with); the players were exercising to their own beats, some earnestly, some listlessly, some not at all; and there was constant teasing chatter, punctuated by many a raucous "shit" and "fuck."

When calisthenics were over and the players began to disperse to various parts of the field, I wandered back to the foul side of first base, where the ancient Luis Tiant was warming up, presumably to pitch his share of batting practice. I had seen Tiant at least a dozen times on television or from a seat at Yankee Stadium, but now, like the only boy at a circus, I could watch from ten feet away the famously eccentric pitching motion. With the ponderous grace of an elephant gyrating on a stool, Tiant extended his arms, grunted, rotated, threw. It was hard to believe that thousands of professional hitters had been confounded by these labored pitches. The famous Tiant magnetism—the reason the Yankees had given a forty-year-old athlete a ten-year contract to pitch and scout for them—was not in evidence here. Even the cigar was missing. Tiant worked expressionlessly. Again and again: grunted, rotated, threw.

Next, I made my way to the batting cage, where some dozen players had assembled to take turns hitting against Tommy John. Pitching through the window of a protective screen set up in front of the mound, John was throwing to a catcher who squatted no more than three feet from the back of the cage. It was possible for an observer to stand directly behind the catcher without risk (unless one was foolish enough to wrap one's fingers around the piping that supported the cage and risk getting them mashed by a ball fouled off backward). From here one could get as close a look at both the approaching ball and the swinging bat as the umpire calling balls and strikes in an actual game.

But Tommy John was not throwing his most elusive pitch, a slow sinkerball whose tantalizing action seemed only to have been enhanced by the effect of the surgery to reconstruct the tendon in his elbow (thus salvaging his career and earning him the title "The Man with the Bionic Arm"). John was simply serving them up straight for the hitters, as were Tiant and Catfish Hunter when their turns came in the pitching rotation.

Nor were the hitters generating much excitement. The horseplay around the batting cage was subdued—except for Mickey Rivers's efforts to needle Cliff Johnson, the large backup catcher with a faintly Oriental look to his features. Rivers's theme of the day was Johnson's appetite for junk food: "I'm gown get me some ribbies [RBI's, or runs batted in] by puttin' a cheeseburger an' milk shake on home plate when Cliff's on base," barked Rivers, suggesting that only food would move the hulking Johnson to run home when Rivers got a hit. "I'm gown put pickles an' ketchup on it. Get me some ribbies." At the plate, the batters swung earnestly but with little effect. Ground balls and line drives mostly. An occasional soft fly to the outfield. Nothing anywhere near the fences. The Yankee bats seemed dead. Or was it just too early in the spring for serious hitting?

I was beginning to feel a little discouraged. The novelty of being in the Yankee training camp was wearing off, and I was starting to feel embarrassed about my shyness. The ballplayers were going about their routines as if I weren't even there. Of course they weren't paying attention to any of the other outsiders either, with the exception of my collaborator, Francesco Scavullo, who'd finally arrived only minutes earlier with two young assistants loaded down with equipment. Scavullo and I had been hurriedly introduced by Tracy, who had reappeared with him. A slight, black-haired fiftyish-looking man elegantly decked out in a white Panama hat and black slacks with a matching tunic, Scavullo was moving briskly about and aggressively sticking his camera into players' faces and firing off his motor-driven Nikon as if it were a machine gun.

I watched enviously as a mere slip of a woman from one of the Miami papers approached the huge Cliff Johnson and asked him how he took care of his catcher's mitt. She seemed not at all disconcerted as Johnson regarded her suspiciously, sighed, and contemplated his glove; all the reporters present seemed accustomed to being treated as intruders. "I put the ball in the pocket, wrap it with tape, soak it in water, then unwrap it. To form a better pocket." This was mumbled in a guarded manner that bore little resemblance to the raucous, jovial Johnson who had been clowning with Mickey Rivers all morning. A few more precise questions, a few more stiff replies, and Johnson was released from his durance. He nodded, let his shoulders sag with relief, and trotted off to greet his buddy Rivers with a swipe of his paw and a crushing bear hug. But at least the reporter was armed with questions and accustomed to the routine of asking them.

Still more self-assured was Sparky Anderson, the former manager of the Cincinnati Reds who was putting in some time as an ABC television reporter until another managing job came along, and who'd just arrived at Fort Lauderdale Stadium. Because the players knew him and respected him, they reacted to him with a few degrees of warmth. Soon he was launched on an interview with Graig Nettles that was lively if not entirely coherent.

NETTLES: What gets me is that it's the flamboyant players who catch the fans' attention and get the big money. I'm not flamboyant.

ANDERSON: Well, you know, Graig, in the opinion of the players and coaches, you've always been the best.

NETTLES: Not to knock the fans, but that's all I've ever cared about.

Even Tracy had gotten into the spirit of things and was eavesdropping on interviews and beginning to ask questions, which made my timidity seem all the more embarrassing to me. But if I'd had a whole armory full of questions and the spunk to start shooting them, I still would have felt disappointed over the absence of small talk and relaxed give-and-take that I'd expected from the Yankees. So I'd withdrawn to the dugout to watch, and was wondering why even Al Rosen seemed to have cooled toward me.

*　*　*

Now, in midafternoon, practice seemed to be coming to an end. Alone or in little groups, the players were lazing off the field and into the clubhouse. The batting cage was removed, and a shiny new car was driven onto the infield to replace it. Men with TV cameras, sound equipment, and light reflectors gathered in an arc halfway between home plate and the pitcher's mound. Graig Nettles, his face glowing eerily with makeup, started trotting back and forth between third base and home plate, periodically slapping the car and calling out, "And don't go home without test-driving the new Supra—the longer, wider, more powerful Celica. See your Greater New York Toyota dealer today." After several repetitions of this, he winked at a bystander and added, "I'd like it, I'd drive it, but I wouldn't buy it." Evidently, Graig Nettles had decided to become more flamboyant.

Soon the diamond was all but empty except for short right field, where Reggie Jackson and Lou Piniella were doing wind sprints back and forth between the foul line and second base, while a man somewhere in the stands behind the dugout kept shouting remarks about Jackson's being a "hot dog" and there not being "enough mustard in the whole world to cover him." Watching Jackson run with muscular strides, I couldn't help agreeing that there was a touch of the show-off in him. He had a subtle way of calling attention to himself that made it difficult not to focus on him even when he was surrounded by the rest of the squad of over fifty men who were in camp at the moment. He had been the first of all the Yankees I had identified in the locker room that morning, and although his nearness to the door could probably be explained by his being the team player representative and therefore responsible for meeting Marvin Miller when he arrived, it had since crossed my mind that with an instinct for his audience as finely tuned as an opera diva's, Jackson had sensed the presence of new people in the clubhouse and was checking Tracy and me out.

He certainly seemed to command the wondering attention of his teammates. The morning's calisthenics session had been ten minutes old before Jackson joined it, loping along the right-field foul line with proud giant strides, like the great Cuban quarter-miler Alberto Juantorena after breasting the tape in victory. No doubt the reason for his tardiness was last-minute business with Marvin Miller. Still, it was an entrance you couldn't help noticing. And it was underlined by a palpable change of mood among the players, a sudden muting of wisecracks and restraint of horseplay, as Jackson lay down a little apart from the group and began a set of elaborate exercises that had nothing to do with what anyone else was doing.

Later, during batting practice, I saw him lecturing one of the younger players—the promising infielder Damaso Garcia—in loud and fluent Spanish. Garcia probably saw it as gracious and humble of Jackson to be offering him instructions, especially considering the difficulty of being a foreign-tongued rookie in an alien culture and the traditional aloofness, if not outright hostility, of veteran players. But if Jackson's intent had been merely to offer advice, he could easily have taken Garcia aside and spoken to him in undertones.

No, whatever Reggie Jackson did was dotted with exclamation points. Now he and Piniella had finished their wind sprints and were standing in front of the dugout about forty feet apart, playing bare-handed catch with what looked like a raw egg—to "soften the hands," Jackson shouted to someone in the stands. I tried to ignore him for a moment and take inventory of what else was going on. There was the hulk of a policeman nearby, vainly ordering some children to refrain from peeking over the rim of the dugout for a glimpse of the now-departed players. There was the bark of a TV crewman directing a small crowd to move about and cheer as Graig Nettles once again trotted home, slapped his Toyota Celica, and exhorted the cameras not to "go home without test-driving the new Supra. . . ." There was the screeching of seagulls overhead, drowned out at intervals by small aircraft buzzing in and out of a nearby airfield.

But not to pay attention to Reggie Jackson was like trying not to think about a hippopotamus for five minutes. Now the egg had broken in his hands and he was toweling himself off cheerfully to the triumphant chortles of Piniella. Now he was at the edge of the stands signing autographs and promising Edith Camp, the woman from *Town & Country*, that he would be right with her. Now he was sitting in the dugout, responding to Mrs. Camp's questions but directing his answers to everyone around him, which included me, Tracy, two other reporters, the policeman, Scavullo's two assistants, and Scavullo himself, who had hunkered down at the top of the dugout steps and started firing his camera, to Jackson's only too obvious pleasure.

. . . I work hard. I can drive what the fuck I want to drive. I drive a Rolls-Royce 'cause I've worked hard for that mother-fucker. All right? I don't want to brag just 'cause I've got a lot of money, 'cause I went out and bought a fucking Rolls Royce. I have never had a vacation in my life; I'm thirty-two years old. If somebody wants to work hard like I do, and work for seven or eight different companies, have seven or eight different jobs, then you might be able to drive a Rolls Royce too.

I thought of Joe DiMaggio and his quiet grace.

I did not spend the evening at a roadside tavern with my favorite Yankees, playing shuffleboard and downing a few beers. Driving back to our hotel in Hollywood, Tracy asked what I thought we should do with our evening. I suggested a visit to the jai alai fronton in Miami, for which I'd seen an ad in the morning paper. Great, he said, but shouldn't we make some attempt to get together with Sca-vullo and his crew? I suggested that we invite them along for dinner and jai alai. In fact, why didn't he call them when we got back to the hotel, and let me know? I'd wait for his call. Then I was going to go for a swim in the hotel pool.

As I was changing into swimming trunks, my phone rang. Sca-vullo's room wasn't answering, Tracy told me. Okay, I said. We'll try him later. Meantime, let's go for a swim. I'll meet you at the pool.

I put on a robe and a pair of rubber sandals, wrapped a bath towel around my neck, and set out through the hotel's corridors in what I guessed to be the direction of the pool. About halfway there, I noticed two small men approaching from the other direction. They were Scavullo's assistants.

"Hi," I greeted them.

"Hiiiiiii," said one of them with an exaggerated manner that puzzled me.

"Uh, do you guys have any plans for this evening?"

"Well, what did you have in mind?"

"We tried to call you . . ."

The second assistant was now nudging the one who had talked to me, and they were both backing away, obviously struggling to keep from bursting into laughter. Suddenly I saw myself through their eyes—my robe, my towel, my flipflops, my bare legs—and caught on.

They had not recognized me as the book's collaborator. They had taken me for an aging faggot on the prowl.

By the middle of the second day I felt so knotted up by my inability to make contact with the Yankees that my perceptions began to go askew. I was hanging around the auxiliary practice area located behind the left-field boundary of the little ballpark, watching various Yankees hit against the automatic pitching machines that were lined up there in a row of cages known as the alligator pit. A few feet away from me, just outside a batting cage, Willie Randolph, the star second baseman, was talking heatedly to Charlie Lau, the batting coach who had recently come over to the Yankees from the Kansas City Royals. Lau had become known for redeeming several mediocre Royal hitters by teaching them to swing down on the ball instead of uppercutting it, though it remained unclear whether this was really a superior batting technique or simply one that took advantage of the artificial pool table–hard surface of the Royals' ballpark. Since whatever Lau and Randolph were discussing seemed to involve the bat that Randolph was holding, I inched a little closer to them, hoping to eavesdrop on Lau's teaching methods. But as I got closer, I thought I heard Randolph saying, "I can't take it no more!" and Lau answering him, "I know, I know, but you've got to." I froze, convinced that I was intruding on a private conversation about some emotional problem Randolph was having. Panicking, I looked for something else to focus on, but could find no other excuse for being so close to them. Suddenly, Lau spun around and advanced on me. Groping for words to explain that I had thought they were talking about hitting techniques, I opened my mouth to speak. But Lau was already raising his hand as if to slap me.

I flinched.

Lau's hand held an unlighted cigarette.

He said, "Excuse me, sir. Can I bother you for a light?"

My hand was shaking so hard that when I fired up the jet I used as a pipe lighter, I burned away a third of his cigarette.

I was too unnerved to stay with them, so I made my way along the row of batting cages toward the auxiliary practice field that lay beyond. In the last cage, a tall, gray-haired man in a Yankee uniform was swinging at and missing pitches served up to him by the pitching machine, while several television cameras focused on his awkward efforts. As I drew closer, I recognized the man as David

Hartman and remembered reading in the morning paper that he was doing a series on spring training for his television show, "Good Morning, America." Hartman was now complaining to whoever was manning the pitching machine that he would never get "the hang of it." The man by the pitching machine, who was difficult to make out at first through several layers of fencing, was assuring Hartman that he was doing just fine and that he should keep on trying. "Just swing level and meet the ball."

The man held up another ball for Hartman to see and dropped it into the pitching machine. The television cameras whirred away. Hartman swung futilely as the ball came flying and plopped against the backdrop. "It's no use, Reggie," Hartman called out. "Keep your eye on the ball," said Jackson, for naturally it was he who had taken center stage of "Good Morning, America."

As I approached the practice field beyond, where some sort of base-running drill was going on, I noticed that off to one side a small crowd of people that included Tracy was gathered around a bench on which Bucky Dent, the shortstop, and Whitey Ford, the former pitching star who regularly coached at spring training, were sitting. While Dent seemed withdrawn (perhaps brooding on his contract problems), Ford was exchanging small talk with everyone who spoke to him.

It was just the sort of casual setup I had been looking for. Yet something froze my feet and kept me from joining the group. At the same time, I began to feel uncomfortable standing where I was. I was the only person alone on the entire field. I thought: people are wondering why I'm standing here stiffly alone while everyone else is either talking or doing something. My self-consciousness began to approach panic. I thought: I have to get hold of myself. I've got to find some perspective. What am I doing here? I'm supposed to be writing a book about baseball. Why me? Because I love baseball and can write a fairly decent paragraph. In fact, unless Red Smith or Roger Angell has shown up while I wasn't looking, I can probably write as good a paragraph of prose as anyone here. That's it, then. If Mickey Rivers is the best all-around baseball player in the immediate two-thousand-square-foot area, I might be the best all-around writer. So get busy and find something to write about.

I took a step in the direction of the Whitey Ford gathering. But my determination had also made me bite down harder on my pipe.

Because I had chewed away the part of the mouthpiece that would normally have formed a grip for my teeth, the pipe shot out of my mouth and went tumbling in the dust about three yards from my feet. Again I froze. I couldn't just leave it there, pretending it wasn't mine; it stood out as prominently in the dust as a freshly deposited turd. Trying to look casual, as if pipes were always flying out of my mouth, I bent over and retrieved it, dusted it off and stuck it back between my teeth, and looked around to see how many of the Yankees were laughing at me.

No one was paying the slightest attention.

That evening, the five of us—me, Tracy, Scavullo, and his two assistants, whose names turned out to be Sean Byrnes and Bill Calderaro—drove north along the coast to Vero Beach, the site of the Los Angeles Dodgers' training camp. On the way, we stopped for dinner at a seafood restaurant that Scavullo knew of from previous visits to Palm Beach. Over the meal we compared impressions of the Yankees. Tracy was still shaken over the experience he'd had asking Reggie Jackson for his autograph.

"It seemed like a good time. He was coming in from left field, walking along with a coach. A comptroller of my company—his son, actually—wanted Reggie's autograph. So I went up to him and said, 'Reggie, would you mind giving me your autograph on this piece of paper.' And he just *glaaaaared* at me, and—wooooh! He signed it, naturally. But I guess it was the wrong time."

"I got the impression the whole team's a little in awe of him," I said, recalling the silence that had fallen over calisthenics when Jackson had trotted out after his meeting with Marvin Miller.

"I asked Whitey Ford if that was so," Tracy said. "He told me, 'Bullshit.' "

"I annoyed Jackson too," Scavullo drawled in his flat, metallic voice. "I annoyed all of them. I like to take my first picture of them when they aren't looking. They hear the sound of the motor drive and turn to find out what it is. So the second shot always catches them looking annoyed or surprised. Then you get them trying to compose themselves. You get some fabulous shots that way."

"Thurman Munson got really mad," said Sean Byrnes. "When we were taking pictures of him, he yelled out, 'Hey, what is it today, the circus?' "

"I got the impression our very presence annoyed them," I put in.

"Well, it's really kind of a boring profession," said Scavullo. "I mean they're all about as good as they're going to be, y'know? So there's not much work or commitment to it, y'know? At least not in spring training. If I were a baseball player, I wouldn't be so happy to have creative people around."

I didn't believe that. But Scavullo's saying it made me feel a little better.

At nine the next morning, we presented ourselves at Dodgertown, the training base of the Los Angeles Dodgers. If the Yankees reminded me of basic training camp, then Dodgertown was a summer resort. I could feel the tension draining out of me even as Fred Claire, whose official title was vice-president in charge of public relations and promotions, invited us into his office for a preliminary briefing.

> There's no question but that we have, I think, the most picturesque camp. I mean when you see Holman Stadium, where there'll be an intrasquad game this afternoon, or walk over to the batting cages . . . [looking at Scavullo] because that's an incredible shot: all this wire and these arm-pitching machines. And there's a nine-hole golf course that's [gesturing] over there in that area, which makes for a rather remarkable setting itself in terms of these guys in there swinging their bat and maybe the golfers or at least the golf course in the background. So there are a lot of very picturesque places—we've got a strange area where the pitchers throw, tennis courts that are just adjacent to that, a swimming pool on back in this area—you know, just in terms of the whole flavor of what this is all about.

Claire was not exaggerating. Dodgertown was picturesque. True, there were parts of the place that were a bit overdone: the little streets named Koufax Lane and Robinson Alley, the globe lamps stitch-marked to resemble baseballs that were mounted in front of each office bungalow, and the swimming pool with black painted script spelling "Dodgertown" diagonally across its bottom (so that you knew where you were if you happened to be flying over it). But the place was a pleasure factory. Everything seemed designed to keep the players happy and, even more important perhaps, to show off their happiness to a happy public—everything from the sound of the Bee Gees' album *Saturday Night Fever* that throbbed out of loudspeakers during batting practice at Holman Stadium, to the lack of dugouts for the players to retreat into, which gave an illusion of their accessibility and eliminated the need for special police to keep the public at bay. "Actually, there are people here who are trained to handle any situation where a member of the public might approach a player while he was trying to catch a fly or otherwise bother a player," Fred Claire explained. "They're not in uniform, but they're around. But mostly it's a matter of trust. And that trust is helped, I think, by the atmosphere we've created here."

And if the Yankees were coldly aloof, the Dodgers were warmly gregarious. When Fred Claire finished briefing us and directed us to a field where all the Dodger players were doing calisthenics, we were greeted with cries of "Scavullo! Scavullo! Take my picture, Scavullo!" ("I guess they've seen me on the TV shows in L.A.," he said matter-of-factly as he prepared to begin shooting his camera.) Steve Garvey, the team's first baseman and cleanup hitter, sat up where he was exercising, ostentatiously pulled a comb from his pocket and went to work with it, calling out, "Hey, it's Francesco Scavullo. Make me beautiful, Scavullo." Tom Lasorda, the Dodger manager, broke from a huddle with his coaches, and said loudly, "Scav*ullo!*" savoring the Italianate sound of the name.

At the batting cage, during hitting practice, Johnny Oates, the warm-up catcher, turned around and warned me politely not to wrap my fingers around the frame and risk getting them crushed by a foul ball. Davey Lopes, the second baseman, upon overhearing Tracy and me discussing the Yankee camp, came up to us and asked how things were going "over there." When I said that the atmosphere seemed "tense, not at all like this place," he frowned and muttered, "Maybe that's our trouble—not being tense *enough!*"—a reference to the Yankees' win over the Dodgers in the previous fall's World Series. Steve Garvey actually came over and introduced himself, asked me what sort of book I was writing, and then made small talk for a while, mentioning along the way how difficult he found it to bring his family to Florida for the five weeks of spring training and create "a semblance of home" for his children.

And if Yankee manager Bob Lemon was a smiling sphinx, then Tom Lasorda was a one-man vaudeville show. I had read reams of newspaper copy describing the insufferable fervor with which Lasorda promoted the Dodger way of life: Dodger blue flowed through his veins and arteries, and he practically believed in a Big Dodger in the Sky. And indeed the pulpiteer in him was evident the moment we introduced ourselves.

"Your blue shirts are okay here," he greeted us, gesturing to those among us who were indeed wearing blue. "Those kids with red shirts over there have got to go. Hey, Fergy, Fergy, Fergy," he yelled at his catcher, Joe Ferguson, who was doing his exercises a little casually. "Fergy, just remember one thing. You're only cheating yourself when you cheat in these drills."

But nothing had prepared me for Lasorda's comic spirit, his boundless energy, and the considerable size of his hambone. "Hey, Lasorda, take it easy, man! Jesus," cried out pitcher Don Sutton with amused concern when his leader nearly hyperventilated laughing at a rather lame joke about the forty-year-old pinch-hitting specialist Vic Davalillo. "Ha, ha, ha, ha, ha, ha! Where did Davalillo go to get his physical? At the A. A.? Hah, haaaaaaaaaaaah! That's funny. Huuu, haaaaaaaaaaaaaaaaaaaah!"

"He's probably wired for that TV special," observed another player nearby (by which he meant that Lasorda was carrying a microphone on his person).

"Yeah, that's gotta be it," exclaimed Sutton. Then, affecting an elaborate air of innocence, he asked loudly, "Uh, is it going to be a Dodger special or a Tom Lasorda special?"

Moments later, when a reporter in the crowd around Lasorda asked if he had a minute for an interview, the manager heaved his rotund figure onto tiptoe, pointed a quivering finger at the sky, and lamented in a mock-tragic voice, "A minute away from this great team? Every minute I'm away from this team—that's sixty seconds of unhappiness I'm going through." "And *it's* going through?" I felt comfortable enough to ask. Lasorda's body deflated and his mobile face collapsed into a comic frown. "Well, I don't know about *that*," he muttered huskily, walking away with his shoulders sagging.

Coming back to the crowd around the Dodger bench after the interview was over, he spotted Scavullo training a camera at him.

"*Scavullo*. Ain't nothing better than an *Italian* photographer. What part of Italy are your folks from?"

"Potenza, which is north . . . it's near Calabria."

"Calabrese, huh? We're Abruzzese, man. You can go all over this country, you go all over the *world*, and never run into a bad Abruzzese. And you can check the jails all over the world. Never been an Abruzzese in jail."

"Never convicted, anyway," put in Tracy.

"Tell you this story about this Italian guy," said Lasorda. "He's going up to get his citizenship papers. So he brings all his Italian friends with him. They're all in the court. The judge says to him, 'Tony, I know how important this is for you, being an American citizen. I'm going to ask you three questions. If you answer them, you become an American citizen. First question is, How many states are there in the United States?' And Tony looks back at all his friends. He says, 'Judge, you've gotta fifty states in thesa United States.' And all his friends applauded, 'Yaaaay, Tony.' Judge says, 'Next one. Who was the first president of the United States?' Tony says, 'Judga, the firsta president of the United States was Georgea Washington.' And all his buddies go, 'Yaaay, Tony. Great!' Judge says, 'Final one. If you answer it correctly you become a citizen. I know how much this means to you. Who shot Abraham Lincoln?' Tony says, 'Judge, I don't know.' And everybody applauds, 'Yaaay, Tony!' Judge says, 'Wait a minute. I don't understand. The first president of the United States, George Washington; you guessed it right; they all applauded. I asked you how many states there are in the United States. Fifty. You were right. They all applauded. Ask you who shot Abraham Lincoln, you say 'I don't know' and they applaud. What's going on?' Tony says, 'Hey, Judge. Don't you know us Italians? We don't squeal!' "

And while answering interviewers' questions, recognizing and greeting old friends in the crowd of bystanders, and kibitzing with any Dodger brass that came around, Lasorda also managed to see and direct everything that was happening on the practice field, even to the point of asking a spectator in the stands please to throw back a foul ball that had landed there. Lasorda was a force of nature and an instant character. No wonder the Hollywood crowd had taken him to its bosom. He was the perfect interface between folk heroism and celebrity.

The Dodgers were even superior in their profanity. Where the Yankees' verbal landscape was a weedbed of "shits" and "fucks," the Dodgers cultivated an occasional attempt at wit. "Hey, Lasorda, how 'bout Dava*dildo*," shouted one player during calisthenics, substituting two *d*'s for two *l*'s in the maligned Davalillo's name and gleefully submitting the result for his boss's approval. "Who?" said

Lasorda. "Dava*dildo*," repeated the player. "Aha hah, Da-hah-hah-hah-va*dildo*! Aw*right*," exploded Lasorda. "Hey, *you* didn't think of that one. No way. That's too brilliant."

Best of all was the attention the Dodgers paid to us. Publicity man Fred Claire took me aside on the practice field and expounded on the history of Dodgertown.

> This was an air-naval training station, and those barracks housed the troops. They were built in 1945 or thereabouts. And then in 1948. . . . The Dodgers had trained in several places. But these barracks were here, and there was a man in Vero Beach by the name of Holman who really initiated the whole thing. They had these grounds, they had this facility, they had a small airstrip here; so he contacted the Dodgers and said, "Would you be interested in coming down here? We'll lease the grounds to you for . . ."—I don't know, a dollar a year? And the Dodgers came down.
>
> A lot of things that are here grew from the thoughts and principles of Branch Rickey, who said "We've got to have a stadium here. We've got to have the batting cages there. We've got to work better." He laid down the principles that we've been subscribing to for twenty-five years—how you trained, what works, the type of schedule that you work with. Other than refining, we're doing basically the same things that Dodger teams did twenty-five years ago. Branch Rickey said that "other teams might have better players, but we're going to work harder than any other team, and if we do, we will succeed more than most other teams. We may not have more talent, but we will work harder, scout harder, put in longer hours, work our players harder, build the right teams, give them the good food, give them the proper rest—and then we will win more than most teams." That was the philosophy that Branch Rickey created.

Tom Lasorda invited Tracy and me to watch the intrasquad game from the stands with him and his wife, Jo. During the game, he exhorted his troops, greeted various visitors, and reminisced to us about the 1978 World Series. "The turning point was when Nettles made those great plays." (In the third game, with the Dodgers ahead two games to none, Nettles had made four acrobatic plays at third base that allowed pitcher Ron Guidry to hold the Dodgers to one run despite giving up eight hits and seven walks. The momentum shifted, and the Yankees won four straight games.) "And there was Bucky Dent, that bastard." (Dent had led the Yankee attack with ten hits and was named Most Valuable Player.) Jo Lasorda talked about Scavullo. "I've got to go get his autograph. I have his books. What he does is not to believe! But just to have his advice would be heaven."

After the game, when we were down on the field, Al Campanis, the Dodger general manager (or vice-president, player personnel, as the media guide called him) was driven up in a golf cart and introduced to us. He immediately began a little lecture.

> I've been writing an article, "How to Observe a Baseball Game." You know that not many people know how to observe a baseball game? It's like football. They watch the ball all the time, but there're so many other intricate things. The guards pulling, the offensive and defensive maneuvers. Just to teach people how to observe a ballgame. What do you look at? Anticipate the manager's wants—what is he going to do? Second-guess the manager. You get people involved. And more women! I give a lot of clinics to college coaches. I go to Japan, Europe. And one of the things a lot of people don't know is the fundamentals of the game. When you should do things. There are various offensive plays: you can take, you can hit, you can hit and run, you can bunt, you can suicide squeeze, you can steal a base. A manager makes over two hundred decisions a ballgame. So this is an interesting game. Do you know how many different decisions a manager can make involving nine players? This'll astound you. It's in the hundreds of thousands.

I tried as best as I could to look astounded.

Hungry for any sort of attention after two days with the Yankees, I enjoyed the experience hugely. I even felt confident enough to conduct my first formal interview—with Andy Messersmith, a pitcher who had played for the Yankees the previous year and was now with the Dodgers. There was nothing to it. You just walked up to the player, asked if he would answer some questions, and stuck your microphone out.

LEHMANN-HAUPT: How does the Dodger camp compare with the Yankees?

MESSERSMITH: I don't know. It's a little different for a pitcher over here, 'cause you do more than just pitch. I mean over there it was just do your pitching and do your running. Here we got fielding, running, batting, that type of stuff. Bunting. Stuff we didn't do over there. I enjoy it more. Some guys do, some guys don't. I enjoy the extra work. Of course I've been here before. I've been here longer than I had been over there. I know most of the guys, so it's easier for me personally. It's easy to come in here. Over there it was . . . most of the guys didn't want me over there to begin with. I think, when they first heard about it, they thought, "What the fuck we doing with this guy."

LEHMANN-HAUPT: But they needed pitchers. Why would they take that attitude?

MESSERSMITH: Well, I don't think they felt like they needed pitchers. You know, the way last year's staff looked . . . the way it ended up they needed pitchers, but the way it started they sure didn't. They had ah . . . shoot, they had a lot of guys. They had Hunter, Holtzman, y'know the guys. They had about seven starters, and there you go, pick up . . . I could see, I can see their attitude. You know, you pick up a guy that's coming off an arm operation. You know, why? And, ah, it was a different attitude. You didn't fit in quite as . . . 'cause you didn't know the guys.

LEHMANN-HAUPT: Do you think anybody fits in over there?

MESSERSMITH: I think it takes a while. It's not something that happens right away over there, that's for sure.

LEHMANN-HAUPT: The atmosphere is so different over there. Everybody works harder here. There's less tension.

MESSERSMITH: I think so. I definitely feel that way. I've been in, let's see, this is four camps now, and this is by far the best camp I've ever been in. Everybody has different . . . you know, what turns them on, and this is a kind of camp that I enjoy. I like the extra work. When you're a little bit older you need the extra work. If you're twenty-five or something, or twenty-two, you just heat up and let it go. I'm thirty-three now, I'm coming off an injury and stuff, so the extra work is good. Over there I didn't get enough work to feel I was in the kind of shape I wanted to be in.

LEHMANN-HAUPT: How's it going so far this spring?

MESSERSMITH: Well, good.

LEHMANN-HAUPT: Coming around?

MESSERSMITH: Yeah, it's slow. But I feel pretty good about it.

When the training day was over, Jo Lasorda took us on a tour of what she called "the campus," and then to lunch in the Dodgers' private dining room. Moments after we sat down, Walter O'Malley in a wheelchair, and his equally senescent wife in what looked like a miniature hospital bed, were wheeled past us to an adjoining table. O'Malley in his late seventies was a far cry from the hard-driving New York lawyer who had taken over the Brooklyn Dodgers, moved them to California, and built them into one of the wealthiest franchises in baseball. But the O'Malleys were still held in awe. When we asked if Scavullo could take pictures, shock waves swept around the dining room and permission was firmly denied. Jo Lasorda looked sad and said she understood how disappointed we must be. It had meant so much to her when the O'Malleys' son Peter had allowed his seventy-one-year-old mother to pose in a group photograph of Dodger "girls." She even wore one of the T-shirts with Frank Sinatra's face that the singer had sent to his friends the Lasordas.

By the time we finally left Dodgertown, I felt euphoric. Steve Garvey had given us the names of his favorite restaurants around Vero Beach. Tom Lasorda had taken me aside and practically begged me to get Scavullo to send along any pictures of him and his wife. "I'd like to have one for the wall of my office," he confided to me. Fred Claire had invited me to Los Angeles. "Anybody who writes a baseball book should be at Dodger Stadium before they write the book."

I liked the Dodgers. I actually liked the Dodgers. Driving away from Dodgertown, I made up my mind to visit Los Angeles and Dodger Stadium. But how could this be? I *liked* the Los Angeles Dodgers? I *disliked* the New York Yankees??

Preoccupied with my confused feelings, I took a wrong turn at the exit from Dodgertown and found myself at the airstrip Fred Claire had referred to. Parked on it was the Dodgers' private jet, a Boeing 720B with the blue Dodger logo painted on its side. I got out of the car to take a closer look. These Dodgers were certainly different from the scruffy, plebeian team I had grown up rooting against. Those Dodgers would have had Willard Mullin's cartoon of a bum on the side of their private jet. Hell, those Dodgers wouldn't have had a jet if they had still been around. They would have traveled around the country in a flying boxcar.

It was an altogether different organization I had spent the day with, so maybe it was okay to like it a little. Well, not an *altogether* different organization. It was still owned by the O'Malley clan, whose patriarch Walter F. had uprooted baseball from Brooklyn. Even I, as a Yankee fan, could see the coldheartedness of *that* act. The Dodgers had prospered, and the symbol of that prosperity now lay before me. But the soul of baseball had been diminished and one had to resent the O'Malleys for doing it. All the same, the Dodgers had been warm and outgoing and eager to please. Most important, they had helped me to relax and take my first baby steps as a sports reporter. I had to be grateful to them for that.

But I still didn't have nearly the confidence I needed. And in the days that followed, with Tracy gone back to New York to attend to his regular business and Scavullo having cut short his tour for a previous commitment, I wandered around various other spring training camps in somewhat of a fog. At the New York Mets camp, in Saint Petersburg, I was told by manager Joe Torre to move back to the other side of a rope divider I'd absentmindedly crossed to get a closer look at a couple of pitchers warming up. "I'd just as soon your not being around the pitchers," Torre said. I didn't understand, but it was just as well because it gave me an excuse to leave. The Mets struck me as an absurd contradiction, a lovable people's team owned by a millionaire aristocrat. Somebody connected with the team had told me that when owner Lorinda Payson de Roulet arrived in Florida that spring she had stayed on her boat and given a cocktail party for the team at the yacht club where she was moored. Most of the players had looked awkward and miserable standing around in jackets and ties. To me that was the whole story of the Mets.

At the Philadelphia Phillies' playing field in Clearwater, I found myself standing in a narrow alley between a batting cage and the trailer that served as the Phillies' makeshift dressing room. While eavesdropping on a conversation between a reporter and the relief pitcher Tug McGraw, I became aware of a short, stocky, long-haired figure in uniform pants and a crimson sweat shirt who must have just slipped out of the dressing room and was now standing next to me surveying the scene around him. It was Pete Rose, the man of the hour thanks to the $3.8 million contract he had recently signed, and the one player everyone had assured me I would not even get close to because of the crowds of worshipping fans and curious reporters that were rumored to be following him everywhere.

There was no bell jar over Rose. If anything, he seemed a little hungry for conversation. Something about his manner made me feel that it would be positively unfeeling not to talk to him even though I was not prepared to do an interview, especially with such a luminary. I groped for a question.

"Excuse me, Mr. Rose."

"Pete."

"I beg your pardon?"

"Pete." He acted as if it was perfectly natural for me to be talking to him.

"Oh. Right. Ah, Pete . . . I'm writing a book about baseball and I wondered, did your signing with Philadelphia . . . that is, was the fact that you stand to break a lot of National League records have anything to do with your signing with the Phillies instead of an American League team?"

"All other things being equal it was. Kansas City was the only American League team in the final bidding for me, and since I preferred the Phillies anyway, I'm just as glad to have the chance to go after the records."

"Because I've always wondered how free agents could throw away the chance to break records."

"What free agents have done that? Name one."

"Well, Reggie Jackson, when . . ."

"Jackson has no chance of breaking any records. He's not even close to the top in what he does best, which is hit home runs. Look it up. I have a chance to break a couple of N. L. records and to finish high up in a couple of others. There hasn't been another free agent in that position."

"Well, I meant . . ."

What *did* I mean? I had lost track of what I was getting at. How did this interview end up here? How did reporters do it?

"I don't want to seem like an egomaniac," Rose continued, perhaps mistaking my silence for disapproval. "The records come second. My main concern has always been to play my best and help my team win. I think I've proved that."

He certainly had. Otherwise he wouldn't be known as "Charlie Hustle," which was exactly why I had asked the question in the first place. What I had been trying to say was that I could never understand how Reggie Jackson had been able to sit out a quarter of a season in Baltimore in 1975, when he might have been compiling records and helping his team to win. Any player's career was too brief for him to waste time, I had always thought. And I had wanted Rose to confirm that view. But I'd gone astray by putting the question wrong.

"Well, good luck with your book, " Rose said, assuming from my silence that the interview was over. Before I could open my mouth again, he had given me a farewell tap on the rump and disappeared back into the locker room.

In Orlando, where I went to watch an exhibition game between Boston and Detroit, not even an awesome hitting display by the Red Sox could focus my mind. I sat in the press box with the journalist J. Anthony Lukas, a friend from boarding school days, who was down from Boston to do a story on a rookie Red Sox catcher, Gary Allenson, for the *New York Times Magazine*. He introduced me to the unkempt bear of a man sitting next to him, George Kimball, who covered sports for an alternative weekly paper called the *Boston Phoenix*. Kimball had an odd way of looking at you, which, it took me a while to figure out, was the result of his having one glass eye. During the game he talked about a tirade he had just overheard delivered by the Red Sox's special batting instructor, the great Ted Williams, who seemed personally affronted by Charlie Lau's theory of hitting down on the ball. Williams reasoned that because of the height of the pitcher's mound, a ball thrown from there traveled downward as it approached the plate, so for a batter to swing down instead of up would seem to reduce his chances of making solid contact. According to Kimball, Williams was so incensed by the illogic of Lau's theory that he had taken to maligning Lau's character to anyone who would listen.

Lukas and I were longtime fellow Yankee fans: in 1949, the year of my first Yankee pennant, we had followed the September stretch drive on the only radio available at Putney, the school in Vermont we attended; it was located in the school's maintenance shop. Now he looked at me solemnly and shook his head. "Geez, Lehmann-Haupt, what a deal!" I felt even worse about my lack of confidence. He said he wished he had time to go see next Monday's exhibition game between the Yankees and the Dodgers, the first rematch of the previous year's World Series rivals.

That gave me an idea. Maybe I'd gotten confused about the Yankees and Dodgers because I'd stopped thinking of them as teams. Maybe seeing them play that game would put things back in perspective for me.

I felt a little better as I drove my rented car down the Gulf Coast and then east along Alligator Alley, the Everglades highway that cuts straight across the lower third of the Florida peninsula. I was headed for another Yankee-Dodger confrontation. It brought back memories of last fall—of Nettles flying left and right to deny the Dodgers maybe five or six runs; of Reggie Jackson stopping a thrown ball with his hip to rob the Dodgers of an out and turn the crucial fourth game in the Yankees' favor. I thought of other happy incidents in the rivalry—of Tommy Henrich's ninth-inning home run to win the first game of the Series in 1949, of Billy Martin's lunging catch of a pop-up to end the Series in 1952, of Don Larsen's perfect game in 1956, of Reggie Jackson's three home runs in 1977. I thought of the catastrophic moments too—of Sandy Amoros's lunging catch of Yogi Berra's drive to save the Dodgers' seventh-game win in 1955; of the bad-hop grounder hitting Tony Kubek in the neck and costing the Yankees the 1960 Series (no, that was against the Pittsburgh Pirates, not the Dodgers, but it still continued to gall me); of Joe Pepitone losing sight of Clete Boyer's throw to first, allowing the winning run to score in the last game in 1963. How could I have felt a moment's affection for the loathsome Dodgers?

But after my race from Saint Petersburg back to Fort Lauderdale, the exhibition game turned out to be a bore, with the Yankees producing three puny hits and Reggie Jackson getting picked off first base. Nothing happened to distract me from my memories of the Dodgers' warmth and the Yankees' chilliness. The play was so dull that up in the press box behind home plate, from where I watched, Red Smith and Steve Cady of the *Times* spent most of the game poring over the record of Ron Franklin, the young jockey who that morning had been retained to ride Spectacular Bid in the Kentucky Derby despite his horrendous handling of the three-year-old colt in the recent Gulf Stream Handicap. I introduced myself to Smith and Cady, knowing that I was going to have to give an awkward explanation for my presence.

"What are *you* doing here?" asked Red Smith

"I'm supposed to be writing a book about baseball," I offered.

"Who's going to review it?" he shot back with a deadpan look.

As I sat in the press box the gusts of wind from the field made the whole structure sway and tremble, which only added to the sense of insubstantiality I was already feeling. Toward the end of the game, Steve Cady glanced off to our right and muttered, "Steinbrenner and Rosen are looking kind of grim." I turned to where he was gazing and saw the owner and his chief executive sitting side by side in a small compartment on the same level as the press box. They looked unhappy all right, but they also glistened in their brightly colored tropical attire like newly minted money. After the final out of the game, I followed Cady and a small band of other reporters across the roof toward Steinbrenner's box, half hoping that maybe Rosen would introduce me to his boss. But he showed no sign of recognition as he stood in front of a closed door with his hands on his hips as if guarding Steinbrenner from us.

A reporter asked why Nick Buoniconti, the agent for shortstop Bucky Dent, had met Steinbrenner and Rosen that morning. Was Dent closer to signing? I had read in a newspaper that day Dent's announcement that if the Yankees didn't give him a new contract by the end of spring training he intended to become a free agent at the end of the season. "Dent has given an ultimatum," I piped up. Rosen looked at me with cold nonrecognition. "Come on," he said with contempt. "Ballplayers don't give ultimatums. Countries give ultimatums. Next question." All I had succeeded in doing was provide him with a diversion.

It was time to go home. As I passed through the gate near the clubhouse entrance, I looked at the fans waiting there in anticipation. They looked back at me blankly, as if I were an obstruction to the view. I remembered my elation when entering the stadium a week earlier, and I felt a flash of despair. I was still closer to them than I was to any of the heroes I was looking for.

On the plane back to New York, I browsed through a program of that afternoon's listless exhibition game. Once again the word *Beowulf* caught my eye. This time it was garnished with details. Beowulf was a restaurant on North Federal Highway, offering "the finest dining with. . . .Your Host: Chet Stumpo, Your Chef: Monroe—Featuring Scampi, Prime Rib & Steaks, Roast Duck, Fresh Fish, Stone Crabs, Barbecue Baby Ribs, Calves Liver, Original Salad Bar."

PLAYING

ON MY FORTY-FIFTH BIRTHDAY, June 14, 1979, three months after I'd flown home from Florida and over a third of the way into the regular baseball season, I found myself watching a game from the photographer's pen at Toronto's Exhibition Stadium. My Anglo-American publisher had decreed that for the sake of its affiliate north of the border, Canadian baseball should be represented in our book. So our little crew had journeyed forth again. Scavullo, knowing his way around baseball players by now, had brought only one assistant, Bill Calderaro. Tracy had come along too, but was spending this particular evening with the pianist Glenn Gould, a Toronto resident, hoping to persuade him to write a book. So now I was sitting in a section of the first-base dugout that had been partitioned off and assigned to photographers. I'd joined Scavullo and Calderaro there for company and to provide help in case they needed it with their heavy equipment. The three of us were watching a night game between Toronto's Blue Jays and the California Angels.

I couldn't imagine how this evening was going to fit into our book. But if my experience so far had taught me anything, it was to avoid anticipating where a given event might lead. Already the young season had produced surprises, both pleasant and unpleasant.

I'd gone to opening day at Yankee Stadium expecting something special. But the Yankees had played listlessly and lost to the Milwaukee Brewers. Because of an invasion of out-of-town reporters I was given only temporary press credentials, which banished me from the main press box to a seat in the grandstand and didn't allow me to visit the locker rooms. So I'd gone home feeling I'd wasted the whole afternoon.

Then, about three weeks later, after the Yankees had issued me a regular full-season press pass, I'd gone to a game expecting nothing more than to wander around and get the lay of the Stadium. It was a cool Friday night in May, and the California Angels had just beaten the Yanks, 4–1, partly because Reggie Jackson had lost a fly ball in the lights. In the visitors' locker room, while watching reporters crowd around the winning pitcher for the Angels, Jim Barr, I suddenly realized that I was standing alone next to Rod Carew, the perennial All-Star and batting champion. He had recently been traded to the Angels from the Minnesota Twins, who were either unwilling or unable to pay him what he wanted. Since he hadn't figured significantly in the game just completed, the reporters were allowing him to dress in solitude.

I felt strongly about Carew. I'd very much wanted him to sign with the Yankees. George Steinbrenner had been interested too, apparently, and if he and Carew had been able to agree to terms, Carew would have been traded to the Yanks instead of the Angels. But something had gotten fouled up in the negotiations. Steinbrenner had then gone public in his inimitable way and said of Carew that if he didn't want to play for the Yankees, then he didn't deserve "the privilege of being a Yankee." Carew had fired back at a press conference he held after signing with the Angels, calling Steinbrenner's remark "a downgrading thing to say. The players on all the teams in the majors are pros; they all do their best to provide entertainment for the fans. You can't take anything away from any club." Later, there had been a story in one of the tabloids claiming that Carew had been perfectly willing to sign with the Yankees. It was Steinbrenner who had put out the word that Carew didn't want to play in New York, because the Yankee owner didn't really want to pay what Carew was demanding.

I wanted to ask Carew about all this when I found myself alone with him by his locker. But once again I couldn't bring myself to speak. Perhaps it was his aloofness; unlike Pete Rose in Florida, he gave no hint that he was even aware that I was standing two feet from where he was dressing. Or maybe I was inhibited by the anger I felt at him for not signing with the Yankees. I could be a little unreasonable about such things: when I'd heard on the radio the previous September that the young star Lyman Bostock had been shot to death in Chicago by a deranged man who'd mistaken him for his wife's lover, my first thought had been, That's what he gets for signing with the Angels instead of the Yankees. Anyway, I couldn't think of what to ask Carew and I left the Angel locker room without saying a word to him. I was so annoyed at myself for this that I'd returned to Yankee Stadium the following Sunday afternoon armed with a list of questions I was determined to ask him, no matter what. After the game, I approached him again. He was standing in front of his locker, naked except for his jockstrap. Perhaps I only imagined it because of my discomfort over accosting someone who was undressed, but again, he seemed aloof. Even when I asked if he'd mind a few questions, he didn't so much as acknowledge my presence. Instead, he rummaged briefly in his locker, then did an about-face and walked away. But as he passed me, I thought I heard him mumble that he was going to "get" something. So I waited by his locker. Pretty soon, he returned and sat down on a stool with his back to me. But there was something about his attitude that suggested he was waiting for my questions. So I started in with elaborate politeness.

LEHMANN-HAUPT: I haven't had a chance to read your autobiography yet, so forgive me if I ask you anything that's covered in it. I just have a couple of small questions. First, what do you think of how Minnesota is doing now?

CAREW: I could care less. I'm really not concerned about them.

LEHMANN-HAUPT: Well, do you think the fact that they're in first place by four and a half games is a temporary thing? Or do you think they're a real threat?

CAREW: I don't think they're a threat.

LEHMANN-HAUPT: I became aware down at spring training of a dispute going on between Charlie Lau and Ted Williams over whether a batter should swing up or down at the ball.

CAREW: I don't know about that. Everybody's got his own way of doing it, and whichever way I feel is comfortable for myself, I do it.

LEHMANN-HAUPT: Are you aware of this dispute?

CAREW: No, I never . . .

LEHMANN-HAUPT: Williams apparently ridicules Lau for teaching hitters to swing down at the ball. He claims—

CAREW: Well, I don't want to get involved in that discussion. I'm not going to say anything that's going to incriminate me because I know how things come out in print. And I'm not going to get myself involved in that.

LEHMANN-HAUPT: Well, do you have a theory of your own about uppercutting or chopping down on the ball? I'm really not trying to trap you in a controversy. I just want an expert opinion.

CAREW: I don't have a theory on it. Some hitters do it each way. That's all I can say.

LEHMANN-HAUPT: I gather you feel there was something of a conspiracy on the part of the Yankees to make you look like the scapegoat in the—

CAREW: I really don't want to talk about that. As far as I'm concerned that's all over and done with. I have nothing more to say about it. It's a situation that's happened and it's over and done with, and I'm not going to keep putting wood on the fire.

LEHMANN-HAUPT: Okay. But maybe you can answer this for me. How come the Twins, or Calvin Griffith [their owner], didn't just go ahead and make the deal with the Yankees when they could have? After all, the Yankees were offering more in exchange for you than the Angels were.

CAREW: Well, let me tell you something. I'm not Calvin Griffith. I don't know how he thinks. I don't know what he was thinking about when he didn't go after it. I'm not trying to be difficult, but . . .

LEHMANN-HAUPT: Mr. Carew, you've got to realize that a book is a little different from the daily press where what you say appears in print the next day. A book takes a longer view of things. I'm really not trying to—

CAREW: What book?

LEHMANN-HAUPT: Beg pardon?

CAREW: What book?

LEHMANN-HAUPT: The book I'm writing. The reason I'm asking you these things.

CAREW: Well, as far as I'm concerned, the Yankee situation is over and done with. I don't want to get in between anything with Charlie Lau and Ted Williams. And I don't know what Calvin Griffith is thinking about. That's the way I feel.

LEHMANN-HAUPT: Okay. Thanks for your time.

Listening to the tape of the interview and reading over the transcript I made of it, I found all sorts of reasons to put the blame on myself for Carew's apparent surliness. It had been hostile to raise the subject of how his old team, the Minnesota Twins, were doing. Sure, I had a right to want to know how teams like the Twins and Baltimore Orioles continued to do well despite losing their stars to free agency, but the way my question came across, I was saying "If you're so great, Carew, then how come your old team is doing well without you?"

I blamed myself for trying to draw him into the Williams-Lau hitting controversy. It was true that in his book, *Carew*, which had just been published, he had gone on for fourteen pages about his theories of hitting and written that he had come up with batting stances for at least five different situations. He was also not exactly the retiring, noncontroversial diplomat he'd insisted on playing with me; he'd written about Reggie Jackson that "success has gone to his head" and that he had "no respect left for Calvin Griffith." But in his book, he'd had control of the context. Talking to a reporter, he didn't know what would be made of a controversial statement. So I couldn't really knock him for playing it close to the vest.

I blamed myself for treating him as if he were merchandise ("After all, the Yankees were offering more in exchange for you than the Angels were"). I blamed myself for failing to mention right off that I was interviewing him for a book. Look, I said to myself, you went into that interview with a chip on your shoulder. You were mad at Carew for not signing with the Yankees. You resented his aloof manner in the dressing room, even though you were imposing yourself on him while he was all but naked. You probably resent how much more money he makes than you. And you may even be jealous that he's published a book when you haven't.

In my defense, I argued that few other players seemed to mind being interviewed while dressing or undressing. Some even seemed to enjoy it. Reggie Jackson liked to wander around the locker room stark naked talking to strangers. In fact, one time when there were women reporters in the room, he'd remained without a stitch on for a full half-hour, though at least he'd had the modesty to pretend that he'd misplaced his underpants. (If I felt mildly awkward interviewing naked men, I found talking to them in the presence of women deeply disconcerting. As the season progressed, it became apparent that while most of the female reporters covering baseball were serious and professional about their jobs, a few of them—"peckercheckers," they were called—had other interests in mind. I was as uncomfortable with them around as I hope I would have been with male voyeurs in a women's locker room.)

As for my imposing on Rod Carew: the players had certain obligations too. Reporters didn't have it so easy, what with tight deadlines, too little space allotted for what they had to say, and subjects who were often suspicious, inarticulate, and oversensitive to criticism. And baseball writers were forced to stay too close to the subjects of their stories. On the road, they practically lived with the players. Under the circumstances, it took guts not to write the sort of puff pieces they used to do in the old days. I'd heard that when Leonard Schecter worked for the *New York Post* and started writing what really went on behind the scenes, he wound up being ostracized by everyone he came in contact with. That couldn't have been easy on him.

Professional baseball was completely dependent on the publicity that the press provided. Back in spring training, Thurman Munson had yelled at Scavullo when he was photographing him, "What is it today, the circus?" Well, a circus was exactly what baseball was, and the ballclubs knew it and even made the most of it. That was why they provided writers free entrance to the ballpark, their own dining room and bar with free food and liquor, a special place to watch the game from with little overhead heating units to keep them warm in cold weather, admission to the locker rooms to "bother" the players the way I'd bothered Carew, and a special room to write their stories in, with typewriters and telephones and teletype machines that told them what the other teams around the leagues were doing.

The smart players understood the importance of the press—people like Reggie Jackson and Pete Rose and Bill Lee, the zany Montreal pitcher known as "the Spaceman." Reggie Jackson talked; the press recorded; and Reggie got a candy bar named after him. The only reason people like Thurman Munson didn't talk to the press was because they knew they couldn't compete with the cannier, more articulate players. No, I might have mishandled Carew, but he needn't have been so surly.

On the other hand, he had half apologized for being so brusque ("I'm not trying to be difficult, but . . ."). Yet whichever one of us was at fault, the experience hadn't exactly given me more confidence in my interviewing technique. My shyness had even been harmful the evening before the game I was now watching in Toronto, which was the second of a three-game series. During the first game, I'd gone up to the Blue Jay press box and found Billy Martin, the former Yankee manager, sitting alone and watching the game. It had taken all my courage to approach him and ask what he was doing there. And when he said he was scouting for the Yankees, I'd thanked him and quickly left. What an opportunity I'd blown! I should have asked him *why* he was scouting this game. Could it be that with the Yankees doing as badly as they were, he was going to be reappointed as their manager in time for the upcoming Toronto series in New York? I should have asked him if I could sit with him and hear his reactions to the game as it was being played. He seemed friendly enough. He probably would have appreciated the company. No, he probably would have told me to shove off. But at least I should have tried. I should have said, "Mr. Martin, you are basically a field manager, and you're used to watching baseball from ground level. What can you tell about the Blue Jays from way up here in the press box?" Of course I may have had in the back of my mind the alarming frequency with which Billy Martin had punched people out. But at least I should have tried.

And the day before yesterday, when I approached Bill Lee in the Montreal Expo locker room to ask for an interview, I actually stuttered—I, who had never stuttered before in my life. "Mr. Lee, wou-wou-wou-wou-wou," I blustered—I'd had to toss my head as if to shake the word loose—"would it be possible for us to get together some time when you're in New York?"

Bill Lee had been friendly too. But still, you never knew. A few moments before the game I was watching now, I had been standing at my now-habitual spot behind the batting cage, absentmindedly watching the Blue Jay hitters take their final warm-up licks. Slowly it had dawned on me that the sports-jacketed figure standing close by and also watching batting practice was Tony Kubek, the former New York Yankee shortstop. I'd admired Kubek for his steady play on the great teams of the 1950s and 1960s. After his retirement in 1965, he had gone on to a television broadcasting career, doing wholesome and enthusiastic interviews with players and fans for Joe Garagiola's WNBC baseball announcing team. A quick look through the Blue Jay media guide revealed that Kubek was now an English-language announcer covering the Blue Jays for Canadian Broadcasting Company TV. But the image of Kubek that stood out in my mind was his play in the seventh game of the 1960 World Series. With the Yankees leading the Pittsburgh Pirates by two runs in the bottom of the eighth inning, and Gino Cimoli on first, Bill Virdon had hit a perfect double-play grounder to Kubek's position at shortstop. But the ball, deflected by a pebble or a rut, had bounced up and hit Kubek in the larynx. He'd been rushed to the hospital, while the Pirates scored five runs, enough to leave them tied at the bottom of the ninth, and to set up Bill Mazeroski's game-winning home run. So, prompted by the pool-table smoothness of the Blue Jays' artificial playing surface, I touched Kubek's elbow and asked him quietly, "What if you had been playing on this stuff?"

It seemed a reasonable question, even a moderately tactful one. It propelled us into the middle of things. It avoided the introduction "Er, Tony . . . ," which I disliked for its uninvited intimacy even though it was accepted practice among sportswriters to call athletes by their first names. It also steered me clear of my more habitual "Ah, Mr. Kubek . . . ," which I was beginning to find uncomfortably stiff.

True, the question touched on a sensitive spot in Kubek's life, since the bad-hop grounder not only had made him the goat of a dramatic Series, but also was supposed to have led to his early retirement, when, a few seasons later, a doctor had supposedly warned him that any aggravation of the injury could do him serious harm.

But the question also showed a knowledge of, and by implication a respect for, Kubek's history. Perhaps it even betrayed sympathy—at any rate Kubek could choose to see it that way.

From his point of view, the question offered unlimited possibilities: a sad shake of the head and a muttered, "Yeah, if only...," should he want to sidestep the whole can of worms; or a brief discourse, given his knowledge of the game and his ability to talk about it, on the advantages and drawbacks of artificial grass—its removal of an element of chance, perhaps ("Suppose that the Senators and the Giants had been playing on Astroturf in the 1924 World Series; think what a loss it would be to baseball lore if that ball hadn't hit a pebble and bounced over Freddie Lindstrom's head and allowed Washington and the great Walter Johnson to win"); or its contribution to the statistical symmetry of the game ("The beauty of baseball lies in its being a game of percentages; any improvement that enhances the game's predictability only serves to make it all the more beautiful").

But instead of taking advantage of the many openings I had offered when I asked, "What if you had played on this stuff?" Kubek looked at me and shouted, "HOW THE FUCK WOULD I KNOW! AND WHAT KIND OF QUESTION IS THAT!?" And then walked away.

All things considered, I seemed to lack a certain touch.

In contrast, on May 16, just three days after my painful interview with Rod Carew, something pleasant had happened. It had begun unpromisingly enough—a few hours before a night game with the Detroit Tigers, I'd approached Reggie Jackson in the Yankee locker room only to find him vigorously shaking his head even before I'd opened my mouth.

"Why are you shaking your head, Mr. Jackson?"

"Because you aren't a reporter. You're not here regularly. Which means you got to be writing a book. And I don't want to be in any more books."

"Why not?"

"Because I always get nailed in books. I don't want to get nailed again. I wish you all the luck in the world, okay? But I won't talk to you. Sorry."

After the game, I'd gone over to Jackson's locker, where he was dressing while being interviewed by a crowd of reporters. The Yanks

had won, beating Mark "The Bird" Fidrych, who was still struggling to recover from an arm injury. The Bird hadn't regained the
form that had made him such a sensation in his rookie season, 1976,
when he had won nineteen games. He'd thrown surprisingly hard
this evening, but he'd given up three two-run homers (two by Nettles and one by Chambliss) in the three and two-thirds innings that
he'd pitched. The reporters were asking Jackson, who'd walked and
struck out against the Bird, for his impressions of Fidrych's performance. I stuck in my own two bits—"Fidrych said he couldn't pitch
the ball low"—because I'd just listened in on an impromptu interview with Fidrych held in the corridor outside the Tigers' dressing
room and discovered an intense and worried young man who was a
far cry from the free spirit who only two seasons earlier had charmed
the baseball world with his enthusiasm and his amusing habit of literally talking to the ball he was about to pitch. In response to my
remark, Jackson gave me an impatient look and said:

> Bird pitched good. He threw the ball well. He threw his fast
> ball hard enough where it didn't really make a lot of difference.
> But his breaking ball hurt him. 'Cause he couldn't keep you off
> balance, y'know? He didn't have any of his breaking ball. And,
> y'know, you don't see a guy like him wild. Y'know, it's just un-
> usual. The guy hasn't pitched, that's all. He'll be all right.
> Ain't no big thing. He ought to be happy as a gay in the
> YMCA, way he threw tonight. Right?

Elated at having been spoken to by Jackson, I decided to leave
before he could somehow take it back. Walking a few feet ahead of
me was Joe Durso, the senior baseball reporter of the *New York
Times*, whom I'd once met years earlier. When I caught up with
him and reintroduced myself, he let out a happy cry, professing to
be thrilled that his paper's book critic had descended to the nether
world of sports. Whether or not he meant this sincerely—I'd once
written a less than wholly enthusiastic review of a book of his—
Durso proceeded to turn the evening into a kind of magic. He insisted I come with him to the reporters' lounge, where he ordered
me a drink and introduced me to everyone standing anywhere near
the bar, including Yankee president Al Rosen, manager Bob
Lemon, coach Yogi Berra, broadcasters Phil Rizzuto and Frank
Messer, and various reporters and minor Yankee officials. Everyone

appeared delighted to see Joe Durso, even people who must surely have seen him only earlier that evening. Al Rosen seemed once again the genial man who'd sat next to me on the plane to Florida. "I had the privilege of flying down to Florida with this fellow," he announced to the people around us. At the crest of the evening, I found myself staring over the rim of my glass at the oval countenance of Mel Allen, who'd made something of a comeback and was now the Yankees' cable TV announcer. Though I found it disconcerting to hear the sound of my own voice echoing the famous brass gong of his, I ventured a question. Did Mr. Allen by any chance recall that game of a long-ago Sunday afternoon in which Joe DiMaggio had hit three home runs against Bobby Feller and the Cleveland Indians—the game that happened to have made an instant and ardent baseball fan of me?

It's strange that you ask that, 'cause that's one of my favorite stories: how I became DiMaggio's batting coach. He had been in a slump. Sitting upstairs where I broadcast—this was before the teams sent people upstairs to watch the players from above, y'know—I noticed something about that famous stance of his, see? I remember saying to one of the people upstairs, "Have you noticed Joe's stance?" Anyway, what it all amounted to, without all the details: we were on the train going from Chicago to Cleveland. I went by his sleeping compartment, y'know; he was reading a book as I went by. I said, "Hiya, Joe, whatcha readin'?" It was some paperback. I've forgotten what, but it wasn't anything terribly deep. It wasn't *War and Peace*. But anyway, I was standin' in the doorway, and I was hoping he'd say, "Come on in," which he did. So I got talking with him about anything and everything but baseball, see. And all of a sudden I said, "Joe, have you deliberately changed your stance?"—like it was a *fait acompli*, everybody-knew-it type of thing. And he suddenly put the book down, looked up slowly, and said "Whatta y'mean?"
"Well," I said, "y'know, you always had that imaginary line that both toes would be touching," I said, "but lately, you've had that right foot pulled back away from the line." He said, "I have?" "Well," I said, "I asked a couple of the guys I work with, and they noticed it too."
Anyway, the old story is . . . course, that may not have had anything to do with it. Long as you can remove a mental block

of some type, a player *feels* that that was it. Anyway, the next day we're in Cleveland, he hit those three home runs. Put the toe back up there. This is true.

Later, when Durso went off to write his story of the evening's game, the people in the lounge seemed to drift away or turn back into strangers again. Still, the evening had lifted my spirits. I hadn't gotten there on my own, but at least I'd experienced a moment in the sun.

So I was learning to take things as they came. And I was beginning to relax a little. In fact, while waiting in the photographers' pen for the Blue Jay–Angel game to begin, a sudden urge actually to play in the game had come over me. Maybe it was the carnival atmosphere of the Toronto ballpark—according to the Jays' media guide, Exhibition Stadium had been built in 1974 on the fairgrounds of the 101-year-old Canadian National Exhibition, and right behind the grandstand was a full-scale amusement park.

Or maybe it was the lowliness of the Blue Jays, who were only four years old and hadn't yet grown out of last place. I'd noticed in my wanderings so far this season that the farther behind a team stood in the pennant race, the more relaxed was the atmosphere of the parks they played in. By comparison with Yankee Stadium, where you began to feel intimidated as soon as you climbed the subway stairs or steered your car off the Major Deegan Expressway, the Toronto ballpark was thoroughly easygoing. Here you could roam almost anywhere you wanted, encountering only an occasional, almost apologetic request to see your press credentials. Since the way to the photographers' coop led right through the visiting team's dugout, I'd actually had to walk between manager Jim Fregosi and one of his coaches as they were going over the Angels' lineup card for the game about to be played.

Or maybe it was my enticing proximity to the playing field. The first baseman was no more than a dozen feet away from where I was watching. Already, during infield practice, several badly thrown balls had skipped past him and bounced against the low fence that screened us from the playing field. There was a good chance that during the game a wild throw from shortstop or third would wind up in my hands. Then, Nolan Ryan was pitching for the California Angels tonight. Nolan Ryan, whose fastball had been nicknamed "Von Ryan's Express," was perhaps the hardest-throwing right-handed pitcher in the American League. At that point in his career he had already struck out over 2,700 batters—which made him eighth on the all-time list, and he was still only thirty-one years old, with a good chance of breaking Walter Johnson's record of 3,508. Some right-handed Blue Jay batter swinging late at Ryan's fastball would hit it right in my direction.

No ball had ever been hit toward me at a big-league game, but I'd never stopped expecting one. It was a game within the game, a chance to connect directly with the action on the field. Of course, everybody in the ballpark anticipated a ball coming his way—everyone, that is, except my father, who once, while keeping a business friend company at Yankee Stadium, had been hit on the head by a foul off the bat of Cleveland's Tito Francona. That ball had raised a big red bump on my father's forehead and lodged Francona's name forever after in his memory, where it shared a lonely compartment with Babe Ruth and May Lott.

Unlike my father, most fans carefully figured the chances of a ball's being hit their way, whether they were sitting in the bleachers, the box seats, the press box, or even the radio announcer's booth. They brought gloves and fishing nets to the ballpark. Trying to catch balls hit foul near the field-level seats, some fans even risked falling out of the stands, or actually jumped, chancing possible eviction from the ballpark. And now, up in Toronto, I was going to get my opportunity. Some right-handed batter was going to hit a Ryan pitch in my direction. True, it might be a grounder, but if it was, I wouldn't have to field it, thanks to the fence in front of me. That was just as well. Ground balls had always been a problem. Ground balls had a way of hopping errantly and mashing your kneecaps or lips. My brother Carl had once admitted to me that the real reason he had volunteered to play catcher for his grade school team was so he wouldn't have to field grounders. Being a catcher presented all sorts of other problems—like learning not to close your eyes when the batter swung or digging pitches out of the dirt when they came in low or throwing out base runners when they tried to steal, or even tossing the ball back to the pitcher accurately (this last Carl told me in the utmost confidence, since it seemed an embarrassing thing to have had a problem with)—but one thing was certain: he would never again have to plant himself in front of a malicious grounder.

Or the ball hit off Ryan's fastball would be a high hopper. That would be okay. High hoppers were the easiest to field, provided that you caught the ball at the top of its bounce. You only had to allow for topspin. But I was ready for that. Though I'd been slow to become a baseball fan, I'd played the game since childhood and flawlessly handled not a few high hoppers in my time.

But most likely the hit would be an uncomplicated line drive, since Ryan's fastball came in hard and straight with not much stuff on it. This was fine with me too. True, a ball hit that hard could sting when you caught it barehanded. But I'd had years of practice at pulling my hands back to soften the impact of the ball. There was nothing to it. Why, I'd seen old men in Florida reach out their withered claws and catch line drives without so much as a wince. Yes, it would be a line drive. Nolan Ryan would wind up and fire the ball with that deceptively easy motion of his. Some right-handed batter would swing late and send a hummer straight to the spot where I was sitting. I would see the ball leap off the bat and follow its flight through the artificially lit night air. Then I would catch it with a backward sweep of my hands and the momentum would carry my body into an unostentatious little pirouette, and I would hold it aloft to the cheers of the photographers in the pen with me and the barely perceptible nods of admiration from the players and coaches who would have leaned out of the dugout to see if the screaming liner had done any damage. Finally, after showing it to the woman photographer seated on my left and the policeman to my right, I would pocket it as a souvenir for my kids. As the game got under way, I was ready.

But the game was no contest. The Angels, bristling with good hitters despite the absence of Rod Carew, who was out with a wrist injury, were too much for the Blue Jays. By the end of two innings they had jumped to a seven-run lead, and Nolan Ryan was still too overpowering for anyone to be connecting solidly, even by swinging late. And then, as often happened even during my actual playing career, my mind began to wander. The climax of that career had been my senior year in high school, when I'd played first base for the Putney School baseball team. Once, during a practice game, I'd caught a throw from the shortstop that pulled me five feet off the bag toward home plate, and in a single motion I'd tagged the hitter out and thrown the ball home in time to nip a runner trying to score from third. In another practice game, when I'd been assigned to play shortstop, I'd broken to my left to cover second base just as the pitcher released a fastball, and arrived at the base exactly in time to catch a low line drive off the hitter's bat and tag out a sliding base stealer for an unassisted double play. Had there been a runner on second too, I'd have had a triple play. As it was, they'd cheered and called me Slats Marion.

But in regular season play that year, I'd hit only .250—four for sixteen—and two of those four hits had been bunt singles. From that point on things had gone downhill. In my freshman year at Swarthmore, having switched to pitching because I was stronger at throwing than hitting, I'd made the junior varsity team as fourth-string relief pitcher. But in the only game I'd gotten into I'd lost control of a fastball and thrown it over the top of the twelve-foot-high backstop. After that the only ball I'd played was softball and stickball. And lidball. In a dusty back room of a publishing house where I was working as a copy editor, my fellow drones and I had invented a game using a foot ruler as a bat, a wastepaper basket as a strike zone, and the paper lid of a soda cup as a ball. It was surprising how difficult it was to hit the Frisbeed lid with the flat of the ruler, and how satisfyingly the lid flew off when you whacked it accurately.

Or when all else failed, I dreamed about playing baseball. At various moments of the day—I might be shaving, or walking to the bus, or opening packages of books—a voice inside my head would suddenly start up, I'd move my lips in submissive synchronization, and out would come an adolescent dream of glory, starring the dreamer himself. "It's the last of the ninth, folks, with the visitors ahead 3–2. There're runners on second and third with two outs. The crowd is looking to the home-team dugout to see if. . . . And yes, folks! He's coming out! He's going to bat even after that catch in the last inning. His left arm is hanging at a funny angle as a result of that collision with the wall, I think, but he's carrying a bat in his right hand. They're going to pitch to him even though first base is open. I don't blame them; he's obviously hurting. Here comes the first pitch. He swings and lifts a soft liner down the first-base line. It's dropping, the ball is dropping fair! The tying run scores. Here comes the winning run! Incredible! He swung late, but he got enough of the ball to win the ballgame!"

Now as I stood dreaming in the photographers' pen up in Toronto, I heard the crack of the bat meeting the ball. And there it was; I could see it so clearly in the night air that I could practically calculate its rate of spin. I could hear it hum as it passed no more than six inches from my left ear. In the split second between its disappearance from my field of vision and its thumping against the dugout walls behind me, I calculated like a pool player the intriguing two-cushion possibilities. I was not surprised, then, when the ball reappeared to my left, bounced smartly off the top of the fence, smacked with an audible report the chin of the photographer to my left, and came to a quivering rest on her lap like an egg plopped onto aspic. From there she plucked it up, flipped it twice into the air like a pitcher waiting for the catcher's signal, and stuck it into her equipment bag—a souvenir to take home.

It had all been so much more comfortable on the evening of May 30, in front of the television set in my kitchen at home. The TV was very small—a Sony 5100, to be precise, with a screen that measured only five inches diagonally. The players were approximately three inches high, the playing field about twelve inches square; the ball was no bigger than a half grain of saccharin—I felt like Gulliver watching Lilliputians. Moreover, the game was being played between two teams I cared about: my own New York Yankees and the Brewers from Milwaukee, who, as in recent past seasons, were this year giving the Yankees some of their stiffest competition. And if the pauses in the game forced my mind to wander, my woolgathering, instead of distracting me from the game, only made it that much more enjoyable. And, as it happened, the game I was watching on my little TV produced one of the most dramatic pauses for woolgathering that I'd ever witnessed.

As a rule, I didn't much like watching baseball on television. I preferred to listen to games on the radio, which demanded only your ears and a small corner of your brain. You could do dozens of other things while listening, like washing a car or tying up a batch of trout flies or even painting the outside of a house—a feat I once accomplished on about eight weeks' worth of games, though naturally that was in the days when most of them were still played in the afternoon. Doing other things while you listened meant that you relieved whatever vestigial guilt you might be feeling about wasting the time it took to listen to a game. This was especially true if the Yankees lost, which always struck me as being a particular waste of time, since I wasn't the sort of fan who took pleasure from a game well played at any cost.

Television, by contrast, required the use of the eyes, and there wasn't a lot you could do without your eyes except talk on the telephone or eat. I couldn't afford the loss of my eyes for the block of time it took to watch the average baseball game. So over the years I'd worked out a routine that allowed me little glimpses at the TV set whenever a Yankee game was being broadcast.

For instance, as a person who read a lot, I'd become a prodigious tea drinker. To prepare myself a mug, I had to go from my study, at one end of the house, through the living and dining rooms to the kitchen, at the other end of the house. Upon entering the kitchen, I had to proceed along the length of a low partition that separated the cooking area from the rest of the room, then around the end of the partition, which happened to lie just opposite a counter on which the little Sony television sat, and up to the stove, where a kettle always stood waiting. When I reached the kettle, I'd lift it to see if it was full of water, and if it wasn't I'd pick it up, turn around, and fill it at the sink while looking out the window to see if there were any humans or animals passing by. Once I turned the flame on and tossed a tea bag into my mug, there wasn't much to do while waiting for the water to boil. It wasn't worth going back to my study for the interval, especially when part of the point of the tea run was to take a break from whatever I was doing there. So I had gotten into the habit of switching on the Sony as I rounded the partition. In the time it took the water to boil, I could catch up on any games or even familiar movies in progress. No time at all was wasted. That was how I got to the Sony on the evening of that unusual Yankee-Brewer game.

Filling the kettle at the sink, a little fuller than usual so it would take a little longer to boil, I looked over my shoulder at the tiny screen glowing greenly in the dark. It was Memorial Day, I realized belatedly. (Since I worked at home on a highly irregular schedule, I tended not to notice less significant holidays.) What a contrast to Memorial Days of the past, when shirt-sleeved crowds would watch doubleheaders that lasted all afternoon and into the early evening. But baseball was a night sport now, and apparently the club owners could no longer afford to give away two games for the price of one.

As I turned the flame on a little lower than necessary, Phil Rizzuto announced that it was the bottom of the eighth inning, with Milwaukee coming to bat. The Yankees were ahead, 2–0, on a two-run homer by Lou Piniella.

Good. The Brewers had been driving the Yankees crazy the past few seasons, especially at home in County Stadium. Better yet, the Yankees were beating Mike Caldwell, who always gave them trouble with a pitch that some suspected of being a spitball, which was cheating. Tommy John was coasting along on a three-hit shutout. Good. I sat down and watched John retire the first two hitters in the bottom of the eighth. Then I got up and turned the flame under the kettle even lower, and went back to the Sony again.

Tommy John's success tonight was especially pleasing. After leaving the Los Angeles Dodgers to become a free agent and sign with the Yankees, he had begun the current season by winning nine games in a row, easily the best start by any pitcher in the major leagues this year. But the last time out, starting against the Cleveland Indians, he had been knocked out of the game in the very first inning. His beautiful string had been broken. He had blamed his failure on an earlier rainfall that had left the pitcher's mound wet and slippery, and now his excuse seemed validated. To judge from the score this evening, he was back in form and using his tantalizing sinkerball to make the Brewers hit grounders for easy outs.

Good. Not only did I want to see a Yankee pitcher go 27– or 28–1 for the season, but I liked Tommy John. It was John who had provided that rare light moment at spring training, when he had jumped and clicked his heels together as he arrived for calisthenics, playing Peter Pan to Reggie Jackson's Prometheus. It was John who had sat in front of his locker at Yankee Stadium and explained to a group of reporters with disarming candor that the reason he was having such a good season was that twelve out of the fourteen American League ballparks used real grass, which slowed down the grounders that his sinkerballs produced and made it easier for the Yankee fielders to turn them into outs.

Besides, John's success was helping to put my baseball world back in order after the confusions of spring training. George Vecsey had laid it all out in a recent Sunday *Times.* It seemed that John was a devoted family man, a devout Christian, and a political conservative who happened to have lived for a time in Yorba Linda, California, the birthplace of Richard Nixon. None of this endeared him to me particularly, but it did seem to make him an ideal match for the straight-shooting Dodgers. Yet when John had grown concerned enough about his future to ask for a three-year contract when his two-year one had run out, the Dodgers had turned Scrooge-like, first by citing the injury to his arm as an excuse not to commit themselves too far into the future, and then, when John blew that argument sky-high with his twenty wins in 1977, by pointing to his advanced age of thirty-six. All of which would have been predictable had it involved almost any other team in baseball. But it seemed out of character for a team that placed such high value on its paternal beneficence.

Then when John had stubbornly played out his option year, entered the free-agent draft, and signed with the Yankees, the Dodgers had sulked, stopped speaking to John's wife, and taken his picture off the wall. "The more I tested them," said John, "the more I realized the Dodger image was all P.R." Besides, he claimed to like New York and the nonfamilial Yankees. For me it was all proof that my deeper instincts might be sound after all, and that I'd been taken in by superficialities during my brief flirtation with the Dodgers.

But I'd hardly had a moment to savor John's success against the Brewers that evening, when Jim Wohlford, their left fielder, singled, catcher Charlie Moore worked John for a base on balls, and Robin Yount, the shortstop, dribbled a single through the left side of the Yankee infield, sending Wohlford home to bring the Brewers within one and moving Moore to third with the potential tying run. Phil Rizzuto now revealed that John had not been all that sharp that evening, having earlier given up a couple of huge fly balls to Sixto Lezcano and Cecil Cooper that only the speed of center fielder Mickey Rivers had prevented from becoming extra-base hits. So manager Lemon was now walking to the mound and signaling for a relief pitcher to face Sal Bando, the hard-hitting Brewer captain and third baseman who was one of the more prominent veterans around the major leagues of that great Oakland A's team that had been built and then disbanded by the mercurial Charles O. Finley.

The kettle was beginning to hiss, but the game was too tense to abandon now. So I decided to let the water come to a whistling boil, even though it meant that my tea would be too hot to drink right away. The problem was that the Yankees had been virtually without relief pitching ever since their bullpen ace, Goose Gossage, had gotten into a locker-room scuffle with Cliff Johnson late in April and torn a ligament in the thumb of his pitching hand. As I'd witnessed down in Florida, Big Cliff was fond of bear-hugging people and roughhousing with them, and what had started with Gossage's playful needling of Johnson had quickly escalated into a major fistfight. Gossage's absence had ignited a firecracker chain of disasters, among them three sickening late-inning losses to the lowly Seattle Mariners, the panicky switching to the bullpen of such valuable starters as Ron Guidry and Tommy John himself, and the banishment to the Chicago Cubs of the once-reliable but recently shaky Dick "Meat" Tidrow, in exchange for an even more erratic pitcher named Ray Burris. With the breakdown of the bullpen, only John's extraordinary string of victories had kept the Yankees in the pennant race, just five games behind the first-place Baltimore Orioles when this evening's game with the Brewers began.

In fact it was Ray Burris who had come in to replace the departed John and was now taking his warm-up pitches. The kettle was whistling loudly, as if blowing steam to take the pressure off the Yankees' situation. But Sal Bando cracked a bad-hop grounder to third, which Graig Nettles fielded with a diving stab and converted into what for him was a routine acrobatic out. The Yanks were out of trouble for the moment, still ahead by a score of 2–1.

It was eleven o'clock now. The water was boiling irritably. With a full inning to go in the game, I could return to my study and read for ten minutes and then come back to catch the final outs of the game. But there was still a fresh wedge of lemon to slice, two saccharin tablets to deposit in my mug, and the boiling water to pour—tasks that would neatly fill the time of the between-innings commercial break. And then it would take at least a couple of batters for the overheated water to get cool enough to drink.

I paced the preparation of my tea to fill the time of the commercials. I put the mug beside the Sony. The Yanks went down without doing anything in the top of the ninth. Phil Rizzuto and Bill White discussed how the Brewers had been complaining to the umpires that Tommy John had been throwing spitballs. This was a switch. Normally when Mike Caldwell pitched against the Yankees, most of the discussion focused on whether *he* was wetting his pitches.

Did Tommy John and Mike Caldwell actually throw spitballs?

The tricky pitch, produced by dampening part of the ball with saliva, sweat, or grease so that it left the pitcher's hand with an extra amount of spin, had been outlawed back in 1920, partly because its unpredictability made it dangerous, but mostly because it tipped the balance of the game too much in the defense's favor. The spitter produced low-scoring pitchers' duels, which seemed undesirable at a time when, in the wake of the infamous Black Sox Scandal of 1919—when several Chicago White Sox players conspired to throw the World Series to the Cincinnati Redlegs—baseball was trying to get back in the public's good graces. When the spitter was outlawed, an exception was made for seventeen pitchers who depended on it for their livelihood—among others, Jack Quinn of the Yankees, Phil Douglas of the New York Giants, Burleigh Grimes and Clarence Mitchell of the Brooklyn Dodgers, Bill "Spittin' Bill" Doak and Marv Goodwin of the Cardinals, Doc Ayers and the original Dutch Leonard (Hubert Benjamin, not Emil John) of the Tigers, Ray Caldwell and Stan Coveleski of the Indians, Urban Shocker and Allen Sothoron of the St. Louis Browns, and Urban "Red" Faber of the Chicago White Sox—but no one else was allowed to throw them, and the shrewdness of the decision appeared to be confirmed when baseball entered what would be known as the Babe Ruth Era, or the age of the home run. But doubts remained about whether the pitch hadn't survived like an underground stream that bubbles to the surface here and there. Was it still in secret use, as managers and frustrated hitters were forever claiming, particularly about such successful sinkerball pitchers as San Diego's Gaylord Perry or the Yankees' Tommy John?

I hadn't had the temerity to ask John about the pitch. But then, I knew its effectiveness firsthand. Once, about the time my brother Carl had taken up his new position of catcher, I'd been pitching to him in the little park next to our apartment. Tickled by curiosity, I'd licked the inside of my first two fingers and thrown what would normally have been a modest fastball. The pitch headed high and slightly to my brother's left, making him rise from his crouch and reach up with his glove. Suddenly the ball performed a most remarkable dip, illustrating the cliché about falling off a table—and it smacked him smartly on the knee. Cursing and weeping, he made me vow never to throw such a thing at him again.

I'd thought of that pitch when I read *Whitey and Mickey: An*

Autobiography of the Yankee Years, a rollicking memoir that Joe Durso had helped Ford and Mantle put together. In one chapter, Ford recalled how just before the 1961 All-Star game in San Francisco, Horace Stoneham, the owner of the San Francisco Giants, had bet the two-hundred-dollar tab that Mantle and Ford had run up at Stoneham's golf club. Stoneham wagered that Ford would not be able to get Willie Mays out if he happened to pitch against him in the game the following day.

"Sure enough," Ford recalled for Joe Durso's tape recorder, "the next afternoon in Candlestick, there I am starting the All-Star game for the American League, with Warren Spahn pitching for the National. Willie's batting cleanup, and in the first inning I got the first two guys out, but then Roberto Clemente clipped me for a double—and then comes Willie.

"Well, I got two strikes on him somehow, and now the money's on the line because I might not get to throw to him again.

"So I did the only smart thing under the circumstances: I loaded up the ball real good. You know, I never threw the spitter—well, maybe once or twice when I needed to get a guy out really bad. And sometimes, Elston [Howard, the Yankee catcher] would help out by rubbing the ball against his shin guards and putting a nice big gouge in it, things like that. But this time, I gave it the old saliva treatment myself and then I threw Willie the biggest spitball you ever saw.

"It started out almost at his chest and then it just broke down to the left, like dying when it got to the plate and dropping straight down without any spin. Willie just leaned into it a little and then stared at the ball while it snapped the hell out of sight, and the umpire shot up his right hand for strike three.

"Okay, so I struck out Willie Mays. But to this day, people are probably still wondering why Mickey came running in from center field now that the inning was over, clapping his hands over his head and jumping up in the air like we'd just won the World Series—and here it was only the end of the first inning of the All-Star game, and he was going crazy all the way into the dugout. It was a money pitch, that's why, and we'd just saved ourselves four hundred dollars."

That cleared up any remaining doubts about illegal pitches still being in use. And just in case we thought that he'd only thrown spitters in exhibition games, Ford went on to describe how he had

82

doctored the ball occasionally in regular-season games too, especially near the end of his career. And so had other pitchers, like Pedro Ramos and Eddie Lopat, although, Ford added, it was just as useful to have the reputation of being a spitballer as it was actually to be one, because it gave the hitter one more thing to worry about.

Recalling Ford's confession, I found myself wondering if a spitball would have made any difference to my own truncated pitching career. In my kitchen, I practiced my old windup, trying to throw the crumpled tea bag wrapper into the little scrap container beside the sink. I missed. On the television screen, the Brewers were coming to bat for their final licks.

Cecil Cooper, the power-hitting first baseman, led off the bottom of the ninth by striking out. But Dick Davis, the designated hitter, lined a single and went to second when a hard grounder hit by shortstop Sixto Lezcano took a slight bad hop and caused the usually infallible Graig Nettles to muff it. I sank into the chair by the television as Paul Molitor hit a grounder that bounced beyond the grasp of a diving Nettles, then ricocheted off the glove of shortstop Bucky Dent and came to rest too far from anyone to stop Dick Davis from racing home with the tying run.

Damn. That meant extra innings at best, and at worst a loss for the Yankees. That was also it for the as-ever-unreliable Ray Burris, though he could hardly be blamed for the piddling hits that had now cost Tommy John the chance for his tenth win of the young season. It looked as if Ron Davis were being waved in from the bullpen. This was food for more unhappy thought. Ron Davis was the remnant of what in the fullness of time had turned out to be perhaps the worst trade the Yankees had ever made, far surpassing in bad judgment the deal they had worked in 1948, paying a lot of cash to the St. Louis Browns for a pitcher named Fred Sanford, who became ever after known as "the hundred-thousand-dollar lemon."

The Ron Davis deal, as I liked to call it, had seemed promising when it was first announced, on June 1, 1976. The Yanks had given the Baltimore Orioles four pitchers and a catcher. The pitchers had all seemed obscure except for Rudy May, who had not performed too impressively since coming to the Yankees from the California Angels two seasons earlier. The catcher, understandably, had not been able to displace Thurman Munson in the Yanks' starting lineup. In exchange, the Orioles had given the Yanks a better-known catcher, Elrod Hendricks, plus four pitchers, one of them no less than Ken Holtzman, a starter and twenty-game winner for the Oakland A's during their glory days in the early 1970s. Good deal, or so it seemed at first glance.

But as time went by, three of the obscure players who went to Baltimore turned out to be Scott McGregor, now an ace for the best pitching staff in the American League; Tippy Martinez, part of baseball's most reliable bullpen; and Rick Dempsey, the O's solid starting catcher. And Rudy May had been shipped to the Montreal Expos as part of a deal that brought Baltimore Don Stanhouse, another top reliever, and Gary Roenicke, one of the team's better reserve outfielders.

Meanwhile, the players the Yanks had gotten in return might have helped them a little to the 1976 pennant, but later they had drifted away through free agency and retirement until none of them was left except an unhappy Ken Holtzman, who, after being allowed to rust for two years, was finally shipped off to the Chicago Cubs in exchange for Ron Davis, the lanky, bespectacled pitcher who was even now throwing his warm-up pitches from the anthill of a mound on my little television set. And Ron Davis, the sole return for a vital part of the Baltimore team that was at present leading the Yankees' division by two and a half games, had until very recently paid the most minuscule of dividends.

But two nights earlier, Davis had come in to stop the Brewers long enough for Mickey Rivers to win the game with a home run in the tenth inning. And now, just as I was about to give up on the game, he threw a pitch that the muscular Gorman Thomas, swinging heftily, grounded into a snappy inning-ending double play.

Tie score. Extra innings. Relief. But now I had to decide whether I was going to give up working for the evening. The arguments against watching the rest of the game were overwhelming. It was only a little after midnight—if I forgot about the Yankees and went back to work, I could get in two more solid hours of reading. If on the other hand, I stayed to watch the game, I not only would in all likelihood waste the rest of the evening, but I'd be tempted to switch from drinking tea to sipping Scotch whiskey, which would leave me not quite so bright and sunny in the morning. Moreover, if I stayed to watch and the Yankees blew the game, as they were likely to do given both the disadvantages of being the visiting team in an extra-inning game and the wretched state of their bullpen, I would be left with the feeling that I'd wasted a couple of hours for nothing.

By the time I was finished weighing my decision, the commercial break was over and Phil Rizzuto was explaining how the previous weekend his friend Yogi Berra had pulled a muscle in his back while reading the newspaper. As I emptied my cup of tea into the sink and fixed myself a Scotch on the rocks with a dash of water, I thought about how one might accomplish Yogi's feat. Well, yes, if one were to try to extract the sports section from the Sunday *Times* while leaning at the wrong angle, one could easily do damage to the lumbar region. When I returned to my seat by the television, the Yankees went down in the top of the tenth—one, two, three.

But to my surprise, Ron Davis in the bottom of the tenth retired the Brewers just as quickly, on three brisk ground balls. Shades of Tommy John, who was probably showered and dressed by now and watching the game in the clubhouse. Then, in the top of the eleventh, Bob McClure came in to pitch for Milwaukee—we were rid of Mike Caldwell at last—and promptly got into trouble. First Nettles singled, atoning for his earlier error. Then big Cliff Johnson worked McClure to a three-and-two count and drew a walk, moving Nettles over to second, to scoring position. Then Chris Chambliss beat out a bunt, moving Johnson to second and Nettles to third, from where he scored when Juan Beniquez lofted a fly to right. The Yanks were up by one, with Johnson on third, Chambliss on second, and still only one out. Thinking of the cigar that general manager Red Auerbach lit up whenever his Boston Celtics basketball team clinched another victory, I added a celebratory half-inch of Scotch to my glass and settled back in my chair to watch the Yankees apply the coup de grâce.

But then something frightening happened. It began when Bucky Dent hit a lazy fly ball to left-center field. The TV zoomed in on the Brewer left fielder, Ben Ogilvie, catching the ball and unleashing his throw toward home to catch Cliff Johnson, who would be tagging up from third. Another camera view showed that Ogilvie's throw would be too late and inaccurate to catch Johnson, who, as yet a third camera now revealed, was highballing home with the second run of the inning. Big Cliff, with his bulging thighs and his Chinese warlord face, was looking out toward the field to see if the throw would arrive soon enough to force him to slide. But Ogilvie's throw was so late that not only did Johnson decide to cross home plate standing up but he was also veering to his right so that he could round the plate in a leftward curve and head for the dugout without breaking his huge stride. This put his path on a collision course with the home-plate umpire, who was crouched by the plate and staring down in case of a close play at home . . .

Omygod! Let's see that again! And no sooner had I asked but they were running a slow-motion replay, and again Johnson was galumphing home—there must have been 220 pounds of him barreling along—and again the little umpire was rising out of his crouch just in time to catch the full force of Big Cliff's careering body head on. It was an irresistible force meeting a rag doll. In slow motion, the two of them seemed to embrace for an instant, then the umpire flew away onto his back, his head jerking back and hitting the ground hard while the rest of him landed loosely and just lay there . . .

. . . and was still lying there when the replay ended. Lying there very still. The other umpires were gathered around him now, and the team trainers, and some of the players. Reggie Jackson was joining the group with a warm-up jacket dangling from his hand. Phil Rizzuto was explaining that they were folding it up to use as a pillow for the fallen umpire; Lou DiMuro was his name. Lou DiMuro had not even twitched.

More replays from more angles. Big Cliff had been hurt slightly too. Stumbling to his left after the impact, he arose groggily with his left elbow cradled in his right hand. I remembered the time nearly fifteen years before when I'd seen on television the collision between Yankee shortstop Ruben Amaro and outfielder Tom Tresh under a pop fly to shallow left field. Amaro had torn up his knee so badly he couldn't play for the rest of the season. I recalled listening to the game in the spring of 1957 when Gil McDougald, the Yankee third baseman with the odd batting stance, hit a line drive that struck the face of Cleveland's Herb Score, shattering his cheekbone, endangering his eyesight, and effectively ending his career, since Score was never the same pitcher again. Then there was "Pistol Pete" Reiser of the Brooklyn Dodgers, who ran into so many outfield walls and got hit by so many pitches that eventually what many thought was the most natural talent in the history of baseball was reduced to an empty husk. And of course there was the most famous accident in baseball history and the only on-field fatality that I could think of: the incident on August 17, 1920, in which submarine-ball pitcher Carl Mays of the New York Yankees had hit on the head and killed Ray Chapman of the Cleveland Indians. According to a newspaper account I'd once read, the ball hit Chapman's head so hard that the report of the impact led the spectators to think the ball had struck his bat. Mays, under the same impression, fielded the ball after it caromed halfway back to the mound, and threw it to first to put Chapman out.

They kept saying that baseball was a game of inches, but they were referring to the margins between fair balls and fouls or hits and outs, not to the delicate line between wholeness and injury. Lou DiMuro lying there so still—the announcers were speculating now that his neck might be broken—was an example of what could happen when the game's delicate symmetry was upset. Perhaps it was even an added attraction that baseball contained such potential for violence and injury. They talked about football and basketball being contact sports, but where in those games was there anything like the danger of a thrown or batted baseball? It had never failed to amuse me the way people referred to a routine line drive. There was no such thing as a routine line drive. To stop with your hand a ball traveling over ninety miles an hour was a miracle of skill and timing, even if your hand was protected by a padding of leather. The entire ballet of baseball was a kind of miracle, and for a moment it had broken down.

But why had it done so tonight? Was it simply an accident? You couldn't fault Cliff Johnson for watching the throw from the outfield or for not bothering to slide when he saw that it had no chance of beating him or even for veering as he approached the plate; he was still well within the basepath. Nor could you blame DiMuro for placing himself to get a good view in case there was a close play at home plate. So it had to be coincidence that they collided.

But then why was Johnson involved in so many accidents? I recalled now that it had been Johnson who at spring training the previous year had misthrown the ball on a play at first base that led to pitcher Andy Messersmith's being injured and put out for the season. It was Johnson who on opening day at the Stadium had broken his bat swinging at a pitch and sent a fragment of it flying into the crowd, where it did enough harm to a spectator to require medical attention. And of course it was Big Cliff who had brawled with Goose Gossage, which was why this game was now in extra innings, you could argue, and why DiMuro was lying there now as still as a corpse.

There was something about Cliff Johnson that made him unaware of the space he occupied in the world. Sidney Zion, my lawyer-reporter friend, had overheard Johnson boasting at a bar in Fort Lauderdale one night that he was really the team's best catcher and that it would be only a matter of time before he would be promoted to first string. This was absurd, considering that Thurman Munson was one of the two or three best catchers in all of baseball. And only a few nights earlier Phil Rizzuto had been saying on the radio that Johnson had recently told him he was probably the team's best bunter, a claim that was instantly cast into doubt when Johnson, even as Rizzuto was talking, managed to foul off three straight pitches in a hapless attempt to bunt a runner to second.

With a little help from the Scotch I was drinking, I began to feel stirrings of distaste for Cliff Johnson, or Heathcliff, as his teammates called him, though he bore scant resemblance to the demonic hero of *Wuthering Heights*. My discomfort went back to spring training, when Johnson had given so little of himself to the woman who had asked how he cared for his glove. The man was simply out of tune with himself. Could it be that he was also unstringing the Yankees? Maybe they were doomed to lose as long as he was around.

On the little television screen, a camera high in the stands picked up the headlights of an ambulance on a highway approaching Milwaukee's County Stadium. Odd not to have one available at the ballpark. After another volley of ads, the ambulance emerged from a runway inside the park and made its way to where DiMuro was lying. With the help of white-coated attendants, the other umpires lifted his still figure onto a stretcher, raised him to the level of their shoulders and eased him into the dark interior of the van. There was still no word on how badly he was hurt, though reports had filtered up to the broadcast booth that he was conscious and feeling numbness in his legs. The doors of the ambulance closed, the vehicle crept away and disappeared through a gateway in the outfield, and soon the television picked up the sound of a siren wailing and the sight of flashing lights rushing away in the distance outside the stadium.

Feeling sobered, I watched the Brewers trot back out to their positions on the field. How could they put their hearts into baseball now? Rizzuto announced that thirty-two minutes had elapsed since the collision, but it seemed like a day. The show had to go on, but the action seemed anticlimactic, and I was not much moved when the Yankees scored a fifth run on a double by Mickey Rivers, or when relief pitcher Ron Davis put the Brewers away for good on three ground balls in the bottom of the eleventh. What if DiMuro had broken his neck?

But when I turned the Sony off and sat in the dark of the kitchen watching the dot of light at the center of the screen fade away, a rush of warmth came over me. DiMuro's back might be broken, but I couldn't deny that the Yankees had won an important game. They had beaten one of their strongest rivals on its home ground. What was more, they might have solved their relief-pitching problem. In fact, the Yankees might have turned a corner tonight. It could well have been the beginning of the push to first place that I'd been waiting for all season. Even if it wasn't—even if they could only hold their present position, as now seemed possible with the emergence of Ron Davis—then it would be only a matter of time before Goose Gossage was back. Then let the rest of the league beware.

In fact it had, on balance, been a successful evening, except of course for Lou DiMuro, who, a phone call to Sportsphone now revealed, was resting comfortably at Mount Sinai Medical Center, awaiting the results of X rays. I'd made a wise investment of my time after all. It was one o'clock in the morning—time to go to bed and sleep the sleep of winners.

It was not as simple to put an end to the evening in Toronto. By the seventh inning, the game was lopsided in favor of the California Angels, and I found it impossible to take any interest in the action. Scavullo had all the pictures he needed. But how to get away? The only way out was through the exit at the far end of the dugout, which could be reached only by stepping out on the field and walking the full length of the Angel bench in front of dozens of players and tens of thousands of spectators. Not only was the stroll an embarrassing prospect, it was also illegal since American League rules held that no nonplayer was allowed on the field while play was in progress. But another of the photographers assured us that so long as one waited until the teams were changing field positions at the end of the half-inning, no one ever seemed to mind. So when Toronto had made its third out of the current inning and the Angel fielders had returned to the dugout, we set out single file, Scavullo, Bill Calderaro, and I.

The journey was more or less uneventful. Halfway to my destination, I passed the Angel second baseman, Bobby Grich, another free agent who had spurned the Yankees. He was leaning against the top of the dugout, handing a folded piece of paper to an usher and telling him to "give this to those two blondes up there in Section Eleven." And just as I was about to step into the exit, I heard somebody ask, "Hey, who's the civilian?" But once inside the runway, I began to relax a little. In fact, I couldn't resist stopping there and looking back. Out at home plate, the Blue Jay catcher was tossing back a warm-up pitch, and the first Angel batter of the eighth inning was advancing to the plate. Right in front of me, maybe five feet away, the Angel manager, Jim Fregosi, was pacing back and forth with his hands jammed into his back pockets, now staring down at the dugout floor, which was littered with what looked like the shells of sunflower seeds, now glancing out toward the field with a frown of concern that seemed unnecessary considering his team's big lead.

It was an unusual view of a baseball game—how many fans got to watch from the dugout?—so I decided to linger at the doorway a minute. Too bad I didn't care about the game that was going on, or even know the exact score. Funny how I could get so involved in the Brewer-Yankee game when it was only twelve inches square and be so indifferent to a contest that I was practically a part of. I formed a small square with my fingers and thumbs and held it up to frame the batter, the catcher and the umpire. Fregosi, still pacing, gave me a sharp look, and I lowered my hands quickly. I watched him scan his bench and wondered what he thought whenever his eye fell on Nolan Ryan, whom the New York Mets had traded for him back in 1971. Fregosi had played for the Mets in 146 games—fewer than a season's worth—and Ryan had developed into the greatest strikeout artist in history. Typical Mets. It occurred to me to ask Fregosi in a whisper for his thoughts on the deal. But it was surely against the rules, and, what with Tony Kubek, I'd had enough of asking spontaneous questions that day.

Still, it was an extraordinary experience to be standing practically in a major-league dugout, watching a game from the vantage point of a manager. It was probably against the rules, but maybe if I took the chance of staying there a little longer I would see or overhear something unusual. I looked back toward the end of the hall to see if I was holding up Scavullo. He was watching Calderaro pack away his equipment and seemed in no hurry. I turned back toward the dugout again.

An Angel player approached me and excused himself; I was standing in front of the water fountain. Relieved that he seemed to take my presence there for granted, I apologized and moved to the other side of the runway.

The next big event in the season was the All-Star game, to be played about a month from now in Seattle. Scavullo and I were scheduled to fly out, cover the game, then visit a few West Coast cities in search of more material. I would take things as they came, let events flow by me, and try to keep my eyes and ears open. And relax. Breathe deeply. Relax. The way I was doing now.

Out on the mound, the Blue Jay pitcher went into his windup as the new inning began. Jim Fregosi stopped pacing and watched.

A voice directly behind me suddenly roared out, "ALL RIGHT, NOW! WHAT THE FUCK IS GOING ON HERE!"

I flinched so violently I actually left the floor of the runway. I spun around, expecting to see a squad of policemen bearing down on me with night sticks and handcuffs.

It was only the Angel player, finished with the water fountain now, exhorting his teammates. "ALL RIGHT, YOU LIFELESS FUCKERS, LET'S MAKE SOME NOISE, LET'S MAKE SOME NOISE," he screamed. "LET'S GET SOME MORE RUNS NOW. LET'S HEAR SOME NOISE!"

STARRING

SUNDAY, JULY 15, 1979; 10:15 A.M.
ABOARD NORTHWEST ORIENT AIRLINES FLIGHT NO. 7,
NEW YORK CITY TO SEATTLE, WASHINGTON

ONCE AGAIN, AN AIRPLANE brought me luck. Or rather a mix-up over my seat assignment did. Having arrived at Kennedy Airport just in time to board my flight to Seattle for the All-Star game, I found that my first-class reservation had been ignored and I'd been booked into tourist class. Normally, I would have resigned myself to the error. But Tracy wouldn't be along on this jaunt, and I knew Scavullo would be flying first class; he would never accept anything less. Since I was hoping to spend some time on the flight getting to know him a little, I insisted that my original request be honored. After a short wait on standby until an empty spot materialized, I paid the extra forty dollars required, boarded the plane, and put my briefcase on my seat. Now it was only a matter of finding Scavullo and persuading either his seatmate to switch with me or my seatmate, who hadn't shown up yet, to switch with Scavullo. I discovered him four rows behind me across the aisle, resplendent in a white linen suit and black silk shirt. But he had Bill Calderaro with him. And when I got back to my seat, I found that my partner was Charles S. "Chub" Feeney, formerly the general manager of the San Francisco Giants and now the president and treasurer of the entire National League. Much as I wanted to visit with Scavullo, this was too good an opportunity to pass up.

As usual, I found it hard to open a conversation, although I'd been introduced to Feeney just a week earlier at the New York Mets annual old-timers' day game. I decided to remind him of our meeting before he could plunge into a paperback copy of Howard Fast's *The Immigrants* that he was impatiently twitching in his hand. But once I'd done so I found myself at a loss. Feeney had a manner, common to people in power, that combined cordiality with remoteness. I was also mildly troubled by his connection to the old New York Giants, which made me think of the heavy-bellied old men with flaming noses that I'd always associated with Giant fans.

The image of those men reminded me that Feeney had recently had a heart attack. An inquiry about his health might be just the polite but straight-from-the-shoulder way to move the faltering conversation into more intimate territory. Feeney responded by handing me the folded piece of paper that was marking his place in the Howard Fast novel. It was a copy of his electrocardiogram.

Well, since directness was in order, why not ask about the progress of contract negotiations with the players? Feeney adroitly shifted to the role of distant observer and blandly agreed I was right to predict that the bargaining would be tough. As he mouthed his platitudes, he reached to the floor for his briefcase, stuffed the Fast novel into it, removed what I instantly recognized as the two most recent issues of the *New York Times Magazine*, and opened one of them to the crossword puzzle page.

In a final attempt at conversation, I shifted the subject to the All-Star game. How had it all got started? Feeney, unable to recall the name of the Chicago sports editor who first thought up the idea back in the early 1930s, called across the aisle to a reporter I'd seen around enough by now to recognize as Will Grimsley of the Associated Press. Grimsley supplied the name of Arch Ward. Feeney added that the club owners hadn't originally thought much of the idea but were forced to go along because the receipts were to go to charity. With that he let the subject die and fell to filling the spaces of his crossword puzzle.

An intermittent puzzle addict myself, I asked Feeney if he minded my kibitzing. Not at all. I tilted my head to get a better view. Feeney worked rapidly and had most of the two puzzles done by lunchtime. I was able to help him with all of four definitions.

SUNDAY, JULY 15, 1979; 1:45 P.M.
IN ROOM 714, OLYMPIC HOTEL, SEATTLE, WASHINGTON

In my tiny hotel room, I found two gifts awaiting me—a bottle of wine and a box of candy, accompanied by a letter from C. Mike Berry, chairman of the All-Star Summer '79/Civic Committee, with instructions on where to pick up working media credentials. Chairman Berry's letter read in part:

WELCOME TO SEATTLE—

As the 1979 All-Star Civic Committee Chairman, I welcome you to the Pacific Northwest, home of the Seattle Mariners. Seattle is proud to host baseball's 50th All-Star Game and I am sure that your visit to our city will be a most memorable one. . . .

Whether you are fighting a king salmon in Puget Sound or skiing down the face of one of the snow-covered slopes of the Cascade range, you will understand why Seattle is the nation's most livable city.

All of us hope you enjoy your stay during the All-Star Game and hope that you plan to visit Seattle again in the near future.

Thanks for visiting us.

Sincerely,
Mike

Though the contents, including the signature, were mimeographed, and though I doubted there would be much time for fighting king salmon in Puget Sound or for anything else of that nature, the letter made me feel part of things, a member of the crew. So did the instructions to pick up my credentials in Suite 205 of the Olympic anytime between 4:00 and 10:00 P.M. So on the dot of four, I trotted down to Suite 205. There I was handed a list of all the reporters

94

who would be covering the game and was asked to sign opposite my name (it was actually there, even spelled correctly). Then I was handed a thick manila envelope with my name Magic-Markered across the front of it, a light blue press tag permitting me "Access to Kingdome, Working Section, Field, Interview Room, Clubhouses" (the name printed here was Christopher Lehmann, but no matter), a cellophane packet containing a metal stickpin of the Mariner team logo (a trident superimposed on a pentagram) with the words "50th All-Star Game Seattle '79" printed on it, and a shiny blue-and-white plastic airline bag with the Mariner logo on one side and the words "Telecasted in Japan by Fuji TV" on the other. The bag was satisfyingly heavy, like a promising Christmas present.

Back in my room, I spread the contents of the manila envelope on my bed. There were maps, bus schedules, restaurant guides, and sightseeing brochures. I unzipped the heavy airline bag. From it I removed:

- a pair of Gillette Twin Blade Disposable Razors
- an aerosol can of New! Gillette Foamy Tropical Coconut shaving cream
- a small box containing a twenty-two-ounce bottle of Cinnebar Soft Youth-Dew Fragrance by Estée Lauder
- a small tin of Johnson's baby powder
- a pair of emory boards stamped Continental Airlines
- a sewing kit in a plastic box imprinted Delta Air Lines
- a handkerchief decorated with the logos of all the major-league baseball clubs
- a pad of paper imprinted "Field notes from the 1979 All-Star Baseball Game. Compliments of the *Seattle Times*, Washington's largest newspaper."
- a plastic pocket penholder marked Sears Craftsman TOOLS THAT HAVE EARNED THE RIGHT TO WEAR THE NAME, with an Ultra Fine Flair Pen stuck in it
- a Styrofoam cup containing two packs of Arctic Lights cigarettes
- a book of matches courtesy of Edgewater Inn, Pier 67, Seattle, Washington
- a deck of playing cards, courtesy of Western Airlines

- a pack of Topps Baseball Bubble Gum cards
- a plastic container of macadamia nuts, courtesy of United Airlines
- a "Punch-a-loon" balloon wrapped in a plastic container printed with instructions how to inflate, hold, and punch it
- a fuzzy orange-and-black bug with free-rolling black eyeballs in clear plastic bubbles, yellow-green antennae, an adhesive underside, and a ribbon tail with the word *Boeing* silk-screened on it
- assorted pens, rulers, bookmarks, postcards, pamphlets, cups and glasses, cocktail coasters, key rings, baggage tags, candies, drink powders, sugar packages, and shopping bags.

SUNDAY, JULY 15, 1979; 7:45 P.M.
IN ROOM 714, OLYMPIC HOTEL

On a yellow Media Information Card ("1979 All-Star Game A–Z"), I noted under "Hospitality" that this evening in the Spanish Ballroom there was to be a cocktail reception. Normally, there were few things that made me more uncomfortable than socializing with a lot of strangers, but I was now determined to follow the routine of an experienced working reporter. Besides, I might spot a familiar face or two if any of the New York reporters had already arrived.

In the lobby of the Olympic I spotted a long table in one corner with several women seated behind it handing out name tags. There was none for me among all those neatly arranged on the table. But that didn't matter. An administrative oversight, no doubt. With a deep breath for courage, I walked into the ballroom beyond the table, ordered a tall Scotch and water at one of the several open bars in the vast room, and made my way to the hors d'oeuvres table at the center of the room, where I loaded up a plate of crab claws and began to chew at them while waiting for my panic to subside.

Then, standing as stiff and undaunted as a ship's figurehead, I surveyed the room. If I couldn't find anyone I knew, I would at least be observing as a good reporter should. The ballroom was rather thinly populated. Moreover there was a surprising number of women and children present. Reporters must use this Western trek to take their families on vacation. Not a half-bad idea. Head north of Seattle and visit the beautiful San Juan Islands or go south to Mount Rainier. Fight a king salmon in Puget Sound with the kids, or ski *en famille* down the face of one of the snow-covered slopes of the Cascade Range. No one was paying any attention to me. Time for another drink. Maybe a few more crab claws.

A bespectacled man of medium stature approached me, extended a hand, and introduced himself as Clifford Kachline. Relieved to have company at last, I returned the courtesy, sneaking a look at the man's name tag. Under his name was written: Society for American Baseball Research, Cooperstown, New York.

"Nice party," I volunteered. "Good crabmeat." I helped myself to another claw.

"Yes," said Kachline. "What brings you here?"

"Writing a book."

"You don't say! What sort of book?"

"A baseball book. About the season, sort of. I was just noticing how many reporters have brought their families with them. Business and pleasure, huh?"

"And you're going to put the contest in your book?"

"The All-Star game? Sure!"

"No. I mean the Pitch, Hit & Run contest. Say, maybe you'd like to come to the banquet. I'm sure you'd be more than welcome."

"I beg your pardon? Isn't this a reception for the press?"

"No, this is a party for Burger King's Pitch, Hit & Run contest. You've probably seen their promotion on television. These kids here are all the finalists. They're here with their families. Come on. I'll introduce you to Bob Landau. He's the fellow in charge."

Docilely, I padded along behind Clifford Kachline, who led me out of the ballroom—the Georgian Room, it turned out to be, not the Spanish Ballroom—and down a corridor into a large dining hall. I was introduced to a blur of people and turned over to a perky young woman, who threw me a look of suspicion (or did I imagine it?) and led me to a table where another cloudbank of names swept over me, the single one I could make out being Robert Landau of Robert Landau Associates, the contest's promoter. Landau's tablemates flashed smiles and burbled politely. I beamed back at them. Reminding myself that anything on earth could fall under the heading of experience, I sat down and began to toy with a slab of pink roast beef.

A series of speakers now began to mount the rostrum at the end of the room. First came Chris Schoenstein, executive vice-president of Burger King, who introduced the eight young finalists in the contest (aged nine, ten, eleven, and twelve), who in turn introduced their families ("This is my mom, my dad"). One of the two eleven-year-olds was Crystal Fields, a willowy black girl from Cumberland, Maryland, who, according to a press release, was "the first female to reach a finals competition competing against boys and girls in the history of professional sports youth programs." The Burger King executive was followed by Mr. Landau himself, who proceeded to announce that there were two celebrities at this evening's gathering. The first was twelve-year-old Andrea McArdle, star of the Broadway musical *Annie*, who would be singing the national anthem at the game on Tuesday. Enthusiastic applause and whistling for Andrea McArdle. As for the other celebrity: "He isn't going to like this," Mr. Landau said, "but we are honored to have present tonight the man who happens to be my favorite book reviewer in America, Christopher Lehmann-Haupt of the *New York Times*."

I rose stiffly, tipped my head in acknowledgment, my face feeling as if it had just come out of a twelve-hour snowstorm, and collapsed into my seat again, while the children and their parents stared at me curiously and applauded politely. It wasn't that I didn't like it, exactly. It was just that it seemed as if I were taking unfair advantage of them.

Landau was succeeded by Bob Davis of the National Recreation and Parks Association, the cosponsor of the competition, who took the opportunity of Crystal Fields's presence to plug the Equal Rights Amendment for his home state of North Carolina. He in turn gave way to C. Carson Conrad of the President's Council on Physical Fitness and Sports, who claimed to bring greetings direct from Jimmy Carter (although one got the feeling he'd never so much as laid eyes on the aforementioned) and gave a rock-'em-sock-'em speech about how "the very guts of the free enterprise system is competition like this one." The children were beginning to yawn, but they came to life again when up to the microphone bounced my old friend Tony Kubek, positively brimming with cordiality. Kubek, who had obviously missed his predecessor's speech, started off by explaining that the competitive aspect of the Pitch, Hit & Run contest was meaningless; "Just being here with your mom and dad is a healthful experience," especially since "families are breaking up in a lot of areas." Kubek then explained that owing to "my bad memory, not because I'm Polish," he would not give a speech but simply field some questions. A silence enveloped the room. I thought of asking Kubek again what his career would have been like had he played on artificial turf, but I decided against it. Best not to expose the children to the language of Kubek's answer.

Kubek was followed by the Burger King clown, who danced among the tables, performing sleight-of-hand tricks. Eventually he bounced over to our table, but seeing only grown-ups he turned and continued his performance facing away from us. In the middle of a difficult behind-the-back maneuver, he glanced over his shoulder and asked me under his breath not to give away the trick. I nodded assurance; he winked back at me. I felt as if I'd found an ally.

MONDAY, JULY 16, 1979; 8:30 A.M.
IN ROOM 714, OLYMPIC HOTEL

Carefully, very carefully, taking precise note of times and places, I consulted the schedule for the day's events.

7:30 A.M.–10:00 A.M.—Media and Player Breakfast (buffet), Georgian Room, Olympic Hotel.
10:30 A.M.–11:30 A.M.—Media Conference (managers, starting pitchers, some other players, honorary captains), Spanish Ballroom, Olympic Hotel.
11:30 A.M.–1:30 P.M.—Media Luncheon (cold buffet), Georgian Room, Olympic Hotel.
11:30 A.M.–1:00 P.M.—Luncheon for Media and Baseball Personnel, Upper Press Area, Kingdome, hosted by Burger King.
12:30 P.M.—Kingdome gates open to public.
1:00 P.M.–2:00 P.M.—Pitch, Hit & Run Finals, Kingdome.
2:00 P.M.–3:00 P.M.—National League Workout.
3:00 P.M.–4:00 P.M.—American League Workout.
4:30 P.M.–5:30 P.M.—Cruiser boats depart (Pier 56) at 4:30, 4:50, 5:10, and 5:30 P.M. Scenic Tour of Puget Sound.
5:30 P.M.–10:30 P.M.—All-Star Dinner (Pacific Northwest Salmon Bake) Media and Baseball Officials, Kiana Lodge, Kitsap Peninsula.
8:00 P.M.—Begin Boarding Boats for Return to Shilsole Bay (Seattle). Buses to hotels.

MONDAY, JULY 16, 1979; 8:45 A.M.
IN ROOM 714, OLYMPIC HOTEL

The game would not begin for thirty-two hours and fifty-five minutes—a lot of time to pass, a lot of milling around to do. But I wouldn't be at a complete loss over how to occupy myself. To compensate for my inability to think on my feet I'd come up with a line of questioning to try out on the players. It had grown out of some obscure late-night ruminations whose details I could no longer recall. And it was predictably unwieldy. What I wanted to find out was the kind of childhood fantasies major-league players had had about becoming professionals, and what the relationship had turned out to be between the fantasies and the reality.

In fact, I'd even tried out the question on Jim Bouton, the former New York Yankee pitcher who was now a television newscaster. Back in May, I'd interviewed Bouton over chicken noodle soup in a diner near his office at CBS.

LEHMANN-HAUPT: Did you have fantasies as a child about becoming a major-league player?

BOUTON: Not only didn't I, it was beyond . . . beyond dreaming. It was just . . . you couldn't do that. We pretended to be guys when we played stickball. My brother would be the Giants, and I would be the Dodgers, and then he'd have to be the Dodgers and I would be the Giants. We were both Giant fans. Then we'd trade off again. And even though I wasn't good hitting left-handed, if I came up in a crucial situation—if it was Whitey Lockman's turn—I would have to go up lefty and do the best I could. That's why when I finally faced the real Willie Mays . . . I mean that was my brother. I mean the first time I faced Willie Mays, it was my brother batting right-handed, trying to imitate his batting stance, y'know?

LEHMANN-HAUPT: Did you pitch to him the way you pitched to your brother in stickball?

BOUTON: [laughing] I remember thinking on the mound, "Hey, I'm pitching to my brother."

MONDAY, JULY 16, 1979; 10:30 A.M.
IN THE SPANISH BALLROOM, OLYMPIC HOTEL

But when I finally located the elusive Spanish Ballroom, the "media conference" held there at 10:30 turned out to be an elaborately orchestrated nonevent. Present and seated at the dais was an imposing array of bubble gum cards—Mike Schmidt, 3B, Philadelphia Phillies; Roy Smalley, SS, Minnesota Twins; Steve Rogers, P, Montreal

Expos; Rod Carew, 1B, California Angels; Joe Niekro, P, Houston Astros; and Nolan Ryan, P, California Angels—along with various officials and the rival managers, Tommy Lasorda of the Los Angeles Dodgers and Bob Lemon, until one month earlier the leader of the Yankees. (The rival managers of the All-Star game were always those of the previous World Series, so Lemon was piloting the American League team even though he'd been replaced by Billy Martin as Yankee manager.)

But very little of substance occurred. Lasorda and Lemon announced their starting lineups and promised they would play to win. Various bubble gum cards said how thrilled they were to have been elected by the fans. Any taint of controversy—such as the perennial question of whether it really ought to be the public that selected the players—was carefully avoided. A thunderhead of clichés built up and rained down yawns. No wonder the press always made a fuss about such All-Star trivia as who the starting pitchers would be or whether the game would be high-scoring or not. There was nothing else to write about.

Indeed I was nearly asleep when the two honorary team captains were introduced—Carl Hubbell, the great New York Giant pitcher of the 1930s famous for his so-called screwball, and Vernon Louis "Lefty" "Goofy" Gomez, the fabled Yankee pitcher equally celebrated for his pitching prowess, his eccentricity and wit, and his anemic .147 lifetime batting average. Though Gomez was supposed to be the clown, it was Hubbell who supplied the first note of spontaneous humor of the morning. The first question he was asked by the assembled reporters was whether he thought Nolan Ryan, the fire-balling pitcher who was to start for the American League, posed any threat to the feat Hubbell performed during the 1934 All-Star game, when he struck out in order the five best hitters in an awesome American League lineup.

Hubbell responded in a scratchy high-pitched voice that bubbled merrily.

> Well, it would be kinda hard to answer that because Nolan Ryan won't be pitching against Ruth, Gehrig, Foxx, Simmons, and Cronin.

So much for the Johnny-come-latelies. When the roar of appreciation died down, he continued in his Pa Kettle voice.

But let me add one thing about that game. In that All-Star game, I wasn't afraid of any of those folks that was up there. So I got through those hitters in the lineup easy. But when I was pitching to Bill Dickey [the hitter who succeeded Simmons in the A.L. lineup] I got to worrying about the next hitter. And that's bad, whenever you're pitchin' against one guy and you're worryin' about the next hitter comin' up. And Dickey gets a base hit! The next hitter was Gomez. I was worrying about him!

To which Gomez responded after he was introduced:

Carl mentioned worrying about me. I can tell you this. I was walking up to home plate, and Gabby Hartnett [the National League catcher] asked me. . . . He said, "Are you trying to insult Hubbell?" And I said, "How?" He said, "Well, comin' up here with a bat." But he was good that day. I know he didn't worry about me and I didn't worry about him either. I struck out.

"King Carl" Hubbell, the "Meal Ticket" of the old New York Giants, besides his All-Star strikeout feat was probably best known as the pitcher with the greatest mastery of the screwball. And Lefty Gomez, "the Gay Castilian," had enchanted a generation of sportswriters with his high jinks: his habit of gazing up at airplanes while he was pitching a game (a base runner once stole home while he was so engaged); or the time he swung his bat to tap the dirt from his spikes (the way the big hitters do before digging in) and accidentally hit his ankle so hard he was laid up for three days (Red Smith wrote that Gomez had finally developed power in his swing); or his advice to a young pitcher that the best way to handle a line drive was to "run in on it before it picks up speed." I was astonished to discover them still alive—Hubbell, lean at the age of seventy-six; Gomez, jauntier yet jowlier at sixty-nine, surprisingly slick and crowd-conscious for a man who was supposed to be so flaky. It wasn't that I hadn't at last accepted that ballplayers grew older as time went by. After all, I was confronted almost daily by the graying image of Joe DiMaggio as a salesman for the Bowery Savings Bank. But somehow in my mind, players like Hubbell and Gomez, who had reached their prime before I was born and who had retired long before I even became aware of baseball, seemed exempt from the normal process of aging. They had been gelled at the peak of their careers and relegated to scrapbooks and the memories of old men who believed the past to be a better time. In my mind, those retired players who were still in the public eye were permitted to age gracefully. Whitey Ford could turn paunchy selling swimming pools, and the M squad, Mickey Mantle and Roger Maris, could appear at Yankee opening-day festivities looking like a pair of heavy-duty fire hydrants. But my image of Christy Mathewson was of the handsome twenty-one-year-old boy I had seen in a collection of old photographs, and Christy Mathewson would remain for me a handsome boy forever.

Perhaps this was why the idea of all-star teams, especially all-time all-star teams, was so appealing despite the difficulty of comparing a Willie Keeler with a Rod Carew or even a Babe Ruth with a Roger Maris. This was why young fans, and even some older ones, argued so passionately over who was the best at a given position. It mattered because somewhere the old players were preserved in their youth, waiting to be called forth to the diamond on baseball's Judgment Day. Who was the best center fielder of all time, Tris Speaker or Joe DiMaggio? I had worried endlessly over this in the first few years of my passion (before Willie Mays or Mickey Mantle had appeared on the scene). I cared about the answer so much that I'd once even gotten up the nerve to telephone a radio sports show and ask the host—was it Marty Glickman?—to name his all-time team, just to make certain that DiMaggio was put in center field. (The call had proved pointless. By the time I could recover from Glickman's response when I told him my name—"Well, let's see if we can 'Haupt' you out!"—he was naming the last three men in his all-time batting order, and I never did find out if DiMaggio had made the team.)

The formal phase of the media conference was now over, and clusters of reporters surrounded each luminary. To my surprise, only one or two people had approached Carl Hubbell, who was still seated at the dais, with Gomez hovering behind him. Could it be, I wondered, that most of the reporters present were unaware of the Hubbell legend: could it be that they shared the attitude of Jack Clark, the young star of the San Francisco Giants, who, when I asked him at a Met-Giant game at Shea Stadium whether he was aware of the great Giant players who had come before him, had said, "Oh, yeah. I know about guys like Mays, Cepeda, McCovey . . . all those guys"—as if Mathewson, Terry, Hubbell, Ott, McGraw, and the like had never existed.

I drifted over to where Hubbell and Gomez were holding forth.

"How do you feel about the designated hitter rule?" a reporter asked Gomez, referring to the American League rule of not allowing the pitcher to bat for himself.

"Well," said Gomez, "I personally would like to see it where they had to send the pitcher to bat, but that's not for me to say." Seeming to sense he'd missed an opening, he added tentatively, "Pitchers, you know, love to hit." Then, putting a hand on Hubbell's shoulder, he spoke up more confidently, "You know who drove in the first run offa Wild Bill Hallahan?"

"That was the first All-Star game," said Hubbell, slipping into the role of the straight man. "1933?"

"Yeah, I singled," replied Gomez, shifting into what appeared to be a familiar routine. "Fast fielding by Wally Berger held me to a single."

Hubbell's eyes widened. "Did the ball hit the bat?" Putting one fist on top of the other, he pantomimed a hitter awaiting the pitch. "You were standing there this way and the ball hit the bat?"

"Yeah," said Gomez, warming to his role, but also speaking his lines like an actor who has gone a little stale in a part. "I looked around behind first base and about eight hundred people fainted. 'Gomez got a hit,' they're yelling. It was like when they declared war." He spotted a friend across the room and scurried away when he was finished, looking a bit like a salesman going after a customer. Hubbell remained seated, ready for further questions. A couple of more reporters joined the gathering. There was a momentary silence.

REPORTER: Ah, do you think the game is easier for players today?

HUBBELL: I'll tell ya, it's a lot easier on the first and fifteenth when you walk up and they hand you that check.

REPORTER: Was striking out those guys in the All-Star game your biggest thrill in baseball?

HUBBELL: Well, it was in a way. I'll tell you: I had to put so much emphasis on ball games that's gonna mean whether you're gonna be in the World Series or not, and then, after you get in, whether you're gonna win or not . . . I mean that is what you play for. Getting into the World Series. That's the whole goal you have in life.

He reflected a moment, his watery blue eyes gazing off into the distance of memory.

Course, that All-Star game was something new. . . . Great for the fans . . . but it was still an exhibition game. Aw, I don't know. I can only play one way. In *any* game, goddamn it, I tried to win. I tried to get the hitters out. It's just pride, just, by God, you was in a contest. You was in a ball game.

Again, he pondered for a moment.

Of course, there was no replay television then. It was broadcast on the radio. But in those days you had photographers running around on the field all the time. This is all during the season. There was no special box for photographers then. There was no telephoto lens. There was nothing. These guys are runnin' around all the time, trying to decide where the next play's gonna be, you know . . . anticipate, so they could get up close . . . a *scoop*, y'know?

The only thing that was moving film was Fox Movietone and Pathé News. That always come on in the theeayters before the feature picture: the Fox Movietone and Pathé News. And those poor guys, they had this big thing on their cameras. Those reels were as big and round as a dishpan, and now he had got to set that down and then focus the camera just right. Then when he starts to take a picture he got to run that film through it. Now this is the damn truth! That poor guy, he had a hell of a time trying to turn around, you know, in the right place and everything else. So by the time he'd get somewhere, the play had already been. So he and the rest of 'em would just have to stand out there. And I saw some film of those three innings I pitched. . . .

I want to mention this: if I'd 'a been a photographer, I'd 'a been exactly where they were. Y'see, they're not like folks now, with a telephoto lens that you can get it from any angle. They got to, y'know . . . they're moving around. Left-handed hitters, they're moving. Right-handed hitters, they're moving. They're takin' hitters' pictures. So they didn't have anyone behind the catcher, which would have shown *me*. But in that whole film, that three innings, there was a picture of me throwing *one* ball. That was all. One shot; one time it showed one ball!

But don't get me wrong! If I woulda been a photographer, I woulda been takin' pictures right where they was. I wouldn't've been taking any of me out there on the mound. Because, you know, with that group of hitters, why you know sooner or later somebody was gonna hit one. And they want to get the picture, you know. Somebody hittin' one over the roof. But you see it was so different than it is now. Hell . . .

His voice trailed off sadly.

SECOND REPORTER: Do you remember. . . . Did you strike those guys out with that screwball of yours?

HUBBELL: [Snapping back to attention now.] Yessir! You think I was gonna throw 'em my fastball? They had been hittin' those for years.

FIRST REPORTER: Isn't one reason those five great hitters struck out that they had never seen that kind of pitch before? Because the American League didn't have a pitcher like Carl Hubbell?

HUBBELL: Well, I don't know if they had any screwball pitchers or not. But I'll tell you this. It wasn't so much the break in my screwball that would fool hitters. I never mentioned too much about this [he laughs softly] as long as I was playing, but even for all the hitters in the National League it was the greatest change-of-pace pitch, because I could [he raises his right arm stiffly and mimes throwing], I could come right over with it, and that motion wasn't any different from the fastball. Y'know, the hitter's lookin' at the pitcher's hand and he wants to see the ball, and he wants to see that motion on that wrist. Well, if you come like that [he mimes throwing hard], y'know, he's gonna be gettin' ready for a fastball. But I could do the saaaaame 'n everything else with it just like that. [He rotates his left hand inside out.] I could just come down like that [snapping hand again] and that would put more spin on it and that would slow it up more. And every one of those guys that swung at the ball swung *ahead* of it. They were swinging too *soon*. They were swinging too *soon*. All but Dickey. He sat down in the batter's circle and he watched me strike out Cronin, and he was figurin' things out. He just slapped the ball to left field. But I got two strikes on him before he did!

THIRD REPORTER: Could you go through those three innings player by player and tell us what you threw on each pitch to each man?

HUBBELL: Oh, no, no. My God, man. That was how many years ago? My goodness, no.

THIRD REPORTER: Gomez says that all he can do now is throw grounders. How about you?

HUBBELL: I can just drop it. All I can do is just drop it. My God, I've got spurs and calcium deposits and everything else. I couldn't throw a ball from here to the end of the table.

LEHMANN-HAUPT: When did you learn that screwball?

HUBBELL: I learned it in the minor leagues, at Oklahoma City. I played a couple of years in the Class D League when I finished high school there in Oklahoma and then I went to the Western League, Oklahoma City club, and one spring training there was an old left-handed pitcher by the name of Lefty Thomas. He had been in the big leagues but he was back down. I joined Oklahoma City for one month at the end of the season. And I watched him pitch a few ball games, and God damn it, he had a good sinking fastball. Those left-handed hitters, y'know, they really like to get that left-hander in the hole 'n get that nice fast one, y'know? And he was just hittin' that outside corner with that sinkin' fastball and there's ground-ball double plays. He wasn't hardly breaking a sweat, and he walked off the winning pitcher. And I thought about that all winter long. God damn.

Well, the only way to learn anything there is monkey see, monkey do. And I picked out my monkey to try to see and do. So next spring I started trying to get that sinker, that fast sinker, and I got it going all right. Then I found out if I could put some spin on it, then hell, I could . . . they started to break.

The more snap you give it, the more rotation you got on the ball, and the better curve that you're going to get. I was gettin' it in one month. I had no problem at all. I could throw a strike with it as good as I could a fastball. And it would break away from a right-hand batter. I didn't know what to call it. The catcher started calling it a screwball. I'd never heard of a screwball.

On the way out of the Spanish Ballroom, I discovered Nolan Ryan, the starting pitcher for the American League, sitting by himself in a clump of randomly disarranged chairs, as if he was resting up from an interview he'd just given and was waiting for whatever would hit him next. Inspired by what a few questions had elicited from Carl Hubbell, I decided to approach Ryan.

LEHMANN-HAUPT: As a child, did you ever play games in which you imagined competing against major leaguers?

RYAN: When you're a Little Leaguer ... I used to play baseball cards, y'know, 'n' everybody had their hero. And so, when you were pitchin' you were so-and-so, and when you were hittin' you were so-and-so. As hitters I always liked Henry Aaron and Mickey Mantle, and for pitchers, when I was really young, Bob Feller was the name, but when I got in high school I saw Koufax pitch a couple of times, I really became a Koufax fan. But where I came from in Texas our exposure to major-league ball was really limited. At that time, Houston didn't have a franchise. It was Triple-A ball then, and that was a big thing. You could go months without exposure. You might watch a World Series, but that was it.

LEHMANN-HAUPT: Well, in a game have you ever stopped to think, "I'm here; I'm playing in the big leagues the way I dreamed of doing as a child?"

RYAN: No, because that wasn't, that was never a childhood dream of mine.

LEHMANN-HAUPT: It wasn't?

RYAN: No. As a kid I never really dreamed about or envisioned pitching in the big leagues. When I signed my first contract I never really thought I was major-league talent, I remember, or that I'd get the opportunity to play in the big leagues.

It was time to take a look at Seattle's ballpark, the controversial Kingdome, where, according to the schedule I'd all but committed to memory by now, the two All-Star squads would be working out this afternoon. Outside the Olympic Hotel, the heat was oppressive—headed for the nineties according to a local television forecast—not at all how I imagined the Pacific Northwest, which I still naively linked to those frosty peaks I'd seen looming up yesterday outside my airplane window. But if the heat struck me as uncharacteristic of the region, something else didn't: the relationship between Seattle's traffic and its pedestrians. At the first intersection I came to, a Volkswagen beetle ground to a stop with its front bumper extending about a foot into the crosswalk. Though I was the only pedestrian around, the driver shifted into reverse, backing up until there was a yard between his car and the walk area!

Farther downtown, I passed three people standing on a corner. Though there wasn't a moving vehicle in sight, they were obediently waiting for the Don't Walk sign to change. I was clearly a long way from New York City, but this didn't stop me from acting by habit. Feeling a little like some corrupt cosmopolitan in a land of innocents, I crossed the street against the signal and turned a corner that brought the Kingdome into view.

Despite its impressive name, it was just another pile of nondescript concrete set down in an environment where it didn't belong. It could have been anything from Shea Stadium in Flushing, New York, to Oakland–Alameda County Coliseum. These cement toadstools lacked the unique character of a Fenway Park, which blended so perfectly into its Boston urban neighborhood that you could arrive at its entrance gate by taxi without ever knowing that you were approaching a baseball stadium. No, the new ballparks made one think that major-league baseball, in the decades of its expansion across the continent, had turned itself into some Bunyanesque bear, who, wherever it sniffed a concentration of people, squatted down and excreted yet another circular concrete stool.

But in Seattle, the bear had gone too far, as I'd been reminded earlier in the day by a talk with Emmett Watson, a columnist for the *Seattle Post-Intelligencer*. He told me how back in the 1960s organized baseball had promised the city of Seattle a major-league team. With this promise in hand, the city asked its citizens to pass a $40 million bond issue to finance a domed stadium. The people duly approved the issue in February 1968, the Kingdome was begun, and the Seattle Pilots were born. But then in 1970, after playing a single season at Sicks Stadium, a thirty-year-old park once used by Seattle's Triple-A team, the Rainiers, the Pilots were shifted east by organized baseball and transformed into the Milwaukee Brewers. Seattle was left with a half-built stadium and no team to play in it.

Instead of letting themselves be pushed around, the city's leaders decided to fight back. They went ahead and finished their stadium, at an escalated cost, thanks to inflation, of $60 million, and they asked the state of Washington to sue organized baseball for conspiracy, fraud, deceit, and violations of antitrust laws.

Apparently the ensuing trial, which was held in Snohomish County Superior Court in January 1976, did not show organized baseball in a flattering light. The state had hired Bill Dwyer, a special assistant attorney general, to represent it in the trial. Dwyer had worked six solid years preparing the case. The trial went on for weeks, with Dwyer conducting a relentless low-key courtroom performance. Baseball's officials, in contrast, behaved high-handedly. In the words of Emmett Watson, who was preparing a column on the whole affair for the next morning's paper, the lords of baseball "were revealed as pious, devious, arrogant, and untrustworthy." Some of the league minutes that had been subpoenaed and offered in evidence turned out to have been altered. Testimony of certain witnesses, most notably Bob Short, the owner of the Texas Rangers, and Joe Cronin, the American League president, contradicted what had come out in earlier discovery proceedings. Despite the visible contempt shown him by such owners as Jerold Hoffberger of the Baltimore Orioles and Charles O. Finley of the Oakland A's, Bill Dwyer kept up his relentless questioning for hours. When Finley finally stepped down from the witness stand and walked past Dwyer on his way out, he conceded him a measure of respect when he rasped, "You've done your homework, haven't you, pal!"

The upshot reflected the skill of Dwyer's performance. Seattle was granted a new franchise, easy financial terms for its owners, a binding twenty-year lease with the Kingdome, and "as a gesture of goodwill," a guarantee that the city would host the fiftieth major-league All-Star game. That was why we were all here to see the game that would be played tomorrow. It was not in timid compliance that the people here backed away from their crosswalks and waited for their Don't Walk signs to change. The citizens of Seattle believed in playing by the rules.

MONDAY, JULY 16, 1979; 1:00 P.M.
INSIDE THE SEATTLE KINGDOME

Once inside it, I found the Kingdome a lot more appealing. The enclosed environment was reputed to be a dismal place for baseball. The field was too small—316 feet along the left- and right-field foul lines (or 52.7 fathoms, as Mariner management had cutely thought to add) and 410 feet to center field. The artificial surface was too hard. The air inside the dome was too thin—or was it too thick? or too still?—so that batted balls tended to travel farther. And the loudspeakers and other paraphernalia hanging from the ceiling formed a veritable obstacle course for high fly balls, though a fact sheet on the stadium insisted that so far only two fair balls had hit speakers in the Kingdome, both in 1979.

Still, I rather liked the setting. It was cool, the air-conditioning having been turned up refreshingly high despite the current energy crisis. A carnival spirit permeated the atmosphere. In and around the dugouts and along the sidelines, players in a colorful variety of uniforms were conducting interviews with reporters or talking at television cameras or striking poses for photographers, among them the slight figure of Scavullo, elegant in a white suit and Panama hat. Everywhere I looked, groups of the famous were gathering and dispersing: Bowie Kuhn, Lee MacPhail, Joe Garagiola, Bill Russell, Tony Kubek, Peewee Reese. On the infield, they were holding the finals of the Burger King Pitch, Hit & Run contest. Pint-sized players in various major-league uniforms were cavorting on the greener-than-green of Monsanto Astroturf. It was as if I'd actually stepped through the looking glass of my TV screen and become a part of Electric Land. Near the third-base coaching box, Danny Kaye, who was a part owner of the Mariners, was explaining to Sparky Anderson, the Cincinnati manager turned TV interviewer, why the New York Yankees had such trouble playing baseball in the Kingdome. "It's the weave of the surface," explained the actor-comedian. "It's different from other artificial surfaces the Yankees play on. Damnedest thing. Graig Nettles can't figure out how the ball is going to hop." Though Kaye's hyperthyroid comedy had ceased to amuse me by the time I got to my teens, I felt flattered that he had included me in his audience, fixing me with his eyes several times as he held forth, even though he couldn't possibly have known who I was. Just for an instant, it occurred to me that I might not really need to find Joe Durso.

But of course I needed to find Joe Durso. Ever since I had first run into the *New York Times*'s veteran baseball reporter two months earlier, my fortunes had shifted 180 degrees, at least whenever he was around. He'd gotten me that interview in which Mel Allen had claimed to have cured Joe DiMaggio of a batting slump and helped him to hit those three home runs. He'd taken me under his wing at the New York Mets' old-timers' day at Shea Stadium a couple of months later and introduced me all around.

Of medium stature and mild-mannered—except when he burst into his manic falsetto cackle of a laugh—Joe Durso exuded a warmth that seemed to light up everyone around him, and a little of the glow inevitably reflected on me. When I once asked him why it was that everyone was always so happy to see him, he blushed and said it wasn't for him to say.

"Come on, Joe. You're a reporter," I taxed him. "It's your *job* to be able to figure these things out."

"Well, I guess it's a matter of trust," he finally admitted. "They know I'm not going to rip them or gossip about them or make hay out of what they say. And I guess they know I don't think sports are the beginning and the end of everything. You know I was a news editor on the *Times* and head slot man on the city desk before I was ever a baseball reporter."

So I'd shamelessly slipped into the role of Joe Durso's pilot fish, if it was possible for a pilot fish to attach itself to a creature as benign and playful as a porpoise.

MONDAY, JULY 16, 1979; 1:30 P.M.
IINSIDE THE SEATTLE KINGDOME

Swimming along with Joe Durso in the Kingdome, I got to meet the following players and ask them if they'd ever had childhood fantasies of becoming baseball stars.

LEE MAZZILLI, OUTFIELDER, NEW YORK METS: Sure I did.

LEHMANN-HAUPT: Have you ever remembered your fantasies while playing in a major-league game?

MAZZILLI: Oh, no.

LEHMANN-HAUPT: Never?

MAZZILLI: No. Game's a game.

RON GUIDRY, PITCHER, NEW YORK YANKEES: I couldn't honestly say if I did or not. I wouldn't remember. I really didn't know enough to be interested in baseball until I was fifteen or sixteen years old. I knew who the players were, but I wasn't *into* baseball.

ROD CAREW, FIRST BASEMAN, CALIFORNIA ANGELS: I never had any heroes.

LEHMANN-HAUPT: You never had *any* heroes?

CAREW: Nope.

LEHMANN-HAUPT: Would that be because you grew up in Panama?

CAREW: Yeah, I guess. I didn't get a chance to see ballgames here. I liked to listen to different ballplayers, but I never imitated anyone. I just wanted to be myself. When you start to copy players—copy their styles—all you do is try to become somebody else instead of yourself. That's the hardest thing to do.

PETE ROSE, FIRST BASEMAN, PHILADELPHIA PHILLIES: I think we all, as kids, maybe acted like people in the big leagues, or something like that . . . stood like people. Sure, everybody does that. Everybody who's around a town where there's a lot of baseball. Like I was around Cincinnati.

LEHMANN-HAUPT: Was that the team that you rooted for?

ROSE: Yeah.

LEHMANN-HAUPT: Did you model yourself after anyone in particular?

ROSE: No. If anybody, it'd have to be Johnny Temple, because we had a lot of similarities. He was very small and I was very small. That was in high school and grade school.

LEHMANN-HAUPT: Did you ever play against him?

ROSE: I played *with* him. He was at Cincinnati when I joined the team. He was my coach, my roommate.

LEHMANN-HAUPT: Did you ever remember during a game that you had once modeled yourself after him?

ROSE: I didn't really model myself after him. It was just that I was small and he was small; he was a second baseman and I was a second baseman. And I think we all have a tendency to know the guys who play the positions that we play more so than . . . y'know, if you're a second baseman, you know more about second basemen than you do first basemen. Or if you're a catcher, you know about. . . . Y'see it was funny in my instance because I was always a catcher, in the Little League and up 'til my sophomore year in high school. Then I was just too small, so I went to the other end of the throw, to second base. So I can tell you all about Smoky Burgess and Ed Bailey . . . Campanella. That was a big deal in those days, when the Dodgers used to come to the park.

TED SIMMONS, CATCHER, ST. LOUIS CARDINALS: You mean pretend you're playing one on one against Lew Alcindor and people like that? I think everyone in baseball did.

LEHMANN-HAUPT: During a game, have you ever remembered doing it?

SIMMONS: No.

LEHMANN-HAUPT: Jim Bouton tells a story that he and his brother used to play against each other imitating all the big-league batters. And the first time he pitched against Willie Mays, he thought, "It's just my brother."

SIMMONS: Oh, wow! No, I've never done that. That's really interesting, though. That really is.

LEHMANN-HAUPT: But you never made such an association?

SIMMONS: No, no. I don't know if I can say this humbly, but I didn't think it was necessary. I mean I felt that it was I who was supposed to be here, not somebody else. Y'know? Not that Bouton didn't feel the same way. I'm not trying to . . . but having those fantasies as a child: I think everyone in this whole place has done the very same thing.

TOMMY JOHN, PITCHER, NEW YORK YANKEES: You mean baseball? Basketball?

LEHMANN-HAUPT: Baseball.

JOHN: Sure, sure. Everybody plays those fantasy games.

LEHMANN-HAUPT: Well, actually, Nolan Ryan never did.

JOHN: Didn't he?

LEHMANN-HAUPT: No. Because they never saw baseball games where he grew up. The city kids tend to do it more than the rural kids, apparently.

JOHN: Shoot, we even played games where we'd take a tennis ball and throw it against the steps of the house, and I'd always be the Chicago Cubs and my brother would be the St. Louis Cardinals, and we'd have these games and we'd have the World Series. Against each other we'd always play teams.

LEHMANN-HAUPT: You'd go through lineups.

JOHN: Yeah.

LEHMANN-HAUPT: Have you ever remembered that while you were playing in a game?

JOHN: No.

LEHMANN-HAUPT: Bouton used to do the same thing with his brother, and his brother did a good imitation of Willie Mays and the first time Bouton ever pitched against Willie Mays, he said to himself, "It's my brother."

JOHN: Well, that's a good story.

LEHMANN-HAUPT: You don't believe it?

JOHN: No.

PEEWEE REESE, FORMER SHORTSTOP, BROOKLYN DODGERS: I wasn't the type of kid that . . . all he wanted to do was play professional baseball. I graduated from high school, I weighed 115 pounds. So I didn't have any idea of playing professional baseball. The only reason I went out for the high school team my senior year was the football coach was a dear friend of mine, Ray Baer, and he had seen me play ball, y'know? But I said, "Mr. Baer, I don't want to go out for baseball. I'm too small." And he made me get in the car and took me out and told the baseball coach. . . . In high school, when the football coach tells the baseball coach to give you a uniform, he gives you one. And I played five games, busted my finger; so I never played like, "Gee, I'm gonna be a professional." When they came to me to sign a professional contract, I couldn't believe it. Of course, I had gotten a little bit larger.

But I can remember: I've told Joe DiMaggio—he was my idol when I was fifteen or sixteen years old; Joe is not that much older than I am. He's sixty-five; I'm sixty-one. But I used his bat. I bought a bat of his. It must have been thirty-six inches long. Shit, I couldn't swing it. But I wanted to be Joe DiMaggio. He was one of my idols. He and Dizzy Dean.

LEHMANN-HAUPT: Did you ever recall while playing in a major-league game, "Gee, there's Joe DiMaggio, the guy who used to be my idol?"

REESE: Yes, yes, yes.

LEHMANN-HAUPT: Actually while playing?

REESE: I sure did. I sure did. I was kind of awed by it all, really, after seeing the Yankees. I was just talking to Carl Hubbell: the Yankees and the Giants played in the 1937 World Series in the Polo Grounds, and here I am, only four year later, playing in Yankee Stadium. I had never seen Yankee Stadium, and all of a sudden you walk into that place, it does things to you. I can just picture myself going the whole Series without getting a hit. I got three hits in the first game, but not too many after that. At least I didn't get shut out.

MONDAY, JULY 16, 1979; 5:30 P.M.
ABOARD A CRUISER BOAT CROSSING PUGET SOUND

"I don't envy you," said Dave Anderson, the sports columnist of the *New York Times*, when I finally met him and told him that I was trying to write a book about the season. I'd seen him from a distance around the office but had never actually talked to him, so when I found a fitting moment in Seattle, I approached him and introduced myself. This was during a relaxed interlude aboard one of the four ferries that were carrying some thousand reporters, baseball officials, players, coaches, front-office personnel, and members of Seattle's host committee across Puget Sound to Kiana Lodge on Kitsap Peninsula for what the schedule called a "Pacific Northwest Salmon Bake." The trip had been advertised as a "Scenic Tour of Puget Sound," but each ferry carried two open bars, and most of the passengers were applying themselves more diligently to the refreshments than to the view. Anderson, a large pink-complexioned man with thinning, light-colored hair, translucent-framed eyeglasses, and a shy, soft-spoken manner, was sitting on a bench with his wife and daughter, whom he'd brought along to Seattle so that the family could take a vacation as soon as the All-Star game was over.

"Most ballplayers are suspicious," Anderson continued. "They won't talk to a reporter until they see what you write about them. Once you build some trust, they begin to open up. With you, they'll never know—at least until your book comes out. And then it'll be too late. So I doubt they'll talk much."

"Yes, I'm finding that. I talked to a whole bunch of people this afternoon. Peewee Reese was the only guy who was friendly and open."

"Don't let it bother you. It's nothing personal. I always try to keep my ego out of it when I deal with the players. The Peewee Reese thing is typical. Once they retire, they change. Then you can't get them to *stop* talking."

"Why is that?"

"I guess they get to missing it . . . the locker-room camaraderie, the routine of the road trips. That's why Yogi Berra keeps on coaching even though he could easily afford to retire. It gets into their blood, and they miss it and want to talk about it. When I ran into Leo Durocher in New York, he said, 'Next time you're in L. A., why don't you give me a call?' And he gives me his phone number. So when I'm out there, I call him. He acts like I'm intruding. When I remind him that he asked me to call him, he says, 'Okay, come on out. But I'm busy. I can only give you an hour.' Naturally, he ends up talking three hours, and I can't get away."

At Kiana Lodge, in the shadows of huge totem poles, I feasted on baked salmon steaks that turned out to be delicious—a surprise considering the huge quantities that were being prepared—and sipped many gin and tonics. The only familiar person I ran into was the woman in charge of herding the kids in the Pitch, Hit & Run contest, whom I remembered from the evening at the banquet. After she and I carried our laden plates to one of the dozens of picnic tables set up for the guests, I found myself sitting opposite Roy

Hartsfield, the manager of the Toronto Blue Jays. The gin and tonics prompted me to describe for him my evening at Exhibition Stadium in June, especially my encounter with Tony Kubek and my lack of one with Billy Martin. "Oh, hell," said Hartsfield, whose glass I'd refilled with Scotch when I'd gone to fetch another round of drinks for the table. "You shoulda stuck with Billy Martin. He and I and Tony Kubek ended up drinking most of that night away."

The woman from the Pitch, Hit & Run contest confided the most dramatic thing that had happened to her so far: Crystal Fields, the girl from Cumberland, Maryland, who was the winner in the eleven-year-old category, had finally released her tension by bursting into tears when told she couldn't get Dave Parker's autograph.

This was my first inside story of the 1979 All-Star game.

TUESDAY, JULY 17, 1979; 12:00 NOON
INSIDE THE EXHIBITION HALL, SEATTLE CENTER

Invocation by Father William Le Roux, S.J.:

First, I would like to welcome the players and fans of baseball, still America's sport. We gather here, just hours before the beginning of the All-Star game, to break bread, renew old friendships, and to make new ones. This midsummer classic has thrilled the nation for over forty years. Who can forget Carl Hubbell's great feat in nineteen hundred and thirty-four? And what a thrill it was when Ted Williams hit that dramatic home run in nineteen hundred and forty-one. We ask You, Heavenly Father, to bless all the participants, protect them from serious injury. Gracious Lord and God, help all of us Americans during these days of crisis and doubt to find the will and the strength to solve our problems, and to rededicate ourselves to the principles and ideals of our Founding Fathers. May we always seek to do Your will, oh Lord, in all our actions. Bless this food and give food to those who have so much less than what we have. Amen.

Joe Garagiola, Master of Ceremonies:

Let's not put on the spotlight. I'd appreciate it if you wouldn't put it on 'cause all these ballplayers will be telling me all night about the glare off my head [which is shiny bald]. . . . Let me officially welcome you to the annual Commissioner Bowie Kuhn Tupperware Club. [Laughter.] A statistical record: this is the most people at a head table on an afternoon before a night game, and if they all stand up so we can introduce them, we won't get finished until Ash Wednesday. I will introduce them, and just like at the ballpark—it used to be when you went to the ballpark, you clapped when you wanted and you sang when you wanted; now you have to watch the scoreboard, when to clap and when to sing—I will ask you to hold your applause and we will all clap whenever I say "clap," and we'll move it on, because we do have a ball game to play. . . . But first of all, let me get my notes together here. Now, for you ballplayers, a portrait presented to first-time All-Star players and the repeat All-Stars who have changed teams. Please pick up the portrait at the end of the luncheon at the back of the hall. Got that, guys? Got that, Cecil? [He's referring to Cecil Cooper, first baseman of the Milwaukee Brewers.] Okay. I saw you nodding a little bit there, Cecil. I just started and he went to sleep. Now, I will introduce the dais guests, because I'd like to know who they are, just like you. Again, please hold your applause. You're going to appreciate that by the time I get through. From the CBS Radio Network, which broadcasts the game around the world, Vice-President for Programming Frank Miller. Frank Miller. There's Frank over there. Okay, Frank. And tonight's telecast will be seen on NBC-TV by some fifty million Americans and countless numbers in many parts of the world, including Latin America and Japan. Representing NBC-TV, the President of NBC sports, Chet Simmons. There is Chet. [Scattered clapping.] Oh, oh, there's a couple guys clapping for job security, huh, coach? We don't have to do that, do we, Lasorda? We're doing good. [Laughter. Lasorda's team, the Dodgers, is in last place.] I'll tell you: I'm not going to pick on him. The guy went to church this morning, lit two candles, and four guys blew 'em out. [Laughter.]

And here's the president of the Hall of Fame, Ed Stack. Ed, I want to give you my new address. I know you've been looking for it. [Laughter] Strictly political, the Hall of Fame. [Laughter.] Yes, it is! . . .

Hey, I gotta tell you something. I don't know if you're like me; the All-Star game means different things to different people. As a player, all the All-Star game meant to me was three days off. That's all it meant. And that I hadn't been traded. But as a youngster growing up—All-Star: it was when the bubble gum cards really came alive. And it is a privilege now, a thrill, a genuine thrill, 'cause in the first All-Star game, this man pitched two scoreless innings. But then in 1934—I want to get these right—in succession he struck out these eventual Hall of Famers: Babe Ruth, Lou Gehrig, Jimmy Foxx, Al Simmons, Joe Cronin. Let me introduce the Hall of Famer—I want you to applaud *him* because I am going to—the National League Honorary Captain, Carl Hubbell. [Thunderous applause.] Ruth, Gehrig, Foxx, Simmons, and Cronin. I once did in one game what it took all those great hitters to do. Struck out five times. . . . [Laughter.]

Now, when Carl Hubbell struck out all those people—and I heard him say this—he finally gave up a hit to Bill Dickey because he was thinking about the next hitter coming up and it broke his concentration. Here's the next hitter, the American League's Honorary Captain, who was the starting and winning pitcher in the first All-Star game, another Hall of Famer, Lefty Gomez. [Applause.] I wish we had time for him to come up here and say a few words. I'll just shoot that one line of his: Lefty's had triple bypass surgery. The first triple of your career, right, Lefty? [Laughter.]

We go to the National League first. Once again, we'll ask them to stand, and they'll remain standing and then periodically we'll applaud them and kind of break the circulation in the hands, but let's don't applaud everybody. I know it's gonna be hard. Here's a very pleasant surprise for the Reds in 1979—and when he stands up you're gonna get the feeling he should be painting the fence, like Huck Finn—relief pitcher Mike La-Coss. Mike LaCoss. There he is, right there. Just hold it, keep standing, Mike. It'll give you a good stretch. Your wife is not here? Where is she? Oh, she *is* here. Theresa is here. Theresa, would you stand and show the folks the best catch he ever made? [Laughter.]

And next to him a knuckleball family, of Niekros—and we

have two knuckleball All-Stars—we have Joe Niekro of the Houston Astros and his wife, Nancy, with us. And I appreciate knuckleballers because they made me what I am today . . . a broadcaster. [Laughter.]

And here's one of my all-time favorites. You'll recognize this guy; last year's National League Cy Young Award winner, at the age of forty, he's a five-time All-Star, three times in the National League, twice in the American League; very likely to become baseball's first three-hundred-game winner since Early Wynn. He's here with his wife, Blanche: Gaylord Perry. [Applause.] I shook hands with him before, and I slipped right off the podium. [Roar of laughter. This is a reference to Perry's reputation as a spitball pitcher.] That's legal, that pitch. It's nothing. He's just got an itch over there where he keeps reaching.

And Steve Garvey, the only player to win the Commissioner's Trophy as the game's most valuable player twice, here with his wife, Cyndy. Steve Garvey. Right over there. They look like they just fell off a wedding cake, don't they, hanh? He's Mr. Clean. Don Rickles says he's the only first baseman who washes his glove. [Laughter and applause.] I'm telling you, you're going to get tired clapping. Why don't we just wait and then we'll give 'em a big one. You sound just like when they used to take me out of a game—that kind of applause. [Chuckles.] This guy, I don't think you'll be able to contain yourself, though; I should have waited. Here's the leading vote-getter in the National League outfield, the host yesterday of many youngsters at his own All-Star party. And, boy, this year, this guy's going to win the Most Valuable Player Award and the Nobel Peace Prize: Dave Winfield. Hey, Dave, wearing that white suit, you're big enough to be a foul pole. [Laughter.] You should see the size of him back here: I've played in handball courts smaller than that. . . .

Boy, here's a guy, just an amazing man, who's baseball's all-time leading base-stealer; he's heading for the three-thousand-hit plateau in 1979. This is the youngest forty-year-old body you'll ever see. And I do want him to say something: Mr. Lou Brock. Lou Brock. [Prolonged applause.]

Lou Brock:

Thank you, Joe. Ladies and gentlemen, it's a pleasure to be here and, of course, speaking for the National League and the fiftieth All-Star game. This game has been described in the past as the game where your pride is on the line. It's also . . . baseball is also described as a sport with a past. It's also very proud of its past. It's just that we players of today are not trapped by the past. We are here today in Seattle for one reason. That is not to live history, but to make history. Thank you. [Applause.]

Garagiola:

Lou, the next time you come to one of these luncheons, try to prepare something, will ya? [Laughter.] I hate to see guys get up and fumble and bumble, and not know what they're saying. [Laughter.] Wasn't that great? We're not here to live history, we're here to make history. Fantastic. Congratulations again. But that doesn't surprise me. What surprises me is that a guy who steals so much as you is honored. Right? See the good fathers over there? Want to go to confession? Want to go to confession? It's all right, Fathers. It's okay. It's legal. So is Gaylord Perry. But anyhow . . . don't put your head down, Commissioner. I'll get the rap for it. You won't. [Riotous laughter and applause.]

Okay! National League coaches. This guy here, he wins some, he loses some, and everybody's got something to say about him. But at playoff time he's usually there, and I say he's one of my real favorites . . . his wife, Ginny, and here's Danny Ozark of the Philadelphia Phillies. [Applause.] And of course the eternal optimist of the Pittsburgh Pirates, described once . . . if he had been the captain of the Titanic, he would have said, "Don't worry, we're just gonna pick up a little ice and take off." [Laughter.] Chuck Tanner of the Pittsburgh Pirates. [Applause.] Okay. Mind you: everything I've said here, by the way, has been written on this card. Came from the commissioner's office; I want to get that disclaimer in. I don't need the job anyhow. . . . And now the American League. . . . From the Texas Rangers, top relief pitcher in the league his first season with the Rangers, three-time All-Star, and—hey, this has been documented: he's the only man on the American League staff who actually—hear this; this is important . . . to get it on the record—actually *ate* the last four pages of *Blind Ambition*, written by John Dean. [Puzzled laughter.] Ate 'em! Jim Kern. Didn't like the guy who was reading 'em, so he just tore 'em out and ate 'em! I like that, Jim. Shows you're fearless . . . and very literate. [Laughter.]

This young man, he's been the American League's leading hitter since Memorial Day, and he is the fan's choice to open up at shortstop. . . . I do want him to say something—Roy Smalley, Jr., of the Minnesota Twins! Roy Smalley, Jr.! [Applause.]

Roy Smalley, Jr.:

I was asked to talk a little bit about what it means to me to be here at the All-Star game. But I'm not really sure that's possible. I have experienced such a myriad of emotions since we got in late Sunday night that I don't think I can sort it out—sort them out—much less articulate them publicly. Suffice to say that this is the biggest thrill of my career. And it occurs to me that the thrill is not so much derived from the immensely first-class three-day vacation that the city of Seattle has hospitably shown us; it's not so much derived from the ego trip of why or how we all got here; or even the tremendous national exposure that working with this great event has. But as I was working out with my American League teammates yesterday, I realized that the most thrilling aspect of this great event is the chance to play alongside such great athletes that I've admired so much from opposing dugouts, to get to know them as people and, for one brief . . . game, to be their teammates in a great game against our National League counterparts. And I want you to know that to be part of this All-Star camaraderie is just absolutely wonderful. Thank you for having me. [Prolonged applause.]

Garagiola:

[Addressing Smalley's father, Roy Smalley, Sr., who is in the audience.] Roy, I have to ask you: Does he talk like that at home too? Camaraderie? Hanh? Myriad of emotions? Counterparts?! I mean the other team is pretty good, y'know? Roy, fantastic! I'm sitting here, wondering: What the hell is he talking about? [Screams of laughter.] [In a mock stentorian voice.] I THOUGHT I'D LIKE TO TELL YOU ABOUT THE MYRIAD OF EMOTIONS THAT I ARTICULATE FOR YOU! . . . That's great, Roy. Just great. Thank God William F. Buckley was your first-base coach. [Laughter and applause.] I really think that we should introduce Mr. and Mrs. Roy Smalley, Sr. They're right over here. Roy, I know you're proud. There they are. I think his parents—we all derive such great satisfaction from what our kids do—it just happens that he's got an All-Star. Something my father couldn't say. [Laughter.] But there were a lot of things my father couldn't say. He couldn't speak English. . . . But let's move this bombastic review swiftly along here. . . .

Here's a local favorite, playing for the Seattle Mariners. And you certainly can applaud him. I know you will. He's been one of the league's leading hitters. He's with his wife, Linda— Bruce Bochte. [Thunderous cheering and huzzahs.] Bruce, enjoy the cheering. You go oh for nine, you'll see what happens. . . .

Here's a guy who's hit three hundred in three of the last four years. He's doing it again this year. He's with this wife here today. With the Milwaukee Brewers, Octavia and Cecil Cooper. [Perfunctory applause.] You're starting to get a little tired. Why don't you rest your hands? Because these guys will be slighted if they don't get all the same, see? You took it all out on Bochte. [Chuckles.] Is that your real name—Bock-tee? What does it mean? You don't know, hanh? Garagiola means "burned-out cheese factory." Did you know that? [Laughter.] It's the truth! It does! I traced the family tree, y'know? You guys haven't got a lock on it there, Kuhn. Y'know, we got our own roots. . . .

Now, the glasses on the table, you get to take them home, everybody. The players, the portraits: you pick 'em up in the back. And we're happy that you came. Thanks to our hosts. And root for the Seattle Mariners when this game is over; it's your home team. Have a good night tonight. So long, everybody. [Prolonged applause.]

TUESDAY, JULY 17, 1979; 2:00 P.M.
ABOARD THE SHUTTLE BUS RETURNING TO THE OLYMPIC HOTEL

FIRST REPORTER: Where was Reggie?

SECOND REPORTER: Jackson? He wasn't on the dais?

THIRD REPORTER: He wasn't at the lunch even.

FOURTH REPORTER: I wonder when he's planning to get here.

FIRST REPORTER: I wonder *how* he's planning to get here.

THIRD REPORTER: He'll probably descend from the ceiling of the Kingdome just in time to be introduced during the pregame ceremonies.

TUESDAY, JULY 17, 1979; 4:00 P.M.
INSIDE THE KINGDOME

Two items of gossip were circulating among the players, reporters, and officials gathered on the playing field of the Kingdome to take or watch All-Star batting practice. I myself was witnessing an amusing little scene when I heard the news. In a crowd of players and reporters milling around the batting cage, Lou Brock—he who was present not to live history but to make it—had playfully grabbed away the tape-recorder microphone of a young reporter and was doing a good imitation of a nervous but aggressive interviewer pressing his subject, in this case the flabbergasted young reporter himself, for his definition of the ideal baseball player. Suddenly, Pete Rose, who had apparently been following this parody while taking his licks in the cage, came charging into the crowd, nudged the young reporter aside, and said into Brock's mike, "And best of all, he's got a great big cock!" It was just at this moment that Joe Durso joined the group and told me the latest scuttlebutt: first, that Al Rosen had just resigned as president of the Yankees, and, second, that Reggie Jackson had at last arrived and was even now changing into his uniform in the American League locker room.

As I took in what Durso was saying, I wondered if there was any connection between the two bits of news. That Rosen had quit was not surprising. He couldn't have been pleased with George Steinbrenner's recent decision to dismiss Bob Lemon as Yankee manager and replace him with Billy Martin. Lemon was Rosen's man. In fact, it was rumored that Rosen had suffered on Lemon's account. Someone in close touch with the Yankees had told me of a scene in which Steinbrenner, while watching a Yankee game with Rosen on television, had screamed abuse at Rosen for what he regarded as Lemon's managerial incompetence. The abuse had grown so ugly that one witness had felt impelled to leave the room. Whether this story was true—and of course Rosen would be too honorable ever to confirm it—it dovetailed with other stories I'd heard about the experience of working for the combustible Steinbrenner, or Stoneburner, as I liked to call him. John J. McMullen, who had recently bought the Houston Astros and was a former minority owner of the Yankees, had once remarked that there were few things more limited than being a limited partner of George Steinbrenner's. As for what it was like to work under him, one close observer had said, "You can tell right away when you walk into the offices whether he's there or not. If he's not, the secretaries and everybody are completely relaxed. You don't even have to ask! But if he's there—what tension! If tension could hit home runs, the Yankees would win every game!" To judge from the turnover in personnel, no one with any self-respect worked very long for him. Rosen had apparently put up with the abuse because he couldn't afford not to. But he was bound to jump ship as soon as a decent alternative came along, and now apparently something had turned up.

Did all this have anything to do with Reggie Jackson's late arrival? Probably not, though for all his public statements to the contrary, Jackson could surely not have been pleased by the rehiring of his longtime antagonist Billy Martin. He was therefore likely to have strong feelings about Rosen's departure, especially if he connected it to Martin's arrival. Whether or not he'd be willing to admit this, it would at least be interesting to hear Reggie's reaction to the rumor of Rosen's defection. I suggested as much to Joe Durso, and he agreed that we should pay a call on the American League locker room.

When we got there, Reggie was sitting in front of his cubicle, still dressed in street clothes. Dave Anderson was just telling Jackson the news about Rosen.

"Is that so?" said Jackson. "Al quit? He's lucky."

"Come on, Reggie," said Anderson. "Tell me something I can write."

"Write that," said Jackson emphatically. "Al Rosen is a lucky stiff."

The small knot of reporters scribbled furiously as Reggie began to remove his street clothes.

"How come you're not in uniform, Reggie?" another reporter asked.

"I forgot my uniform," Reggie explained, looking a little sheepish. "I brought it home to Oakland after our last game with the Angels in Anaheim, but I came up here without it."

"Was that a Freudian slip?" Durso asked. Reggie grinned and shrugged.

"What are you going to play in?" I asked.

"I called a friend in Oakland to fly my uniform up here. I just hope it'll be here by game time."

At this point, Lee MacPhail, the American League president, entered the dressing room. "Come on, Reggie," he said. "They're getting ready to take the team photo."

"I'll be right there," said Reggie.

An equipment man handed a Seattle Mariner uniform to Jackson, who hung it in his locker and continued removing his street clothes.

"You mean you're going to appear in the All-Star team portrait wearing a Seattle Mariner uniform?" I exclaimed.

"That's right," said Reggie, removing the Seattle blouse from its hanger and thrusting an arm into its sleeve.

"Boy, I want to see the reaction to this," I said, turning to leave.

"Fuck you!" called Reggie cheerfully to my back.

("*Gee, Reggie said 'Fuck you' to me*," I thought. "*We've certainly come a ways since he refused to talk to me.*")

"Hey, Reggie," somebody asked, as I arrived at the locker-room exit side by side with Dave Anderson. "If you played for Seattle, would they name a salmon after you?"

"Yeah, they'll name a salmon after him," muttered Anderson as we passed through the door. "A *schnook* salmon."

TUESDAY, JULY 17, 1979; 5:38 P.M.
IN THE GRANDSTAND OF THE KINGDOME, HIGH ABOVE THE FIRST-BASE SIDE OF HOME PLATE

It was now just a couple of minutes until game time. Former President Gerald R. Ford had taken his seat in a box behind third base and had bitten into a hot dog for the benefit of the photographers who had gathered directly below him. Among them was Scavullo, whom I'd barely glimpsed in the past two days. Ted Giannoulas's chicken had mounted the roof of the National League dugout and commenced his hyperkinetic routine. I'd climbed to my bench seat in the temporary press section so high up it was close to the rafters of the Kingdome, my status being correspondingly low among the four hundred accredited reporters said to be in attendance.

The starting lineups had been introduced, as well as the remaining members of each All-Star squad. The honorary captains, Lefty Gomez and Carl Hubbell, had toddled out to home plate from their respective dugouts and shaken each other's hand for probably the fiftieth time in the past two days. Andrea McArdle had become the youngest person ever to sing the anthems—Canadian and American—before an All-Star game (it being the International Year of the Child). And she had sung them as well as I'd heard them sung in a season of innumerable anthems. The large crowd in the Kingdome had settled into a slightly sticky state of expectancy, the air-conditioning having been set at seventy-eight degrees in compliance with President Carter's energy-saving guidelines. Across the land, an estimated fifty million television viewers were perched before their sets.

Now Danny Kaye would throw out the first ball, since he was, according to a press handout, "the United Nations' Ambassador to the World's Children." As Kaye walked to the pitcher's mound accompanied by some fifty children clad in yellow jump suits, I thought what fun it would be if in further tribute to the children, a Burger King winner were used as a pinch-hitter at some point in the game. It would never happen, unless of course Bill Veeck were in charge. Still, what Danny Kaye and his entourage did when they reached the mound was a satisfying substitute. As All-Star catcher Darrell Porter waited squatting behind the plate, fifty-one people went into their windups and fifty-one balls came bouncing weakly toward Porter's waiting mitt. It was Kaye's best moment since *The Kid from Brooklyn*.

As the National League All-Stars took the field, I thought of the fifty million video watchers. I recalled having read somewhere that during commercials on major sports telecasts, the flushing of toilets sent the water pressure dropping all over America. It was one of the few arguments I could think of for having lots of commercial breaks.

Just think what it would do to the nation's plumbing if there were only one or two.

TUESDAY, JULY 17, 1979; 9:00 P.M.
IN THE KINGDOME INTERVIEW ROOM

When the game was over, I drifted in a stream of reporters to a room somewhere in the depths of the Kingdome, where a microphone, a table set on a platform, and a forest of chairs had been set up for postgame interviews. When I commented to my neighbor that surely four hundred reporters couldn't be crammed into the room, I was told that the interviews would be piped to loudspeakers in every press section of the ballpark.

And indeed they had certainly made it easy for reporters. The rival managers were brought forth to give their impressions of the game; and the starring players were trotted out to describe how they felt while performing their prodigies. Every mumbled word of every question was repeated loud and clear by either Bob Fishel, the secretary and assistant to the president of the American League, or Blake Cullen, director of public relations for the National League. And just in case anyone should miss anything that was said, Thermofaxed sheets carrying all significant quotes were issued within minutes of the words leaving their speakers' mouths. You could be a regional monthly's backup stringer bombed out on ballpark beer and still file a story that read as if you had been in the heart of the combat zone.

On the other hand, the complexity of the machinery seemed to discourage hard questioning. Maybe I was projecting my own timidity, but it struck me that to be an aggressive reporter under the circumstances would be almost literally to bite the hand that fed you. At any rate, in the exercise that followed the questions were soft enough to evoke such responses as: "It's just a great honor to play in the summer classic" (Dave Parker of the Pirates); "It was a treemendous game from the fans' standpoint" (American League manager Bob Lemon); "It was the type of ball game that could have gone either way" (National League manager Tommy Lasorda); and "I hit the home run for my folks. I'm proud I did it for them" (Lee Mazzilli of the Mets).

There was, incidentally, a baseball game that was played before the interview session. As usual, the National League won—7–6 this time. Objectively, it was probably a pretty exciting game, a seesaw battle, as the saying went, with the winner overtaking the loser in the later innings, on a home run sublime and four bases on balls ridiculous. There was a decent amount of power hitting (six doubles, two home runs, and a triple), though not as many homers as had been predicted for the lively little ballpark. There were two assists on whirling-dervish throws from the outfield by Dave Parker (an All-Star game record); as manager Lasorda put it, "He displayed an instinctiveness that you want to see in a ballplayer." And a yellow sheet of "Post-Game Notes" could report the following additional items of interest about the game: "The 3:11 game time was one minute longer than the previous record for a nine-inning game, which was set in Cleveland in 1954"; "Only one other pitcher has won two successive All-Star games, as Bruce Sutter did for the National League. The other was Don Drysdale, of the Dodgers, who did it at Anaheim in 1967 and Houston in 1968. Curiously, each man's second victory was under a dome"; and "Carl Yastrzemski's start at first base was his first defensive experience since June 30, because of a leg injury." (The last item on this note sheet said that "an eleven-year-old girl, Crystal Fields of Cumberland, Maryland, showed her heels to the boys in the Pitch, Hit & Run finals, which preceded the game." This seemed a slightly peculiar metaphor to choose for a contest that only partly involved foot-racing (and that against the clock). But then, "roundheeled" in Elizabethan parlance was an epithet applied to women who were easy to seduce. Was male chauvinism subliminally rearing its porcine head in response to Crystal's victory?)

But I'd been interested in the game only as far as it had engaged my rooting interest in the Yankees. And in that respect, it had proved a dud. The American League, in which the Yankees played, had lost. The Yankee players had not done well. Tommy John had not played in the game at all, Reggie Jackson had grounded into a fielder's choice out in a key situation, and while Graig Nettles had fielded flawlessly on the Astroturf that had so often stymied him in the past and had gotten a clutch single in the eighth inning with Brian Downing on second, it had been on this play that Dave Parker had thrown Downing out at home plate. As for Ron Guidry: it was "Louisiana Lightning" who had been called in with the bases loaded in the ninth, only to walk Lee Mazzilli and force in what turned out to be the game's winning run.

I was furious about the use of Guidry. It was bad enough that he'd been the "goat" of the game. It was even worse that the man he'd walked was a player for the lowly crosstown Mets. But most irritating of all was Guidry's being called on in the first place, as well as the circumstance under which it had happened. Guidry had pitched eight and two-thirds innings against the Angels the previous Sunday, and any fool knew that with only two days' rest Guidry's arm was usually as weak as an incubator baby's. Certainly Bob Lemon, Guidry's former manager, ought to have known. Yet he'd not only called in Guidry at the most critical moment, he'd done so after ordering Guidry to warm up no less than three times earlier in the game. Guidry's arm must have been so weak by the ninth inning that he wouldn't have dared to give Mazzilli anything decent to swing at. No wonder he'd walked him!

Now it was true that Lemon was asked during the postgame interview about his handling of Guidry:

REPORTER: Bob, you brought in Guidry in that situation there. He did do some relief work earlier [in the season], but you had other relief pitchers in the bullpen. Why a guy who's principally a starter?

BOB FISHEL: [Repeats question.]

BOB LEMON: Well, I saw him relieve when he was comin' up [a reference to Guidry's having been used as a reliever earlier in his Yankee career]. I saw him relieve this year for me in New York. And he's a strikeout pitcher. And that's sure as hell when we needed a strikeout.

REPORTER: Do you think he lost anything warming up so many times? He warmed up three times.

FISHEL: [Repeats question.]

LEMON: Well, Ron is an experienced reliever, and he could tell by the situation. . . . If you noticed—I watched him—he was throwin' easy. It only takes him a few pitches to get it hot. When I start walkin' out there, he unloads a little bit and then he gets the extra eight pitches when he comes in and he's ready.

But this failed to confront the issue of Guidry's being weak in the first place from having only two days' rest. I wanted to press Lemon further, but timidity and the elaborateness of the interview process inhibited me. So as soon as the formal interviews were over, I headed for the American League locker room to see what Guidry had to say. He was surprisingly outspoken:

GUIDRY: I didn't have all that much to start with.

LEHMANN-HAUPT: Aren't you usually . . . after only two days' rest, aren't you usually pretty tired?

GUIDRY: Yeah, well, that's the thing, y'know. I pitched Sunday, and I threw about 140 pitches. But y'know, to get up three times—three or four times in a night. . . . The first time would have been all right, or would have been a little bit better. But after that you just don't have any more.

LEHMANN-HAUPT: So you were tired when you went in?

GUIDRY: Yeah, I passed by Nettles and I told Graig I didn't think I had very much when I was going in.

I was elated by Guidry's candor. He'd all but come out and criticized Bob Lemon for his handling of him. That he would confide his disgruntlement to me seemed to show a level of trust between player and reporter that usually took years to develop and was especially unusual in Guidry, who had impressed me so far this season as being particularly reserved. Had he finally recognized me after half a dozen meetings? Had he perhaps read the few paragraphs I'd been asked to do on him as a caption for a Richard Avedon photograph that had appeared the previous April in *Mademoiselle* magazine? Or had I spent so much time with Joe Durso that some of the polish of a veteran reporter had begun to rub off on me? Whatever the explanation, I felt a surge of confidence I hadn't felt before, and I proudly conveyed what I'd gotten from Guidry to the reporter who happened to be my seatmate on the bus that was taking us back to the Olympic Hotel.

"Guidry was pretty unhappy with Lemon," I said.

"Yeah, so I heard," said the reporter.

"He feels he was mishandled," I went on.

"I know he does," said the reporter.

I was puzzled. How could he suspect Guidry of being disgruntled when the Yankee pitcher had confided his personal feelings exclusively to me?

Before going to my room, I stopped by the working press room, the Olympic Bowl, to see if any last-minute press releases might have been distributed. On the long table I discovered a pile of pink legal-sized paper that hadn't been there earlier in the day. I picked up the top sheet and read:

MEDIA INFORMATION
ALL-STAR POST-GAME QUOTES
Tuesday, July 17, 1979
SEATTLE KINGDOME

Ron Guidry

Ron Guidry warmed up three times in the bullpen: second inning, sixth inning, and eighth inning.

"I didn't have nothing when I came in and said so to Graig (Nettles) when I walked by him going to the mound."

"When you don't have nothing, you don't lay the ball over the plate, not with these hitters."

"I can't finesse hitters . . . I'm not a finesse pitcher."

"I'm still recuperating from pitching on Sunday and my muscles are still tight." (Guidry normally pitches with four days' rest.)

When asked if he was tired or disappointed, he said:

"I'm both, but disappointed first."

"This is the lowest position you can reach, coming in and walking a guy in that situation."

So much for Guidry's confiding only in me, and so much for my scoop. As I read the release, it flashed in my mind that maybe I had been bugged while talking to Guidry. But then I saw the glaring flaw in my logic. The revelations printed in the press release were even more intimate than the ones he had given me.

CHAPTER

SUPERSTARRING

IF SEATTLE'S ALL-STAR CELEBRATION was cool, clean, new, stream-lined, synthetic, antiseptic, and so well organized it was hard to draw a spontaneous breath, Portland's old-timers' day was the exact opposite. Even the Portland mascot was pathetic, especially com-pared to Ted Giannoulas's frenetic chicken. Where the chicken was slick, sassy, and funny enough to deserve its national celebrity, the Portland Beaver was a bumbling, sluggish nonentity, looking for all the world, with its sad apologetic eyes and its shabby moth-eaten hide, like an uninvited guest who knows he has halitosis. To top off the sense of things gone wrong that pervaded Portland's Civic Sta-dium, my tape recorder broke down within a few minutes of my ar-rival. It was as if some presiding evil spirit didn't want a record made of the evening. So I was forced to recall events from memory, an ex-ercise I found not unlike remembering a hallucination.

I had driven down from Seattle to Portland with Scavullo and his assistant, Bill Calderaro, because Jim Bouton had told me about the old-timers' celebration that was to succeed Seattle's All-Star game by a day. Bouton had been sure that he would be the only player there that I'd know of. But I had decided that we ought to include at least one minor-league town in our itinerary, and the Portland Beavers had held a special interest for me ever since my high school days at Putney, when my history teacher, who came from Portland, had made a habit of fending off my enthusiasm for the Yankees by asking almost daily how the Portland Beavers were doing, as if anyone in all of New England had the slightest inkling of the answer to that one.

Besides, Jim Bouton had made the Portland baseball scene sound highly colorful. He hadn't played for the Portland Beavers; he'd been with a team called the Portland Mavericks. What was the difference between the Beavers and the Mavericks? As Bouton had described it over a bowl of soup with me back in May:

BOUTON: I don't know the exact date that the Portland Beavers became extinct, but I think it was somewhere around 1974. They weren't drawing fans anymore, or not enough to support the team. So they dropped out of the league. That's when a local guy named Bing Russell started up an A Team in Portland to play in the Northwest League. This was going to be a new kind of minor-league team—actually a very old kind of minor-league team—a team that's not affiliated with any organization, and anybody who could make the team would play.

So the Mavericks came into being. And since they weren't affiliated, and since a lot of the guys were castoffs of organizations that had given up on guys that nobody wanted, and since they had open tryouts and kids would come all the way from every part of the country after hitchhiking and riding a bus and a train, and they had dozens and dozens of guys out there, some of them with no baseball ability whatsoever—they had just read about it in *The Sporting News* and figured, "Hey, I can do that!" you know, 'cause they once played in junior high or something like that, so you had all sorts of . . . y'know, you had butchers out there and deliverymen, and then you'd have a guy who'd just got released from Double A, and then you'd have a couple of troublemakers—it was sort of like The Dirty Dozen of baseball teams. And those were the Mavericks. They played there in Portland for about. . . . Well, I hooked on with them in 1975, I think, and I played for them the last part of the 1977 season when I was trying to make a serious comeback. I played parts of those two seasons. So I know they were in existence for that period of time.

What was interesting about the Mavericks was that they drew fans. Lots of them. They would draw two to three thousand fans at a normal game; if there was any kind of a special game, there would be five to ten thousand people there. And there was a certain spirit to the team—the fact that it was being run by Bing Russell, who had some creative ideas, and the writers sort of adopted the Mavericks like the New York writers adopted the Mets. The only difference was that the Mavericks won games; they were very exciting to watch. There was a lot of crazy things about the Mavericks, but the thing that I liked best about them was that they were willing to let me play on the team.

LEHMANN-HAUPT: But at some point they became the Beavers again, didn't they?

BOUTON: Well, what happened was they were drawing; they had one of the highest attendance records in organized baseball. So organized baseball began to look at the territory again and say, "Hey, wait a second; maybe this place is coming alive now." And in the National Association—which is what all minor leagues are part of, including the Mavericks, they were part of the National Association; they were a member of the Northwest League—a senior league is allowed to adopt a territory. The Triple A said, "We want that territory again." So they moved in; they wanted it back again, 'cause they saw that it was doing well at the A level, and they thought, "At the Triple A it'll do even better," right? So they ended up barging in there, and of course they had to pay. Bing Russell took them to court and said, "I want to get paid for them taking my franchise." He ended up winning something like $380,000. He took 'em for a big sum of money, and organized baseball is, I'm sure, very upset about having to pay that out.

So now they're Triple A again and they can't draw flies because they just don't have that kind of magic that the Mavericks had, with their bright red uniforms and a bunch of guys nobody wanted and daredevil baseball, and it was . . . it was fun to watch the Mavs and it wasn't fun to watch the Beavers.

I'm the only Maverick to be invited back to the Beavers' old-timers' game. I mean this is really old-timers' day for the Portland Beavers. The Mavericks have always been looked upon by the Beavers with great dis. . . . "Who are these crazy kids who played here in this stadium for four years?" And yet we—I mean the Mavericks; I wasn't there the whole time—we were the ones that really turned that town upside down. And their own Beavers could never understand that. They sort of resented the attention that the Mavs got. And now here is the Portland old-timers' game, but it's being run by the Beavers. They were talked into including me because the owner, Dave Hersh, felt I would draw some people to the ballpark. That's why I'm invited back. I'm the only Mav, Maverick, who'll play in a Beaver old-timers' game. But it's because I'm Jim Bouton, the former major-leaguer, not because I was a Maverick. The Mavericks won't be able to buy a ticket to that game. The old Beavers didn't want to have anything to do with 'em.

But the Mav years were wonderful years. The parts of two years that I spent there were just great. They had some nice traditions on the team. They traveled around in a school bus that was painted red, and it was a *very* red bus—even the bumpers were red—and the main feature of the bus was the loudspeaker on the top. Why they had one there I don't know. It was just one of these old buses that happened to have a loud-speaker on the top. And from inside the bus you could talk into a microphone and whatever you said would boom out over the loudspeaker. So the Mavericks would . . . we'd pull into some town like Bellingham, Washington, just like the old barn-storming teams of years ago, and we would drive through the downtown area and what we would do is we would challenge the people on the streets. We would announce our presence: "The Portland Mavericks are in town. The big, bad Portland Mavericks. Get your women and children off the street." Y'know? And we'd pull up to a stop sign at a very busy inter-section and somebody would say, "Hey, you. You in the blue shirt. Yeah, you heard. What did you mix in the salad?"—if somebody was really overweight, or something. Or: "You, lady. In the red dress. That's disgusting." Just say gross things to the people. All kinds of lewd things to the girls. And it was very funny to hear some of these things being blared out of the loudspeaker. And of course the townspeople then all wanted to come to the ballpark and watch us get creamed by the local team. So it was great for building fan interest. And then we would drive out to a motel. Each time we'd pull into a town we'd have to stay farther outside of town because the motel wouldn't let us back again, and we ended up staying thirty-five miles outside of Bellingham. That's the closest we could get to the town. Because we'd been kicked out of three motels in two years. One time we took a motel room and just filled it with beer cans. I mean, it was just literally . . . you opened the door and beer cans came out the door.

And they would insult the other team, the other players. They had a tradition where any time the opposing pitcher got knocked out of the game, and the manager would come out to the mound and take him out, the entire Maverick team would stand in front of the dugout and they would sing very loudly, "Happy trails to you, until we meet again. Happy trails to you. . . ." And we would get into arguments with the fans. I remember one argument: there were just a lot of obscene and gross things being hollered back and forth, and the umpire came over to our bench and said, "Hey, come on you guys. Knock it off. You have more class than that." And one of the guys said, "Oh, yeah? Who says?" It was a lot of fun. Those were the Mavericks.

Anyway, there had been signs along the way that Bouton might be wrong about his being the only familiar player in attendance. Among the many people Joe Durso had introduced me to at the old-timers' celebration at Shea Stadium on the Saturday before the All-Star game was Hank Aaron, who had let it drop that he planned to be in Portland on the following Wednesday.

I was surprised because of what Bouton had told me, so I tried to pin Aaron down.

LEHMANN-HAUPT: You'll be in Portland?

AARON: Yeah, right.

LEHMANN-HAUPT: Why are *you* going to Portland?

AARON: Goin' to play in their all-star game.

138

LEHMANN-HAUPT: Did you ever play for them?

AARON: No, no. I was just invited back there, is all. I've . . . uh, left . . . some people out there . . . some friends of mine. . . . They've got an all-star game out there.

LEHMANN-HAUPT: I thought it was going to be an all-star game for the Portland Beavers.

AARON: [With a trace of irritation in his voice.] I don't really know what it is. I haven't the slightest idea. All I know is I was invited, and that's. . . . [Recovering.] I go out there all the time to do salmon fishing.

LEHMANN-HAUPT: Oh, I wanted to do that, but I won't have time. Where do you go?

AARON: [Recovering his good humor.] I go out there in Portland and pick up a friend of mine who I met there two years ago, and he and I go out about twenty miles and do a lot of salmon fishing.

LEHMANN-HAUPT: In the Columbia River?

AARON: Yeah, right!

LEHMANN-HAUPT: Do you wade?

AARON: We wade, and every other thing.

LEHMANN-HAUPT: Are the salmon running this time of year?

AARON: Not this time, no. Not this time. I just know these people . . . and that's why I'm going out there.

LEHMANN-HAUPT: Oh, I see . . .

But I didn't see at all, because Oregon seemed a long way to go to visit fishing buddies and not go fishing. But Aaron's attitude made me feel I'd best not push the matter.

There was something oppressive—even ominous—about Portland's Civic Stadium. Maybe it was simply the overwhelming afternoon heat, which made the air difficult to breathe. But the hollow echo of our footsteps in the empty wooden grandstand, the way the shadow of the stands divided the dusty field into areas of yellow and brown, the sight of a dozen or so old men in red satin shorts cavorting stiffly on the patchy infield, the huge blankness of the high concrete wall in right field—all combined to make me feel the mysterious dread conveyed by the early surreal paintings of de Chirico.

But it was no time to sink into the quicksand of lassitude. Too much was happening down there on the playing field. In front of the Beavers' rickety dugout, a whirling mob was stirring up a visible cloud of dust. When we got closer to it, Scavullo began shooting pictures, while I tried to figure out what was going on. Two gray-haired women wearing pedal pushers and holding hands were tipsily asking everyone in sight for his autograph. Children were craning their heads over the roof of the visitors' dugout and screaming for attention. Television technicians were dragging thick snakes of cable to and fro through the rust-colored dirt. And in the midst of the crowd, a young man wearing a light blue double-knit suit with a red carnation in the lapel and waving a huge black cigar between his thumb and forefinger was pacing in aimless circles and shouting un-heeded orders: "Move the cameras over here, please! Hold the crowd a little, please! Won't you move back into the stands, boys and girls, ladies and gentlemen? Please!"

What was the purpose of all this confusion? Once I'd plunged into the mob, I noticed a pattern to it. Here and there, people were gathered tightly into smaller clusters. Working my way into the middle of one, I discovered men with microphones talking to a player in a Los Angeles Dodger uniform. It took me a moment to realize that it was none other than Maury Wills, a little grayer and paunchier than the original article, but unmistakably the great Dodger base stealer. And in a neighboring clump was the former third baseman Pete Ward, wearing a blue-gray Yankee road uni-form. And a few steps away, in Yankee pinstripes, was Whitey Ford, talking to the great Cleveland Indian fastball pitcher "Sudden Sam" McDowell, who was dressed in the red satin uniform of the Port-land Beavers.

I was reminded of the thrill I'd felt when I first arrived in the Yankees' spring training locker room. It was like seeing your bubble gum card collection come to life, as Joe Garagiola had put it at the All-Star banquet. But now I had a very pointed question to ask them. What in the world were they doing here in Portland's dilapi-dated stadium?

Elbowing my way into the group surrounding Whitey Ford and Sam McDowell, I waited for another interviewer to finish, and then asked, "Excuse me, Mr. Ford. But how come you're here?"

He looked at me and narrowed his eyes a little. "Flew out to see some friends," he said a little brusquely.

"You flew all the way from the East Coast to the West Coast just to see some friends?"

"It's no big deal. Didn't even have to change my watch from East Coast time." He held his forearm up, rotating his wrist. Sure enough, his watch was set at 8:40, three hours ahead. Then he strode away, descended the steps of the nearby dugout, and leaned against the wall in the classic position of a manager surveying the field. I watched him for a while inconspicuously. When he thought no one was looking at him, he retrieved a bottle of beer he'd apparently left on the floor, took a draft from it, put it down again, and clapped his hands as if he were cheering on his players.

I spotted Jim Bouton walking in from the outfield. He looked slight and boyish in his bright red Maverick uniform.

"Hey, Jim. I thought you were going to be the only player I'd recognize."

"Yeah, well, I didn't know. They seem to have made other arrangements."

"Who else is here?"

"Mays, Banks, Aaron, Johnny Lipon, Charlie Silvera, Dino Restelli, Larry Jansen."

"Willie Mays? Where?"

"Some of them are still in the dressing room."

"How come they're all here?"

"I don't know. You'll have to ask Dave Hersh, the Beavers' owner." Bouton pointed to the young man in the blue suit, who was still walking in circles and waving his cigar.

"He's the *owner*? How old is he?"

"Twenty-four, somebody said."

But Hersh was too busy issuing commands, so I ducked through the home-team dugout and into the clubhouse. Making my way through rooms like ancient catacombs, I finally turned a corner and found myself standing at the end of a room-length bench. It was crowded with men in various major-league uniforms. Near one end was Willie Mays, and a few feet away from him, Hank Aaron. Still in my unselfconscious state of excitement, I approached them.

"Excuse me, Mr. Mays?"

"Yeah?" He looked at me with flat, suspicious eyes.

"What brings you here?"

He regarded me a moment unsmilingly. "They call me," he said.

"You just got on the plane and flew here 'cause they called you?"

Mays's eyes shifted back and forth between my face and some point beyond my shoulder, and finally focused in the distance. "Ask him. Ask Chris."

"Chris? Chris who?"

"Hey, Chris," he shouted, his voice going up half an octave to the famous "Say, Hey" register. "Chris! This guy want to meet you." He looked at me again. "Go talk to him," he said coldly. "He'll tell you."

"What's his last name?"

"Pelekoudas."

"Chris Pelekoudas?"

"Right."

I turned away from Mays and approached the man he had called to.

"How come these guys all came out here today?"

"They were invited by the Portland Beavers. It's a Hall of Fame game. These are Hall of Fame players. Potential Hall of Famers, and . . . ah . . . Hall of Famers that have already been named. They just wanted to put on a show for the people. It's a hell of an idea."

"What's your connection?"

"My son works for Dave Hersh, the owner."

"I see. Your name is very familiar. I apologize for not being able to place it."

"National league umpire."

"Oh, yes. I remember."

Turning to the bench where the players were sitting, Pelekoudas cried out, "It's nothing till I call it! Right, Aaron?"

"Huh?" said Aaron.

"It's nothing till I call it!"

"That's right," said Aaron.

"Nothing till the sign goes up! Steerike!"

There was a chorus of cheers and laughter.

I turned to Aaron. "Mr. Aaron? We met at Shea Stadium? The Mets' old-timers' day? We talked about fishing?"

Aaron regarded me gloomily. "Uh-huh."

"Are you going to do any fishing while you're out here?"

142

"No, I'm leaving tomorrow morning."

"I'm told the steelhead are running in the Columbia."

"That right?"

"They say the salmon are so thick in Puget Sound you can hit 'em over the head with a canoe paddle."

Aaron looked blank.

"You didn't go to the All-Star game last night, did you?"

"Nah." Again, the blank and hostile stare.

There was an awkward silence, then Aaron looked away grimly, leaving me to stare at his profile. I began to feel a little crestfallen and thought of what Dave Anderson had said on our ferry ride about not letting your ego get involved when talking to the players.

"What're you doing here?" someone called out.

I looked in the direction of the voice. A man in a Chicago Cubs uniform was staring at me with eyes that danced mischievously. It had to be Ernie Banks, the Cub who had played so well for so long that Chicago had actually erected a statue in his honor.

"I'm writing a book about baseball."

"You—are—writing—a—book—about—baseball?" he said with what seemed like mock deliberation, though his face had an appealing warmth to it. "Are you coming to Chicago in September?"

"I don't know. I hadn't planned to."

"You better be in Chicago in September, because the Cubs are going to win the pennant this year!" He elbowed the players on either side of him. "YOU CAN'T WRITE A BOOK ABOUT BASEBALL UNLESS YOU COME TO CHICAGO IN SEPTEMBER," he sang merrily. "BECAUSE THE CUBS ARE GOING TO WIN THE PENNANT THIS YEAR."

"Yessir," I said, saluting him. His patter was not unfriendly, but it was hard to take seriously since the Cubs, while still within striking distance of first place, did not look anything like the class of their division this year.

"I'm telling you," Banks sang at me, "you better be in Chicago in September. You'll see. Don't forget I told you!"

"Right, right," I said, giving him a grin and turning to leave. He had bailed me out of my awkward position with Aaron and simultaneously gotten rid of me. It was a skillful performance, I thought, as I left the locker room and groped my way deeper into the tumble-down clubhouse. A short hallway led to an open doorway on the right. When I reached it I found myself peering into a small room, a cubicle almost, which looked at a glance to be the team trainer's quarters. The few shelves on the wall were crowded with bottles and bandage rolls. An examining table all but blocked the entranceway. Seated on the near edge of this table, with one foot dangling and the other resting on the floor, was a gray-haired man dressed in gray flannel trousers, a blue single-breasted blazer, and a rep tie. He was alone in the room, completely absorbed in signing his name on a baseball. I experienced that moment of disorientation one invariably does when encountering a famous public face in private. But even before I had gathered my senses, a loudspeaker was booming in my head that I had better shape up and be at my best, because I was now alone in a tiny room with Joe DiMaggio.

My first coherent thought was to turn around and walk back to where I had come from, as if I'd stumbled on the place where my Christmas presents had been hidden and could undo my transgression by reversing my movement. Then I opened my mouth to apologize, but, luckily, no sound came out. DiMaggio finished signing the baseball he was holding, put it down, and picked up another from an open box beside him on the table. Now I began to recall all the lore of DiMaggio's legendary reticence. The man simply didn't talk to strangers. When Gay Talese had tried to interview him for an *Esquire* magazine profile, DiMaggio was supposed to have told him, "You're invading my rights!" Talese had had to write his piece without ever talking to his subject. Legion were the stories of reporters who had approached DiMaggio with an elaborate question, only to be fobbed off with a single unsatisfying sentence and left in that numbed state of embarrassment I'd just experienced with Hank Aaron. It was said that DiMaggio could fill whole rooms with cold black silence. Hadn't Marilyn Monroe testified at their divorce hearing that he would sink into such dark moods that he would tell her to leave him alone when she tried to penetrate that darkness?

Even gregarious people found DiMaggio intimidating. A photographer with *Sports Illustrated* once spent an entire evening in his company without ever working up the courage to address him directly. Even my friend Sidney Zion, whose reputation as a man of the world had been won with his determination not to be cowed by people of fame and social muscle, had confessed to being tonguetied in the presence of the Yankee Clipper. A companion of Zion's had once dragged him to DiMaggio's table at a restaurant, and he'd stood dumbstruck for a moment before blurting out, "Joe, you gave me such thrills!"—an utterance so at odds with Zion's fabled capacity to be hip under pressure that he continued to blush at the memory of it for decades afterward.

Still, I had within the past twenty minutes been cold-shouldered by some of the most famous players in the game. I might as well risk adding my ultimate hero to the list. If by some slim chance he didn't act standoffish, it would more than compensate me for every last snub I had encountered in this baseball season.

"Excuse me, Mr. DiMaggio. My name is Christopher Lehmann-Haupt. I'm the book reviewer for the *New York Times*. I'm writing a book about baseball. Would you mind if I asked you a couple of questions?"

DiMaggio looked up slowly, stared at me in what I at first took to be astonishment at my audacity, put down the pen and baseball he was holding, smiled, and reached out to shake my hand.

"Lehmann-Haupt! Of course not. Glad to meet you."

Wondering for a moment whether he actually had recognized my name, I shook the question off and plunged ahead: "Ah, what brings you to Portland?"

"Well, I was at the game up in Seattle and I have some friends in this town. So it was convenient to drop by."

He gave me a long, direct look. "Also," he added, "the Beavers made it worth my while."

"I see. Aren't you going to put on a uniform, then?"

"No. Even if they had one that fit me, I can't put on baseball spikes anymore." He gestured at his feet, which were shod in loafers. "Those feet are so full of bone spurs from having balls fouled off them, I can't even wear laced shoes anymore. Anyway, they've made me the manager of the all-stars for some reason. Come on."

He stood up, put a hand on my shoulder, and gently turned me back toward the door, guiding me into the corridor. I floated, as if on an escalator, as we moved through the clubhouse, up the dugout steps, and into the tumultuous crowd that greeted us. I felt as if I'd won a role in some movie of the 1940s—*The Babe Ruth Story* or *The Pride of the Yankees*.

On the field, we were surrounded by a surging crowd of reporters, photographers, and fans. It was embarrassing to be caught in the wash of attention that was rolling in on him, but it was also thrilling. There was Scavullo, aiming his camera at us, smiling and gesturing with a sideways tilt of his head for me to move closer to DiMaggio so that he could frame us together. I leaned toward DiMaggio, despite being certain that he'd had enough of me by now. I looked for an escape, but the crowd pressed closer around us.

"What sort of book are you writing?" he said, continuing to concentrate on signing autographs.

"You mean, what's my angle?"

"Well, I didn't want to say that." He was tearing the top off a cellophane bag of peanuts that someone had handed him. "Okay, what's your angle?" He held the peanuts out to me.

("*I'm thrilled because Joe DiMaggio is offering to share his peanuts with me!*" I thought. "*I'm actually thrilled!*")

"Uh, no thanks. Well, so far the book is about a typical fan who suddenly finds himself having to be a reporter. Obviously, the fan is me."

"I see. Good idea."

"I think it's going to have to be one of those books in which the author is the hero, or antihero. Sort of like Norman Mailer writes."

"I haven't read Norman Mailer."

"He's a good man."

"I'm sure he is."

(Later, when the appalling clumsiness I'd showed in mentioning the controversial biographer of Marilyn Monroe to her former husband had finally dawned on me, I wondered if DiMaggio hadn't said, "I *don't* read Mailer" instead of "I *haven't* read Mailer." It was too bad my tape recorder had broken down.)

"As a matter of fact," I now ventured almost in a shout, "what made me a baseball fan to begin with was a Sunday afternoon in 1948 when you hit three home runs against the Cleveland Indians. Two of them were off Bob Feller. Who the other pitcher was I've forgotten."

"Bob Muncrief."

"I was about to ask you if you remembered that afternoon."

"I sure do. And so does this guy, I'll bet." DiMaggio gestured to his right, where a middle-aged man wearing a Cleveland Indian uniform was now also signing autographs. I blinked and looked again. It was Bob Feller, who appeared to have materialized at DiMaggio's command. He looked up and smiled at both of us.

146

"This is the *New York Times*'s book man," DiMaggio said to Feller. "He just reminded me of that game in 1948 when I beat you guys with three home runs."

"I remember," Feller said.

"And Don Black," DiMaggio added, "the starting pitcher in the second game that afternoon, threw me a fastball right down the middle that I should have killed. But instead of hitting a fourth home run, I fouled it off."

A growing crowd was still surging around us while DiMaggio continued signing autographs. Yet he went on listening to me as if we were still alone in the training room.

"I wondered . . . uh, I asked Mel Allen about that game, because of course he announced it. He remembered it right away too, and told an interesting story about it. He said you'd been in a slump, that on the train from Chicago to Cleveland he'd stopped to talk to you in your sleeping compartment and pointed out that you'd moved one of your feet back from where you normally placed it. He didn't exactly take credit for helping you out of your slump, but . . ."

"Well, it makes a good story."

"Just a story, huh?"

"I think so."

"He was never in a slump against me," put in Feller, laughing.

"I think I went about five for ten in that Chicago series, with at least a couple of home runs," DiMaggio went on. "Not exactly a slump. But no single piece of advice ever gets a hitter out of a slump. I remember there was a woman who told me that my back looked different when I wasn't hitting well. People always give advice like that. The greatest danger is to listen to them. My great fortune as a hitter was that I hardly ever had a slump that lasted. Did you see the All-Star game?"

"Oh, yes. I spent three days in Seattle."

"Anything interesting happen?"

"The usual things, I guess. Oh, Reggie Jackson showed up without his uniform. He said he forgot it."

"No kidding!"

"Yeah. He had to have it flown in from his home in Oakland. It arrived barely in time for the game. He wore a Seattle Mariner uniform for the team picture."

"Is that so!"

"How's that for Yankee pride? He didn't seem the least upset by it."

"Y'know, I wonder . . ."

"What."

"I wonder if he got that from me."

"I beg your pardon?"

"A couple of years ago when Reggie was still with Oakland, the team was playing in Seattle and they had an old-timers' game that I attended. They didn't have a Yankee uniform that fit me, so I wore a Seattle uniform. Reggie saw me, I know. I wonder if he had that in mind . . ."

"It would certainly explain his nonchalance."

"Yes, it would. Well, I'm supposed to manage this old-timers' game. Have to go and fill out my lineup. Will you excuse me?"

"Of course. Thanks so much. Say, is it possible I could talk to you again some time? Over a drink or a meal? May I give you a call?"

Looking over his shoulder as he headed through the crowd, DiMaggio smiled. "Well, you can always call." He made his way slowly toward first base, stopping dutifully to sign autographs every step of the way. As I watched him go, somebody thrust a piece of paper and a pen at me. I stared at them uncomprehendingly.

The stands were almost full now. The noise in the stadium had risen to a steady roar. Boys and girls were screaming for attention from on top of the dugout roof, while down below Whitey Ford stood in a corner and surreptitiously sipped his beer. Out on the field the festivities had picked up. The Hall of Famers were driven onto the field in a line of classic cars from the 1950s and were introduced over the public-address system. A home-run hitting contest began, in the middle of which the boy-owner Dave Hersh announced over the loudspeaker that he'd just decided to offer a bounty of five hundred dollars to any old-timer who hit a ball out of the stadium. Moments later Hank Aaron rifled a shot deep over the left-field stands. Next came the old-timers' game, Hall of Famers against the all-star old-time Beavers and one lonely Maverick, Jim Bouton. In the game, Willie Mays, still quick and trim, managed to scamper out of a rundown and steal home. The crowd cheered politely, as if the maneuver were routine.

During the game, reporters and spectators continued to mill along the sidelines. In their midst, Dave Hersh strutted to and fro, now trying halfheartedly to clear the field ("Everybody into the stands, please!"), now fending off inquisitive reporters ("What brought these great stars to Portland? *Mucho dinero* is what brought them! It wouldn't be appropriate for me to say how much, but Portland is as good a baseball town as there is in the country, and the fans deserve this.') All the while, Ernie Banks kept clapping his hands and singing, "Hey, yes. Baseball is great! Baseball is fun! Fuuuuuuuuun! Hey, yeah! Baseball is good for you. Baseball is fun." Clearly, he was experienced at laughing in the face of adversity.

But I was oblivious to it all. I was ecstatic over my encounter with DiMaggio. Never mind that the Clipper was probably only doing the job he'd been paid to do—coming out and mingling with the fans. Nor did it matter that he wasn't exactly the Yankee Clipper of my dreams anymore, but instead the highly paid promoter of banks and coffee whose aging face you saw almost daily on television or in the newspaper. It made no difference. DiMaggio had been kind. He'd confided his thoughts. He'd offered to share his peanuts. So I was no longer troubled by the sight of Aaron and Mays performing like trained seals, signing autographs and answering questions without enthusiasm. And when Scavullo insisted we leave the old-timers' celebration—"The whole scene reminds me of a geriatric ward," he kept complaining; "it even smells like old people here"—it didn't bother me that I would be missing the regular game of the evening, the Beavers against the Tucson Toros, which would cost me a look at some players I'd wanted to see—Dale Berra, the son of Yogi Berra, Lenny Randle, the infielder who had punched and broken the jaw of Texas Ranger manager Frank Lucchesi, Vance Law, the son of the great Pirate relief pitcher Vernon Law, and Jim Willoughby, who had pitched a few crucial innings for the Boston Red Sox against the Cincinnati Reds during the seventh game of the great 1975 World Series. Joe DiMaggio had made my day. In fact he had provided a climax for my season.

Around ten o'clock that evening, I left a restaurant in downtown Portland, where I'd eaten dinner with Scavullo and Calderaro and consumed my full share of the alcohol available. Leaving Scavullo the car we had jointly rented, I wandered the deserted streets looking for a taxi to take me to the restaurant where there was supposed to be a party for the Hall of Famers, a place called The Book Shelf or The Book Rack—ironically, I the book reviewer couldn't remember. For the mile or so I walked there wasn't a moving vehicle in sight, let alone a taxi, but just as I was beginning to get leg-weary, a topless green Triumph convertible roared into view and stopped at a red light close to where I was walking.

"You look lost!" the blond woman at the wheel called out, gunning the motor while she waited for the light to change.

"I'm looking for a taxi."

"Not much chance of finding one at this hour. Where you headed?"

"To a party, I think."

"A party? What kind of party."

"It's a party for baseball players."

"Baseball players? Gee. What baseball players?"

"Hall of Fame players, actually. Hank Aaron, Willie Mays, Whitey Ford, Bobby Feller."

"No kidding. Where's it at?"

"Some restaurant called 'The Book' something. 'The Bookshelf'? 'The Book Rack'?"

"The Book Vault?"

"That could be it."

"Would you trust me to give you a lift?"

"Sure. Would you?"

"Why not. The party sounds like fun."

I climbed into the little car. The woman raced her motor again and roared off, shifting the gears of the Triumph briskly. The wind roared in my ears, obscuring whatever the driver was now shouting, a sentence with the word *Portland* in it.

"I came to see a baseball game," I shouted back, guessing what she had said.

"From where?" the woman yelled, pushing the car up over fifty.

"New York City."

"Wow. Worth it?"

"Absolutely. I met Joe DiMaggio."

"You met who?"

"I met Joe DiMaggio. I talked to him."

The woman stared at me for a long moment, then laughed, looked back to the road and slammed the little car into high gear. I felt as if I were being tilted back in a barber's chair and let my eyes drift up to the sky. All I could see was the underside of tree branches reflecting the occasional streetlamps—an arch of softly glowing green that tunneled its way into the cooling wind.

We raced into the night, looking for a place called the Book Vault.

6

LOSING

THE BOOK VAULT WAS DARK. Nor was there any sign of life at the Book Rack. Portland was closed. As we steered through the empty streets, the woman explained that she had been driving home from a feminists' meeting and thought it would be both appropriate and refreshing to pick up a man. But now it was getting late and she had to report early in the morning to her job, so we had better throw in the towel. She dropped me off at my hotel.

It turned out that I hadn't missed much.

"The party never really materialized," Jim Bouton said when I reached him by phone in the morning. "It was just an empty room with Henry Aaron at one side, sitting at a table and autographing a ball for a guy standing there with his son. Everyone was waiting for Joe DiMaggio to come, but I don't think he ever did. Willie Mays didn't show up either. It was like the great nonparty."

So it was just as well we hadn't found it. It would have tainted what had been a perfect day.

Still, I woke up with a hangover, which made even Scavullo's few laconic exchanges with Calderaro on the drive to the airport sound like dishes breaking inside my head. And there turned out to be more to my irritability than the amount I had drunk during dinner the evening before. When my headache finally cleared during our flight from Portland to Los Angeles, I felt that after my experience with DiMaggio there was no longer any point to what I was supposed to be doing. There was nothing left to look forward to.

This feeling nagged at me for the rest of our trip through the West. One baseball stadium began to seem like another—the California Angels' Anaheim ballpark, the Oakland–Alameda County Coliseum, San Francisco's Candlestick Park; one suburban pile of bear droppings after another, inside of which faceless fans cheered raucously as one anonymous batter after another emerged from the dugout, ambled to the plate and swung, hit, swung, missed, swung, took a pitch for a ball, swung, fouled one off. I was bored. By now I was actually bored with baseball.

Even my long-anticipated visit to the Dodgers left me cold. I'd suspected even as early as spring training—when Dodger publicist Fred Claire had laid down the law that a baseball book would not be legitimate without a call on Dodger Stadium ("Feel free to come. . . and we'll show you what happens here")—that the atmosphere might not be so hospitable if all was not well with the Dodger family. And indeed all was not in the least bit well now that the hopes and promises of spring training had dissolved in the grim realities of the pennant race. By the time of the All-Star break, the Dodgers had just finished losing twenty-six of their last thirty-five games, including eleven of fourteen to the Atlanta Braves, who were, aside from the deplorable New York Mets, the weakest team in the entire National League. On the day I arrived in Los Angeles, Thursday, July 19, the Dodgers stood dead last in the National League West, seventeen and a half games behind the front-running Houston Astros.

What was more, the Dodgers were losing with a signal lack of grace. Rumors of dissension filled the gossip columns of the local sports pages. It was said that manager Lasorda had lost control, that certain players weren't getting along with their teammates, that certain other players had accused center fielder Reggie Smith of being a quitter and dragging down the rest of the team. (Smith had spent the All-Star break on a fishing trip with his family. He'd wasted most of it trying unsuccessfully to get the engine of his motorboat to start.) In fact, Lasorda, with the hope that the rising tension could be eased, had called a pregame clubhouse meeting for the very evening I happened to be visiting.

So it didn't really surprise me that when I called Fred Claire to announce our arrival in Los Angeles, he was unavailable. An assistant came to the phone and assured me somewhat vaguely that press credentials would be ready when Scavullo, Calderaro, and I arrived at the ballpark that evening. It didn't surprise me when I presented myself at the press window at Chavez Ravine early that evening—after being directed to park a good quarter-mile away with the result that I had to help lug Scavullo's equipment over virtual acres of empty parking lot to reach the press window—that no one had heard of us or my application for passes, and that it took a good half hour for temporary credentials to be grudgingly arranged. It didn't surprise me that it was a subdued, almost surly, Lasorda who greeted reporters in his den after the game—even though the Dodgers had beaten the Montreal Expos, 7–3, with some of the more sparkling baseball they had played in months. It was a Lasorda who kept muttering monotonously that the pregame meeting had been "very productive, the best we've had all year; we all got a lot of good out of it." This despite the scuttlebutt that was already circulating among reporters that no one had proved willing to accept Reggie Smith's challenge to step forward and identify himself as Smith's accuser ("Would *you?*" one player asked a reporter rhetorically, undoubtedly with Smith's size and nasty temper in mind), and despite the news that second baseman Davey Lopes had resigned as team captain after the meeting—"to make everyone equal," as he explained somewhat cryptically.

It was in fact a Lasorda who showed signs of animation only twice during the evening—once when a TV interviewer appeared and put the Dodger manager on camera, whereupon the friendly clown of spring training emerged briefly from his summertime discontent; and once when a newspaper reporter mumbled a question, prompting Lasorda to bawl out the pitiable young man for speaking with his hand in front of his mouth. So I spent my time in Lasorda's office looking at the cluttered walls—there were so many photographs, documents, and cartoons on it that I wondered where Scavullo's photographs would fit if they ever found their way there—and left without exchanging more than a word or two with its occupant.

It didn't even surprise me when Fred Claire tried to excuse the evening.

"It's too bad you couldn't have spent some time here," he said when I ran into him in the press box.

"Well, I've been in Los Angeles all day."

"I mean," said Claire, "it's too bad you couldn't get a true impression of Dodger Stadium."

"I got a strong impression of something."

"I mean . . ." said Claire. He didn't finish, but I knew what he meant. It was too bad the Dodgers were losing, and too bad that in their misery they'd become just like any other last-place team.

A few months earlier—maybe even a week before—this fall from grace might have been disillusioning. But it left me indifferent. I'd nearly forgotten the unpleasant experience by the time I got back to my hotel that night. And the evening after that, which I spent in San Francisco watching a dull game between the Giants and the Philadelphia Phillies, I'd forgotten my impressions of Candlestick Park almost before I'd reached the local airport. I continued to feel indifferent as we flew back across the country on the Redeye Special just in time to attend a pompous old-timers' day celebration at Yankee Stadium. The most piquant moment of it for me was seeing up close the wrinkles of advancing age on the back of Mickey Mantle's enormous neck—not wrinkles so much as cracks like the fissures in the parched soil of the Oklahoma dust bowl where Mantle grew up. Maybe a vacation would revive me; I hoped so as I drove my family north for a month on Cape Cod. Maybe after I relaxed a little, something would come along to get me going again.

I lay in the sun and walked by the sea with my wife and played with my son in the surf and wrote postcards to my daughter at camp a few states away and ate dinner with friends in Provincetown and read the Boston newspapers. Occasionally, when there wasn't any special plan for the evening and my mind had slowed to such a sluggish pace that there was nothing better to do with it than drape it in front of the television set, I watched the loathsome Boston Red Sox play baseball.

I watched the Red Sox, who for years had pestered the Yankees, though with rare success, I was happy to reflect. How, I wondered, could so many intelligent, literate people that I knew continue to cast their emotional lots with this persistently good-hit, bad-pitch team? Even in the brief time I'd been watching them, the Sox seemed to be undergoing their habitual late-season fade by playing .500 ball and falling rapidly from three and a half games back to seven full games behind the red-hot Baltimore Orioles. Someone had once observed that all the most literate people were Red Sox fans, and indeed off the top of my head I could think of John Cheever, John Updike, George V. Higgins, Roger Angell, Jonathan Schwartz, John Leonard, Jonathan Yardley, and A. Bartlett Giamatti. (Even my old friend Tony Lukas—once the most passionate Yankee fan I knew but now growing rapidly fed up with George Steinbrenner—had lately found himself leaning more and more toward the Red Sox—or so he'd admitted to me a few months after we'd met in Florida, when it finally dawned on me to wonder why he'd picked Gary Allenson, a Red Sox rookie, to write about for the *New York Times Magazine* instead of some Yankee player.) Was it the Red Sox's tragic destiny—their talent for snatching defeat from the jaws of victory—that attracted thoughtful people to root for them? Or was it simply that all the intelligent people on the East Coast of America came from New England or went to Harvard or summered on Cape Cod or Nantucket Island or Martha's Vineyard and had picked up the Red Sox habit the way you picked up head lice?

But watching the Red Sox didn't help. In fact, things got worse as my vacation progressed, though it wasn't exactly my imagination that was to blame. First, I got a telephone call from Tom Tracy informing me that he was leaving the publishing house that had underwritten our baseball project. Henceforth it would be handled by the publisher himself, one Laurence Dent. Then, a few weeks later, I was informed that Dent too would be leaving, and from now on we would be guided by the managing editor, Marion Wheeler. It was beginning to look as if the book were in trouble.

And then on the evening of August 2, while I was waiting in front of the TV for a game between the Red Sox and the Milwaukee Brewers to begin, it struck me that in addition to the fulfillment of meeting Joe DiMaggio there was another good reason for my loss of interest in the baseball season.

It didn't hit me all at once. It began with a news bulletin. On the TV screen there appeared the sketch of an airplane in flight; it was the outline of a one-engine prop trainer, a Cessna or a Piper Cub.

The voice of the announcer said, "The New York Yankee baseball team, which has not been having a happy season thus far this summer, suffered a tragic setback today." (*"Oh, no!"* I thought, *"something else, like Goose Gossage getting hurt, to ruin our chances of winning this season."*) "Their star catcher, Thurman Munson, was killed this afternoon when the plane he was piloting crashed while trying to land at Akron-Canton Airport in Ohio." (*"Well, what the hell,"* I caught myself thinking half-consciously. *"That's not so terrible. Munson's knees were supposed to be hurting him so bad that he wasn't going to be the regular catcher anymore."*)

Then my mind broke out of its fantasy. "OhmyGod! What am I thinking? The man died. A person died, not a bubble gum card!"

If I continued to feel guilty about my first reaction to Munson's death, I more than atoned for it with the tears I shed the following night during the late news, which showed scenes of the memorial service held earlier at Yankee Stadium—the weeping ballplayers, Munson's image flashing on the scoreboard, the fans applauding for minutes on end. And I was further stricken the following Monday, when, in a Vermont country inn where we were staying while visiting our daughter at camp, I timed a late-night visit to the television lounge so that I caught, in fifteen minutes of channel-hopping, a news report on Munson's funeral in Canton, Ohio, earlier that day, and then the last of the ninth of the Yankee game in which Bobby Murcer, whose tear-choked eulogy could be heard on the news, drove in his fourth and fifth runs of the game to cap a come-from-behind win over the Baltimore Orioles.

And yet, while sitting alone in that lounge, I couldn't help wondering at how many people had wept for Thurman Munson, who had turned a surly, unpleasant face to the world outside his intimates, and who could only be appreciated, his close friends on the Yankees kept insisting, if you understood what an intensely private man he was. The truth was, we were all of us—or those of us over forty, at least—in a continuous state of grief over our mortality, and public deaths offered occasions for public mourning, a ritual outlet for our sorrow. Though you had to feel anguish for the sake of his family and friends, it wasn't Thurman Munson in particular we were mourning; it was the death of a young athlete. It was the loss of youth.

But Munson's death did have a crasser meaning for me, that two-dimensional one that I'd caught a glimpse of in my first reaction to the news. With the loss of Munson, the Yankees really stood little chance of winning the pennant now. They were out of it, already fourteen games behind on the day of his death. Like him, they were dead.

And that was the other thing that had gone wrong with the season. This was another year the Yankees weren't going to win the pennant.

Looking back now and trying to figure out exactly how the season had come apart for them, I thought of the slow start they had gotten, the slight but nagging injuries that had briefly sidelined Ron Guidry and Reggie Jackson, and the crippling loss of Goose Gossage. Yet they still seemed to have a chance as late as June, especially considering the previous year's spectacular comeback. And then they'd played a game that had effectively killed them. Come to think of it, I'd been a witness to the team's demise.

The odd thing was, I hadn't gone to the game because it was an important one. My real purpose had so little to do with the pennant race that it would have been better had the game been meaningless. I'd been working on an incidental project all season—to see games at Yankee Stadium from as many different vantage points as possible. Years of rooting for the team had taught me the average fan's point of view: I'd seen games from the distant bleachers, from the general-admission seats in the grandstand, from behind the columns that used to support the stands before the stadium was renovated, from the seats high up behind home plate, and even from one of the boxes behind the visiting team's dugout, when a friend had gotten hold of a pair of his company's season tickets.

So far this season I'd watched games from every imaginable reporter's point of view. On opening day, I'd been forced by the large crowd of reporters covering the game into the auxiliary press section far behind home plate. But ever since, I'd pretty much had my run of the press accommodations. I'd eaten pregame meals in the Stadium's basement cafeteria. I'd watched games from the press box and explored, like a curious child backstage in a theater, the various adjoining facilities—the special section of seats where Yankee management and its guests watched the games, the television and radio booths, and the tiny compartment where the organist played. It filled me with wonder to watch the organist waiting for his cues. And it somehow disappointed me to discover that behind the kingdom of infinite dimensions that Mel Allen's magic voice had once created was nothing more than a narrow cell where two men and a technician fidgeted, yawned, smoked cigarettes, drank coffee, kibitzed with each other, and generally carried on like normal people doing a routine job of work.

Finally, I'd several times trailed the regular beat reporters as they made their late-inning trek from the press box, along the corridor in back of the stands, down a special elevator used mainly by Yankee executives, and back to the cafeteria, which had now been turned into a bar. There they would watch the final inning or so of the game on television, then scurry to the nearby locker rooms to conduct their postgame interviews, and finally dash to the press room to type and file the stories they had already begun back in the press box with the game still in progress. I'd even gotten into the habit of wandering around the locker rooms, listening in on interviews conducted by radio and print reporters, and then drifting back to the bar, where Al Rosen and Bob Lemon (when they were still with the team), or Billy Martin, Yogi Berra, and various players would often mingle with veteran reporters over a nightcap or two.

But there was one vantage point I hadn't yet achieved, though I'd grown increasingly curious to do so. That was the view afforded a privileged guest of the Yankees, or rather a privileged guest of the Yankees' principal owner, George M. Steinbrenner III. At the start of the season, it had never occurred to me to consider the role of the guest as a special category. What did it matter if an assembly-line foreman from Steinbrenner's Ohio-based American Shipbuilding Company was to come to New York from time to time and be given free tickets behind third base, so close to the field that he could count the freckles on the neck of the third-base coach? What was the big deal about that? How was this spectator different from anybody else with the clout or the luck to get good seats along the foul lines, a feat that even I'd pulled off once or twice in my life?

But as the season progressed, I'd come to understand that to be a special guest of the Yankees was to fall into a hierarchy of privilege as complex in structure as the ringside seating arrangement at a heavyweight championship fight. Combining the gossip of various reporters and my own experience over the season, I'd fantasized a picture of how life at the Stadium really worked. I'd tried it out on a friend with contacts in the official Yankee family, and he'd pronounced it reasonably accurate.

My fantasy went like this. On a given August evening, with a hot attraction like, say, the Kansas City Royals in town and the Stadium bulging with over fifty-thousand people, the American Shipbuilding foreman and his wife might think themselves lucky to be in a box right next to the field. But if they knew enough to look across the way to the boxes behind the Yankee on-deck circle, they might see a party made up perhaps of an assistant to the athletic director of a university that one of Steinbrenner's children was attending and the doctor who'd recently rendered medical service to a member of the boss's family. If the American Shipbuilding foreman and his wife knew enough to recognize these fans as other privileged guests of Steinbrenner's, they might envy the doctor and the assistant athletic director for getting seats right next to the Yankee dugout.

But their envy would be slight compared with what the doctor and the assistant athletic director might be feeling. While they can almost count the pores on the noses of the Yankee batters waiting their turns at the plate, they don't really have that good a view of the field. The right-hand side of the field is obstructed by the back of the dugout. Certainly it's not as good a view as the one from the box *behind* the dugout, which this evening happens to be occupied by a former high elected city official who's gathered some of his cronies to kick around the possibility of a run for the U.S. Senate seat that will be coming up for grabs next year. But the cronies may not be so happy either. They may suspect that if their leader were alone at the game this evening—or just with his wife—he wouldn't be there in the pits with the plebes, but up in those seats to the left of the radio booth, right in front of the owner's executive suite.

And even up there, where a few of the Yankees' limited partners happen to be watching the game this evening, an edge of nervousness prevails, because "George" isn't present. "George" is somewhere else. And wherever "George" is is a better place to be. That better place this evening is directly underneath the press-box level. There, among the bank of luxury boxes that curves gently above and behind home plate, is Suite 332, the second one in from the third-base end, where even at this moment the guests are relaxing in air-conditioned comfort with beers or Scotches, among them perhaps Roy M. Cohn, the controversial lawyer; A. M. Rosenthal, the executive editor of the *New York Times*; Elaine Kaufman, the restaurateur; Jason Robards, Jr., the actor; Mike Forrest, a furrier who befriended the boss when he first arrived in the Big Apple without a crony to his name and who's been doggedly loyal ever since; and, not least conspicuous in the group, stuffed into his standard-issue blue blazer and gray flannel trousers and sporting a navy blue necktie dotted with the Yankees' NY logo, none other than the owner of Suite 332, in fact the owner in a manner of corporate speaking (the actual owner of Yankee Stadium being New York City) of all nineteen of the luxury suites (except, in a sense, Suite Number 324, but we'll come to that particular complication in a moment), the owner of owners who manipulates all these Machiavellian seating arrangements, Mr. George Michael Steinbrenner III himself.

Indeed, the minions of the former elected official may almost feel the eyes of the occupants of Suite 332 boring down into the backs of their necks, and it takes almost all the character they can muster to concentrate on the game being played in front of them and not look back over their shoulders to see who's sitting in the really good spots. Up above, in the executive seats, the limited partners shift their haunches nervously, wondering if "George" will pay them a visit. For all these guests—from the assistant athletic director to the limited partners sitting next to the radio booth—the sound of tinkling cocktail ice nearly drowns out the roar of the fifty thousand spectators. Or maybe "George" is *nowhere* present this evening, which makes even the occupants of Suite 332 a little uneasy, because they can't be absolutely sure that there isn't an even better place to be, a place they've never heard of (although the knowledgeable among them are reassured that Roy Cohn is present in Suite 332, because they know that wherever Roy Cohn is sitting is probably as good a place to be as there is).

The plain fact was, I was dying to penetrate this world of hierarchy and privilege and watch a game from Suite 332. If pressed, I could have thought up a couple of respectable reasons why. I could have said that I wanted to visit Suite 332 just because it was there, like the only missing space on a page in a stamp album. Or I could have said that I wanted to experience something unusual. Suite 332 was said to consist of an enclosure holding about a dozen seats and, behind it, a living room so comfortable and homey that sometimes guests forgot they were at the ballpark. Sometimes, when the company was especially lively, the atmosphere in the suite was like that of a party, and only occasionally did you bother to glance through the plate-glass wall at the front to see what was happening out on the playing field or look up at the TV set above the bar to catch a glimpse of the closed-circuit broadcast of the game. Sometimes, things got so entertaining that you even forgot there was a game at all. That seemed particularly intriguing, considering that whenever I was at a party when there was a Yankee game going on, I found it difficult to forget even if there was no way at all to check on its progress. Just imagine a crowd of people sitting in the best seats in the Stadium, carrying on as if they were at a cocktail party. I wanted to see that for myself.

All this was partly true. But it wasn't the whole truth. The kernel that was missing—the part I didn't like to admit even to myself—was that I wanted to be in Suite 332 just because it was a privileged, exclusive place to be. Like meeting Joe DiMaggio, it would exalt me.

But putting vanity aside, I told myself that it was part of the job of a reporter, one of the hardest parts, to be an intruder. You had to push your way into places, positions of confidence, networks of information where you weren't wanted and didn't belong. So much of a reporter's energy was spent trying to get "in" that it was easy to fall under the illusion that simply to gain entry to exclusive places was all that was required of him, never mind what solid information such places might actually yield. Never mind too that the better sports reporters were perfectly content to write their stories in places penetrable by everyone. The best reporters of all, like Red Smith of the *Times* and Dick Young of the *Daily News*, could write colorful, newsworthy copy based only on what they saw on a television set. *They* didn't need to sit in luxury Suite number 332. I knew this perfectly well, but I still wanted to do it. It was a stage I had to pass through, I told myself. I was going to do it if I could, and I was going to get my little thrill from it.

Anyway, even if it was a flaw in my character that made me hunger for the privileged vantage point, I could at least say that my snobbery was egalitarian. Not that I was in favor of doing away with hierarchy. Hierarchy lent spice to living. It gave one something to strive for. But I believed in the American ideal that the privileged places should be accessible to all the people, even if only a few of them could occupy them at a time. In principle I believed that every baseball fan in the city should be allowed to spend an evening in Suite 332. There ought to be some sort of system. But until there was, I yearned to be invited to the party I'd been hearing so much about. I would somehow manage it. All I needed was to find the right strings to pull.

But my plans misfired. In arranging an invitation to Suite 332, I neglected to mention that I preferred to be asked to a game that the reporter in me could safely ignore while the bon vivant in me was enjoying the party. It was assumed that for such an extraordinary occasion I would naturally want an extraordinary ballgame. So when arrangements were completed, I found myself invited for the evening of Friday, June 29, when the Yankees would be playing a key game with the Boston Red Sox!

As it turned out, the game could hardly have proved more dramatic for such an early stage of the season. Of course, any game between the Red Sox and the Yankees was special. As the sports pages kept reminding one, the rivalry between these two teams went deep into baseball history. It had begun way back in 1904 when, in what was sometimes called the first exciting pennant race of the twentieth century, the Boston Pilgrims, as they were then known, beat the then New York Highlanders on the last day of the season, on a wild pitch thrown by the Highlanders' forty-one-game winner (still a modern record), the spitballer Jack Chesbro.

The rivalry had deepened in the 1920s when, to finance his theatrical ventures, the Boston owner Harry Frazee proceeded systematically to sell all of Boston's most talented players to the Yankees, including the incomparable George Herman "Babe" Ruth, then an outstanding pitcher but soon to be the game's first great home-run hitter; Carl Mays, whose errant submarine pitch had killed Ray Chapman; Waite Hoyt, the pitcher about whom Brooklyn newsboys were later to cry famously, "Waite Hurt Hoit"; and sundry other great players like Herb Pennock, Wally Schang, and "Jumping Joe" Dugan. That pillaging had left the Red Sox in ruins for a decade or so, but the rivalry had renewed itself in the late 1930s and grown and grown until the Yankees finally fell apart in the mid-1960s. For a time after that, the Red Sox had been cocks of the walk—although even without the Yankees to threaten them they could never entirely shake off their capacity for self-destruction—but then the Yankees had revived once more, and only last year, 1978, as if to insure that the Sox would never forget their tormentors, the Yanks had made one of the great comebacks in baseball history (while, conversely, the Sox suffered one of the great collapses of all time) and beaten Boston for the pennant in what was only the second playoff game in the history of the American League.

Moreover, as if sports history weren't enough to arouse my interest in this game, the Boston–New York rivalry had worked itself deep into my personal history. In 1949, the first full season I'd followed professional baseball with passion, the two teams had chased each other down to the last two games of the season, for which the Sox had arrived in town ahead by a single game in the standings. Then the Yankees had proceeded to beat them twice, winning the pennant on the final day in a game that impressed me so powerfully that for years I could recall how every player had performed every time at bat that day.

Now, in 1979, the two teams were at it again—or almost at it again, since in actual cold fact the Yanks were in fourth place, nine and a half games behind the first-place Baltimore Orioles, while the Red Sox were in second, four games in back of the Orioles, three and a half games ahead of the third-place Milwaukee Brewers, and five and a half games ahead of the Yankees.

But there was a sense of drama building around this game, and I wasn't the only one who felt it, since the Stadium was sold out this evening. Things might be coming together at last for the Yankees. There were signs both symbolic and real. Billy Martin was back as manager, and the team had won seven out of ten games since he'd taken over for Bob Lemon a week and a half before, although admittedly these games had been played against two cream-puff teams, Toronto and Cleveland. Bobby Murcer, the aging outfielder, was back with the team too. The Oklahoma kid who as a young player was supposed to take the place of Mickey Mantle (as Mantle had once replaced DiMaggio) had been picked up from the Chicago Cubs for cash and a minor-league pitcher. Why would the Yankees want Murcer back after trading him in 1974 because he had never quite played up to expectations? That issue had been hotly debated in the press box. Some argued that the Yanks were the only team willing to pay Murcer's $320,000 annual salary, and anyway George

Steinbrenner had always liked Murcer and wanted him back, or so he said. Others theorized that the acquisition was designed to throw a scare into Reggie Jackson, who had been acting contentious over the return of Billy, whom he loathed, and anyway, since Murcer could play right field, Reggie's position, Steinbrenner was trying to buy a little insurance in case things got out of hand and Reggie had to be traded. Still others dismissed all these fancy theories and claimed that Steinbrenner had made the move to generate publicity and divert attention from the team's lackluster play. You could take your pick. But Murcer still had some games in him, and his presence might just give the team a lift.

More tangibly, some of the team's injured players were returning at last. Reggie, who had been out for three weeks with a bad leg, was ready to hit if not field, so he'd be the designated hitter against the Red Sox. Ron Guidry, who had missed two starts because of a muscle strain in his back, was going to pitch against Boston's Mike Torrez, which of course called to mind last season's famous playoff game, when these same two pitchers were matched up and the Yankees won all the marbles. Maybe lightning would strike again, even if there were now two teams to overhaul (three, if you counted the Brewers). Why not? The Yankees had only nine and a half games to make up instead of fourteen and a half, and only five and a half against the Red Sox, whom they'd beaten in eight of their last ten meetings. As Lou Piniella had been quoted in Friday afternoon's paper:

> I think this series will have a big bearing on what'll happen later in the season. If we do well this weekend, we're fairly close to them. We've got to start playing good, start making up some ground, and then we'll be in good shape and get in the race later in the summer. I just don't think Baltimore is ten games better than us.

True, there was more hope than logic to his statement, but it added to the growing excitement.

Certainly I could feel it when I drove to the ballpark early Friday evening. Traffic was already jammed on the Major Deegan Expressway by 6:30, and the press parking lot had been closed because of the sudden arrival of a crowd of "Mr. Steinbrenner's friends," as the attendant at the gate explained as he turned me away. In the cafeteria, where I went first to eat a dinner of lemon sole, wild rice, peach pie, and coffee, the rank and file of Stadium workers were giving each other thumb's-up signs and murmuring about tonight's game being "it." Next door, in the press's working room, a couple of Boston writers were talking on the phones with their editors. I recognized one of them from back in spring training as George Kimball, the writer Tony Lukas had introduced me to in Orlando. He was the one who had tipped me off about the feud over hitting techniques that was going on between Boston's special hitting instructor, Ted Williams, and the Yankees' batting coach, Charlie Lau. As Kimball mumbled into the phone, he looked at me with one eye and gave me a glassy stare of nonrecognition. I assumed he didn't remember me until I recalled that the eye in question was in fact a glass one. Indeed, as I'd learned since spring training, Kimball's glass eye was famous. He'd once been asked by a friend in Greenwich Village's Lion's Head bar to "keep an eye on" his drink while he paid a visit to the john. When the friend had returned he'd found Kimball's artificial eye lying at the bottom of his glass.

When I got to the playing field, I found a large crowd of reporters assembled behind the batting cage to watch the Sox take their batting-practice licks. The Stadium appeared literally to have shrunk from the tension of the evening; the white foul pole in the corner of right field now seemed only a few dozen feet away. This illusion could be explained either by the buzzing crowd that seemed already—though it was only twilight—to have filled every seat in the park, or by the balls that Carl Yastrzemski was hitting high and deep into the right-field grandstand on almost every second swing of his bat. At the same time, off on the third-base side of the batting cage, Reggie Jackson, the lone white-uniformed figure among the blue-gray flannels of the visitors, was entertaining a group of Red Sox, among them their manager, Don Zimmer, with an elaborate parody of Yastrzemski in his peculiar batting stance, which over the years had come to resemble a small boy with theft on his mind peering around the corner of a building to see if the fruit-stand owner's back was turned. Jackson's fraternization with the Sox only served to heighten my anxiety. If Reggie was working to charm the team whose season he'd helped to wreck only a year earlier, then his relationship with Steinbrenner might have deteriorated even more than the papers had been speculating.

When I grew tired of watching batting practice, I made my way to the press box to see what was going on up there. A crowd of reporters was pressing at the door, which two attendants were holding all but a few inches shut. Consulting a pair of lists they held—one of them short, the other longer—they would open the door wider for an occasional petitioner whose name appeared on the short list, while directing those on the longer to an auxiliary press section that had been set up in the stands for the evening. My name was missing from both lists, an understandable oversight since I wasn't a regular in the press box. Still, I used the unintended snub to gird myself for the act of elitism I was about to commit. With a shrug I turned my back on the crowd of reporters and set out for the elevator that would take me down to Suite 332.

When I got there I knocked on the door and was quickly admitted by a man in a bartender's outfit who introduced himself as Angie and offered to fix me a drink. Ordering a Scotch on the rocks, I began to inspect my surroundings. I was in another world—a little living room decorated with chairs, hassocks, a desk, a five-piece sectional, a coffee table and wall-to-wall carpeting—that glowed softly like a movie set. The back wall consisted of a bar-refrigerator complex crowned by a closed-circuit television set that was already turned on. The two adjoining walls were light blue and covered with memorabilia. There were paintings of Babe Ruth, Lou Gehrig, and Casey Stengel. There were action photos of Bucky Dent, Tommy John, Thurman Munson, and Ron Guidry. There were pictures of Pope Paul VI performing his 1965 mass at Yankee Stadium, and of the New York City skyline at dusk. There were plaques recording the Yankee performances in the 1977 and 1978 playoffs and World Series. The fourth wall was glass from ceiling to floor. Through it I could make out a disorienting scene—the small bank of upholstered seats below, the overhang of the grandstand above, and in between the brilliant green of the playing field, the sparkling yellow of the arclights, and the deep aquamarine of the twilight sky beyond. It made me feel as if I were standing in the gondola of a luxury zeppelin—the *Hindenburg?* the *Steinbrenner?*—coasting silently in for a landing on the lawn of a vast estate.

A knock at the door interrupted my reverie. It was my old friend Sidney Zion, the lawyer and journalist, who greeted Angie familiarly and ordered a Scotch. Next to arrive was Roy Cohn. Though I'd been trained by long years of association with liberals to despise everything Cohn stood for, his arrival confirmed for me that Suite 332 was indeed *the* place to be this evening. Anyway, I'd long since learned that people ritually despised by liberals often turned out to be more interesting than the liberals themselves. Besides, Cohn was a friend of Zion's, who was possessed of such catholic tastes in his acquaintanceships and political associations that he was probably unique in being able to boast that he'd once held a telephone conversation with Cohn while simultaneously having Cohn's archenemy, Robert M. Morgenthau, on hold. It looked as if a good party were about to begin.

Soon I found myself in such engrossing conversation with Zion and Cohn that I hardly noticed the hyperdramatic strains of Robert Merrill booming out the national anthem over the Stadium public-address system. Other guests had arrived: Yankee limited partner William Rose, his wife, and a friend. Laughter tinkled in the gondola of the Graf *Steinbrenner*. More drinks were served. I felt pleasantly insulated from my addiction to baseball. The voice inside my head that usually nagged at me over how the Yankees were doing was completely still. I reflected almost proudly that of all the people in this room, I was probably the least interested in the game that would shortly get under way.

Yet even as this thought occurred to me, some tiny leak seemed to have sprung in the party. The atmosphere of revelry was beginning to subside. I'd just asked Roy Cohn if it was true, as I had been told, that he'd attended one of the same schools as I had, Fieldston in the Riverdale section of the Bronx.

"No," said Cohn. "Horace Mann."

"Oh," I said, surprised, because I'd heard it said a number of times. "Not Fieldston?"

"Well, I went there briefly when I was a kid. My parents sent me there on the advice of a friend. I don't know why. And the next thing I knew I was learning how to knit and sew. Basics were out in that place then, and if they didn't have parents day, who knows how I might have turned out? Of course, such a modern school did believe in involving parents, and the first chance my father had to make one of those days, he caught me doing knit one, pearl two. I was out of there in no time flat and into the Horace Mann School for Boys. Some of my schoolmates were Si Newhouse of Condé

Nast, Gene Pope, the publisher of the *National Enquirer*, Allard Lowenstein. . . .That was about enough."

This seemed a lively springboard for talk, especially since I had a daughter at Fieldston Lower, but everyone in the party was beginning to move toward the glassed-in end of the room. Some had already gone through the door to the seats outside. When I trailed after them, I saw that the people in the Stadium crowd were rising to their feet and cheering expectantly. Ron Guidry was standing on the pitcher's mound peering at the catcher for a sign. A Red Sox batter—probably the leadoff hitter, shortstop Rick Burleson—had stepped up to the plate and begun to flex his bat.

That's right, I thought with a mild sense of letdown as I followed the little crowd to the bank of seats, it's Ron Guidry making his first start since he hurt his back a week or so ago. We should know right away if he's going to be okay. As I slipped into an empty seat next to Sidney Zion, Burleson waved futilely at an explosive Guidry slider and struck out. The conversation between Zion, Cohn, and me flickered to life again. Cohn remembered that another member of his class at Horace Mann was Anthony Lewis. Maybe it had occurred to him that the *Times*'s liberal columnist and its daily book reviewer were birds of a feather. "Anthony of Arabia," muttered Zion contemptuously, referring to several recent Lewis columns that had been sympathetic to the Palestinians. "His father's name was Kassel Oshinsky in those days," Cohn added. "He owned a garment-center firm called Crown Fabrics. Tony and I were best friends then, even though we didn't agree politically. He was the right-winger and I was the left-winger." "No kidding!" Zion exclaimed, but at that moment Guidry slipped a third strike past second baseman Larry Wolfe, and the conversation faltered again. "Guidry doesn't seem to have lost his zip," I mumbled, whereupon I remembered Guidry's recent tendency to burn out suddenly after starting off strong in a game. As I visualized the way his pitches came in high when he began to tire, Fred Lynn, the Red Sox center fielder, struck out swinging at another slider. Guidry had fanned the side—one, two, three.

While the teams were exchanging field positions, John Lindsay, the former mayor, and his wife, Mary, came down the aisle and took seats in front of me. I was again distracted from the game. Several years earlier, I'd reviewed a novel by Lindsay based on his experiences as mayor. I'd hated the book and said so. True, I'd hated the grin that had played on Lindsay's handsome face when, long before the novel's publication, I'd asked him out of politeness at some party how it was coming along, and he'd replied that "they," meaning the publisher, "were working on it now, fixing it up," as if a novel were a Tinker Toy that could be put together by a committee. But the book when it appeared had done me the favor of being even worse than I'd anticipated, and so I was able to write in all honesty that it made me regret having voted for Lindsay as mayor, meaning to suggest by this absurd confusion of realms the degree to which Lindsay himself had mixed up his categories. The former mayor had apparently found the review hard enough to take in itself, but what had aggravated the experience for him, or so a mutual acquaintance had told me, was having to hear it read over the phone by Mary Lindsay, who was upset by it to the point of tears.

Now, as Guidry strode to the mound to pitch the top of the second inning—the Yankees having gone down meekly in the bottom of the first—the very same Mary Lindsay turned slowly in her seat in evident preparation to address me. I braced myself. Had someone pointed me out to her? Was she about to berate me for my malevolence?

"What did the Red Sox do in the first inning?" was, however, all she wanted to know.

"Guidry struck out the side . . ." I replied.

"Oh, good," said Mrs. Lindsay.

". . . Burleson and Lynn swinging; Wolfe on a called strike. His slider's breaking a foot."

"Oh, Good. Good."

"Not necessarily. Sometimes when he's got too much to begin with, he loses it all later on. It's better when they hit him a little at the beginning."

"Really!"

During this exchange, Guidry struck out the Red Sox's cleanup hitter, Jim Rice, eliciting a roar of approval from the crowd, all the more lusty because the previous year Rice had barely defeated Guidry in the vote for the American League's Most Valuable Player award.

"That's four straight strikeouts now," I said.

"Oh? What's the record," Mrs. Lindsay asked politely.

"I think it's ten. I think Tom Seaver of the Mets struck out ten in a row."

"My! Are you professionally involved with baseball?" she asked.

"Not really. I . . ."

But now the next Red Sox hitter, Bob Watson, was stepping up to the plate, and everyone's attention was focused on whether Guidry could keep his string going. With one strike on him, Watson hit a fly ball deep to Mickey Rivers in center field. The crowd sighed with disappointment.

And so it went. Every time something interesting developed in Suite 332, something more interesting happened out on the field. The game gradually developed into one of those tense scoreless duels in which a swing of the bat or two can settle the outcome, and the least scratch hit or base on balls is magnified threefold. So it took no more than a walk and a stolen base by Willie Randolph in the third inning to divert the suite's attention from a sudden visit by George Steinbrenner and Lee Iacocca, the embattled leader of Chrysler Corporation. The two industrial moguls moved briskly down and up the little aisle, shaking hands with us guests as if they were running for office. I caught myself wondering for a moment where *they* were watching the game and whether it might be a better place, but I cut this short with the reassurance that Roy Cohn after all was here, practically beside me.

In the fifth inning, when Cohn began to complain about the high cost of running a law firm these days, Carl Yastrzemski silenced him with a line single to center field. But neither the Yankees nor the Red Sox could move their occasional base runners along. At the end of seven innings, the score was 0–0, with both starting pitchers still going strong.

Then, to break the tension and maybe change the pattern of the game, Sid Zion suggested a visit to his friends in Suite 324, which belonged to Ed Arrigoni, the founder and owner of the private bus line that runs between Manhattan and Co-op City. Still hoping that the party would come alive, I trailed along with Zion and Cohn. In the corridor, Zion fell into step with me and quietly explained that Arrigoni's suite was really better than Steinbrenner's since it was located right near the middle of the bank of suites and offered a better view of the field, as well as more of a chance to catch foul balls.

"I think it bugs George that it's better," Zion said. "In fact, I think there was even trouble over it."

When we arrived, Zion introduced me to Arrigoni, a lean, relaxed-looking man in his forties dressed casually in red slacks, a yellow short-sleeved blouse, and loafers.

"He's writing a book about baseball," Zion said.

"No kidding," said Arrigoni brightly. "Hey, put me in your book. You see this suite? It's different from George's. See how it's decorated? Steinbrenner wanted me to make it like all the others, but we wouldn't do it. We fought him and we won. Right, Roy?"

Suite 324 was indeed different. The walls were white instead of blue. The sofa was bright red instead of black. As well as the standard-issue photographs of Guidry, Munson, et al, the wall was cluttered with pictures of various friends and family members, and one of a Kansas City Royal outfielder leaping vainly for a ball flying into the stands, with the inscription "Best Wishes, Ed, Chris Chambliss" scrawled in the corner. (It was obviously the home-run ball that Chambliss had hit to win the 1977 American League pennant.) Above a long table loaded down with cold cuts, bread, fruit, and a huge bowl of candy bars, there was a large translucent plastic segment of a baseball with stitches and seams painted on it in red along with the words New York City Bus Service. Set before the glass wall was a pair of highchairs for grown-ups, obviously the perches from which the captain of the suite and his mate watched their games. The atmosphere here was lighter and more congenial than that in Suite 332.

I wanted to take Roy Cohn aside and ask him what had happened between Arrigoni and Steinbrenner, but once again that party I'd been looking forward to seemed to be shaping up. The crowd now included Zion, Cohn, Arrigoni and his wife, Helen, Mario Merola, the Bronx district attorney, Stanley Friedman, a partner in Roy Cohn's law firm, and several other men and women whose names I failed to catch when they were thrown at me. I was instantly engaged on two conversational fronts. A discussion between Arrigoni, Merola, and Friedman had focused on the contest for the Bronx borough presidency that was being fought between City Councilman Stanley Simon and State Assemblyman Oliver Koppell. Simon was the regular Democratic candidate, and he was being backed by Stanley Friedman, who as well as being Cohn's law partner was the

Bronx County Democratic leader. Friedman, who talked around a cigar jammed wisdom-tooth deep into his mouth, was heaping anathema on Oliver Koppell's head, and practically everyone in the room was gleefully echoing him. Since I happened to be an acquaintance and supporter of Koppell's, as well as a backer of Simon's opponent in a previous campaign for City Council, and since silence on my part now would make the condemnation of Koppell unanimous, I felt a small obligation at least to identify myself as his supporter. But conveniently, before I could frame words in Koppell's defense that would not sound belligerent, someone just out of my sight, but not my hearing, mumbled something routinely polite about my skills as a book reviewer. At which Roy Cohn chimed in, "Except for the leads! Right, Chris?"

This charmed me considerably, not because of the attention it focused on me—though I didn't mind that in the least—but more for the gem-rare honesty of the insight. As a matter of fact, the openings of my reviews had been troubling me for as long as I could remember—they were fuzzy, prolix, and generally uninviting—and here perhaps was a chance to talk about it to someone with enough perception and honesty to bring it out in the open. But before I could even so much as acknowledge Cohn's remark, someone over by the window let out a sound of alarm. Everyone immediately turned to look at the playing field, where Red Sox runners were now standing on first base and third. The scoreboard registered only one out. Once again the air was leaking out of my party.

All conversation died now as Guidry, obviously tiring, faced second baseman Larry Wolfe, hitless so far in the game. Before any drama could build, Wolfe cracked a hit to center to score the runner on third. Though Freddy Lynn ended the inning by hitting into a bang-bang three-six-three double play, a collective sigh was the only sound that could be heard in the room. The Yankees were one huge run behind, with only two tiny innings left to go.

Since we had obviously hurt the Yanks by switching from one suite to another, part of the group now headed back to 332 to see if the team could at least get a run to tie the score in the bottom of the eighth. I hoped I would get a chance to ask Roy Cohn about the Arrigoni-Steinbrenner business. But he had disappeared.

(Later, when I got him on the telephone, we had the following conversation:

COHN: George originally wanted Arrigoni out of the whole place. He didn't want him to get the box, the suite, the pictures, the men's room, the rugs, nothing.

LEHMANN-HAUPT: Why on earth . . . ?

COHN: Because George just took the position, "Screw him. I got a list a mile long, and, ah, tell him to buy a television set." And that was that.

LEHMANN-HAUPT: But Arrigoni . . .

COHN: Ah, now, you've got to know George. George, when he says something like that, he usually doesn't mean it, 'cause George is basically a very good-hearted person. And, ah, he likes to make a big initial fuss and then—wow! All right. You know. And that's exactly what happened here, and, um, it just straightened out.

LEHMANN-HAUPT: Arrigoni made it sound as if it was just the decorations.

COHN: Yeah. Eddie Arrigoni—they're both good friends of mine; George is better, I suppose—Arrigoni plastered his whole suite with all those pictures and snapshots of, you know, him and Joe DiMaggio and him and Babe Ruth, you know, all that shit, like if you and I had the box, the first thing we'd do is pull everything off, and so that's what caused the whole thing.

LEHMANN-HAUPT: Well, how was it settled?

COHN: I don't know that it was settled at all. I think George just allowed it.

LEHMANN-HAUPT: You were not involved?

COHN: [Irritably.] Sure I was involved. I was involved in every move in the whole thing. I don't record it mentally as being among the more important events of my life. But I remember it was totally resolved.

LEHMANN-HAUPT: It didn't go to court or anything?

COHN: No, it never went to court.)

Suite 332 proved no better for the Yanks. Though Willie Randolph drew a walk with one out and moved around to third on a single by Bucky Dent, neither Mickey Rivers nor Thurman Munson could do anything to get him home. To make matters worse, Jim

Rice, the Sox's most powerful slugger, led off the top of the ninth by poling a long home run against relief pitcher Ron Davis, who had come in to replace Guidry. So the Yanks came up in the bottom of the ninth trailing by two enormous runs. For me, there was no longer any question of ignoring the game for the sake of the party. In fact, like a floating figure in a Marc Chagall painting, my psyche had left Suite 332 and was hovering over the field. The voice inside my head had come to life. It was urging the Yankees back from the edge of disaster; it was willing the Red Sox pitcher to start missing the plate; it was pleading with Bobby Murcer to do anything—walk, single, get hit by a pitch. *Just get on, Bobby!*

Which Murcer promptly did, with a single up the middle of the infield. *Way to go, Bobby. Now all we need is a walk, a sacrifice, and a hit, and we're even. Who's up? Piniella! Come on, sweet Lou. Oh, shit! Double-play ball. It's over!* But the Sox third baseman, Butch Hobson, muffed Piniella's grounder, and there were runners on first and second with nobody out, and the big man, Reggie Jax, coming to the plate. *Come on, Reggie Martini! You can win it with just one swing. Do it, Reg!* But Reggie struck out swinging, his third K in the game and fourth consecutive out, and it was up to Graig Nettles now. *It's not going to happen,* said the voice inside my head, louder now to me than even the polite cries of encouragement that were beginning to come from here and there in the nineteen suites. *The Yankees are not going to make it tonight, or this year. It's just not going to happen!*

But Nettles rocketed the ball on a line to right field for a single that scored Murcer and moved Piniella around to third. That was all for Torrez, as manager Zimmer brought in reliever Bill Campbell to pitch to first baseman Jim Spencer. Spencer grounded the ball into the hole between first and second, and Yastrzemski stopped it with a diving stab and flipped to the pitcher at first in time to beat Spencer, but it was too late to catch Piniella coming home or Nettles moving on to second. So the score was tied with two outs and the winning run in scoring position, and Willie Randolph was coming to the plate. Bright prospects. But of course with first base open, they were not going to pitch to Randolph. So Willie got an intentional walk, and who was striding to the plate but . . . Fred Stanley! "Chicken" Stanley! Easily the weakest hitter on the entire ballclub!

"Why is Billy letting Fred Stanley hit?" I moaned aloud.

"Where's Bucky Dent?" Sidney Zion cried out.

"That's it!" I said. "Roy White ran for Dent in the eighth. There's nobody to play shortstop except Stanley. Martin is in a box. That's why Stanley's hitting!"

"Why not move Nettles to short?" Zion demanded, pounding his hand on the seat in front of him.

"Then who plays third?" I asked.

"There's gotta be somebody!"

"Juan Beniquez. I think Beniquez can play third."

"How about Murcer at short!" Zion exclaimed triumphantly. "Murcer started out as a shortstop, didn't he?"

"And used to throw the ball into the seats behind first," I added.

"My goodness," said Mary Lindsay.

"Anybody but Stanley," whimpered Zion. "Let Chambliss hit. Let Catfish Hunter play short. Anybody but Stanley."

But Stanley it was, and Stanley grounded weakly to the second baseman, who threw him out with ease. *I knew the Yankees wouldn't make it,* said the voice. *I told you so.*

But it was 2–2 and extra innings, and there was now no longer any question of a party. Nothing could distract me now, not even the manic hilarity that swept through Suite 332 in the top of the tenth inning. Actually, it started on the field when Dwight Evans, the Red Sox right fielder, led off the inning with a long fly ball to the right-center field wall. Mickey Rivers snared the ball with a running over-the-shoulder catch, but his momentum carried him full tilt into the wall and left him stretched out on the dirt warning track, apparently unconscious. While Rivers was being tended to by the Yankee trainer and then slowly helped to the sidelines, a fan jumped out of the stands and began to race around the outfield with a rapidly growing band of security guards in hot pursuit. Finally, one of the guards nailed the runaway with a flying tackle near third base, but the guard knocked himself unconscious hitting the man. The game could not begin again until seven other guards had carried away the wildly struggling renegade, until the guard who had tackled him regained his senses and left the field, and until Juan Beniquez had trotted out and taken Rivers's place in center.

Meanwhile, back in Suite 332 a furious mock argument had erupted between Zion and Bronx D. A. Merola, both of whom had retired to the bar to refresh their drinks and watch the melee on television. From my seat outside, I couldn't tell how the discussion got started. Apparently Zion had been trying to find someone to blame for Rivers's accident, for suddenly Merola could be heard to shout, "What the fuck do you want me to do, Zion, indict the wall?"

"No," Zion squealed in outrage, "but maybe you should indict whoever built the wall."

"And who would that be, wise guy?" asked Merola.

"I dunno." Zion was quiet for a moment. "Who was the mayor when the Stadium was renovated? You should indict whoever was the mayor!"

The discussion stopped dead as it apparently dawned on both Zion and Merola that the man they'd decided to indict was sitting no more than twenty feet away from them. An instant later, Zion emerged from the den and hunkered down in the aisle next to John Lindsay's seat to tell the former mayor that he was being held responsible for Mickey Rivers's costly injury and would be hearing from the Bronx D. A.'s office first thing in the morning. Both Lindsay and his wife dissolved in amiable laughter.

Throughout all this, as well as through the next uneventful inning and two-thirds, I sat gloomily trying to will the Yanks to score the winning run. I'd now become convinced that the entire season rode on the outcome of this game. At last, in the bottom of the eleventh, my efforts seemed to pay off, as the Yanks loaded the bases on a single and two consecutive intentional walks. There was a good reason for the two free passes, though, for with two out and the winning run on third in the person of Lou Piniella, who should come striding to the plate again but the feeble-hitting Chicken Stanley. I could imagine what Billy Martin must be muttering to himself over Steinbrenner's failure to supply him with enough backup infielders to take Stanley's place on the field. But Martin's hands were tied, and, as the crowd muttered ominously, Stanley fulfilled everyone's expectations and struck out swinging.

After the Red Sox subsided in the top of the twelfth, Zion suggested that with the Yankee luck running the way it was, another visit to Arrigoni's suite couldn't possibly do any harm. I disagreed but reasoned that with the Yanks coming to bat, the worst that could happen was that they play dead for another inning. And who knew if the jinx hadn't switched now from Arrigoni's suite to Steinbrenner's? This appeared for a moment to be the case when, a few moments after we'd arrived back at Suite 324, Bobby Murcer rifled a two-out double past first base along the right-field foul line. But that threat ended quickly as Piniella skied an easy one to Evans in right field.

While I was standing at the buffet table, fixing myself a sandwich, Ed Arrigoni approached me and started up a conversation about prospective buyers for the New York Mets, who were strongly rumored to be for sale. I cared so little about the Mets that I wasn't even interested in who would own them, unless it was to be Yonkers industrialist Robert Abplanalp, in which case, it was amusing to think, Abplanalp's buddy Richard Nixon might come to be associated with the team. Maybe he would even be designated the Mets' mascot, replacing their present one, the donkey named Mettle.

"I'd like to buy the Mets," said Arrigoni.

"No kidding!" I said, surprised. "Is there any chance of that happening?"

"No way. Abplanalp is going to get them. Do you want to know why?"

"Sure."

"Because . . ."

But Arrigoni was interrupted by a groan from the crowd, which was echoed by several onlookers within the den. When I stepped to the window, I saw that a Red Sox runner, Rick Burleson, was dusting himself off at second base. He was there with only one out and Jerry Remy heading for the plate. I considered dashing back to Suite 332 in time to reverse the Yankees' luck, but before I could move, Remy hit a grounder that found its way between first and second for a single. But there was still a chance to stop the Sox from scoring, because when right fielder Bobby Murcer scooped the ball up, Burleson had barely rounded third base. I jerked in empathy as Murcer unleashed his throw. I groaned as it flew toward the plate.

In another season, a winning season—last season even, when the Yankees caught the Red Sox after being so far behind—the ball would have bounced on a true line as it approached the plate, and Munson would have had it in time to put the tag on the sliding Burleson. But in this season of losing, the ball hit the infield turf with the wrong spin on it and kicked off slightly toward the foul side of the plate; Munson had to reach to snare it and then lunge back at the sliding Burleson; and his tag got to its target just inches too late.

A sick feeling came over me—a feeling that always came when the Yankees lost, a feeling I'd sworn a thousand times I'd never allow myself to have again. It was a feeling that seemed impossibly remote when the evening began so long ago.

There was no point in returning to Suite 332 now, even though the Yankees had one more time at bat. I knew the ending now, of the game, the series and the season even. Everybody in the ballpark knew.

So I continued to stand in Arrigoni's suite, staring out at the field through the glass wall as Reggie Jackson took a called third strike for his fourth whiff of the evening and his sixth time at the plate without a hit. I felt alone now, drained and barely able to urge Nettles to get hold of one and tie the game instead of bouncing weakly out to first, which was what he did. I became aware that I was seeing the action on television as well as live on the field. In fact, as if I'd been hit on the head and my vision damaged, I could now see three versions of the game at once—one live, one on the TV set over the bar, whose reflection I could make out on the glass in front of me, and one just below it on the set placed in front of the seats for Arrigoni's guests to watch instant replays on.

But no replay was needed now as Jim Spencer hit a soft pop-up out toward left field and, in three places simultaneously—on the field, in the reflection, and on the little screen just below, as if the point needed to be made with triple emphasis—Rick Burleson caught the ball, lowered his glove, and trotted happily toward the dugout.

7

WINNING

THE YANKEES WEREN'T ALONE in being out of it. A few weeks after returning to New York City from Wellfleet in September, I got a phone call from my latest editor, Marion Wheeler. Though she had been the managing editor when I first signed up with Methuen, and was by now apparently running the whole show, I'd met her only once or twice in passing and had little more than a dim impression of an intelligent-looking, intense woman in her early forties. But Tracy had several times alluded to what he regarded as a rivalry with her, and I had a sense that she didn't entirely approve of our baseball book. Whether or not this was the case, the news she now delivered to me was bleak. Methuen had just reached an agreement with Scavullo that he would no longer be part of the project. It was basically my fault: judging from the three chapters I'd submitted so far, I wasn't writing the book they'd expected, and their mounting investment would not be justified by the book I *was* writing. Of course, they'd like me to continue alone, but they were going to have to cut costs before expenses got any further out of hand. I had the feeling that I was aboard a fast-sinking ship.

In a state of shock, I drifted aimlessly for several weeks. I remembered certain promises I'd made to myself when Tracy had first approached me. One of them was to fly up to Boston to see my first game at Fenway Park. I went the night after Carl Yastrzemski had gotten his three thousandth career hit, so there was a trace of anticlimax in the air. Still, it was comforting to wander around the old ballpark, which, with its many layers of paint and rectangular shape, put one in mind of a well-used ocean liner. Though it was meaningless to both teams by now, there was a measure of satisfaction in watching the Yanks trounce the Sox behind Ron Guidry. I ended up the evening at the press-room bar with Yogi Berra, a man so uncharismatic and comfortable in his own skin that we were able to stand drinking together, exchanging only a quiet observation or two about what a recent windstorm had done to our respective houses.

The other promise I'd made was to visit Bill Veeck, now the owner of the Chicago White Sox. I telephoned Red Smith to find out how to get in touch with Veeck. "Just call him," said Smith. "He answers his own phone." So I called Comiskey Park in Chicago, asked the switchboard for Mr. Veeck, please, and sure enough found myself talking to him.

"Can you be here at four o'clock?" he said when I asked him for an interview.

"Today? I'm calling from New York."

"Well, how about tomorrow?"

"I'll be there."

Veeck received me in his "office," which was nothing more than a table in the cafeteria-bar of Comiskey Park, known as the Bards Room. He had before him only a telephone, a pitcher of beer, and copies of Chicago's afternoon papers. We talked and drank until about two-thirty the following morning, making due allowances for the playing of a baseball game and consultations with various members of the White Sox family, including Veeck's wife, Mary Frances; his manager, Tony LaRussa; his vice-president, Roland Hemond; his scout-at-large, Jerry Krause; and assorted investors, players, and visitors.

As the evening went on and the beer went down, the topics we discussed congealed into matter of such dense specificity that in the morning I found myself with a black hole in my head. In time some of that night's lost particles came back to me: that California's last payment to Rod Carew would be made in the year 2015; that Todd

Demeter, the Yankees' top choice in the amateur draft that year, would never make it as a major-league player; that Veeck's favorite writers at the moment were Philip Roth and William Styron; that manager Tony LaRussa had felt chagrined over a wrong decision he'd made during the game that evening; that Veeck had several times voted for Norman Thomas; that the White Sox had a terrific bunch of young pitchers coming up through the minors; that the reason Reggie Jackson signed with the Yankees was that he truly believed George Steinbrenner was going to be his friend; that Tony LaRussa had completed two-thirds of the work on his law degree; that Comiskey Park had a drainage problem because no plumbing contractor who had ever been employed there over the years had left records of exactly where beneath the playing field he had done his work; and that, in Veeck's opinion, baseball writers should report in their stories only what had happened on the field of play, never mind all the ridiculous clubhouse gossip. But overshadowing everything else in my mind was the memory of Veeck clambering about Comisky Park on his artificial leg like a benign Captain Ahab aboard the *Pequod*.

But as the month of September dragged on, I reached such a state of confusion and despair over where my book was headed that I ended up retreating into the world of my baseball cards.

Back in May and June of the current season, I'd gone on a spree of buying baseball bubble gum cards. One of the prices I'd paid for becoming a fan so late in life was missing out on the baseball-card stage that so many kids go through between the ages of seven and eleven. Anyway, I couldn't have been a collector even if I'd wanted to. As I learned years later, because of wartime shortages virtually no baseball cards were even published between 1941 and 1948.

So I'd never traded with my friends—five Snuffy Stirnweisses for one Ted Williams, or a Ted Kluszewski for a Hank Sauer. I'd never gotten to flip cards competitively, odds against evens. I'd never been able to bury away in shoeboxes tall rubber-banded stacks of cards, which, dug out decades later, might contain treasures worth hundreds, even thousands, of dollars, not to speak of an afternoon's worth of Proustian evocativeness. (The most valuable baseball card in existence, the famous T-206 depicting Honus Wagner, the "Flying Dutchman," was now worth in mint condition fifteen thousand dollars.) So even at the age of forty-four, I found it hard to look at a package of bubble gum cards without feeling a little of the sense of deprivation that had brought me to baseball in the first place.

Now I had a good excuse to indulge in this long-deferred pastime.

One afternoon early in the current season, when the garish display of baseball cards on the counter of my local stationery store had as usual caught my eye, I found myself explaining to the two proprietors my need to do some intensive research in the field of baseball. Even though they looked at me a little curiously, I scooped up about five dollars' worth of cards and paid for them along with my afternoon paper.

I was interested to see how my collection would evolve. I had often heard that it was the practice of Topps Chewing Gum, Inc. to print proportionately fewer cards of the better players. How else explain why the ones that had increased in value most over the years were the Cobbs, Ruths, DiMaggios, and Mantles? Scarcity of supply had to be at least a part of it. The theory had even been asserted in print: in a quirky 1977 memoir called *Baseball and the Cold War: Being a Soliloquy on the Necessity of Baseball*, the author, one Howard Senzel—a disillusioned veteran of New Left politics but an unreconstructed fan of his hometown baseball team, the Rochester Red Wings—claimed actually to have seen the uncut sheets of cards that his father, an employee of the firm that did Topps' printing, would occasionally bring home from the office. Sure enough, Senzel insisted, on each sheet of cards some of the players' images were duplicated. The game was rigged!

So I assumed that as I accumulated cards by buying random packs every time I went into my stationery store, the least represented players would be the Steve Garveys, the Willie Stargells, and the Rod Carews, while those who piled up the quickest would be the nonentities who played for weaker teams like the Toronto Blue Jays, the Seattle Mariners, the Atlanta Braves, and the San Diego Padres. But that wasn't the way it worked out.

By the end of May, I'd collected about 2,500 cards. Putting them in order had given me something to do while listening to the late-night broadcasts of Yankee games from the West Coast. There was a total of 726 different cards in the series, and if, contrary to my assumption of weighting, they were printed and distributed in equal quantities, then a random selection should have given me a theoretical 3.5 of each number.

But the dispersal of the cards was far from uniform. It looked at first as if my collection were heavily weighted with lesser-known players, since among the most frequent repetitions were Mike Phillips of the St. Louis Cardinals (12 duplicates), Tucker Ashford of the San Diego Padres (11), Barry Bonnell of the Atlanta Braves (11), Jim Mason of the Texas Rangers (10), Tom House of the Seattle Mariners (9), Balor Moore of the Toronto Blue Jays (9), and Wayne Gross of the Oakland A's (8). All these players were obscure, at least to me. In fact, out of the 765 most common players in my collection, 567 could be described as either journeymen or relative nonentities. Or to define the matter more precisely: the more prominent players were represented on those cards with numbers divisible by 5 (for instance, #25 was Steve Carlton, #30 was Dave Winfield, #35 was Ed Figeroa, #40 was Dennis Eckersley, and so forth), while the superstars were portrayed on cards with numbers divisible by 100 (#100 was Tom Seaver, #200 was Johnny Bench, #300 was Rod Carew, #400 was Jim Rice, and so on). Since 567 of my 765 most common cards represented numbers in between multiples of 5, then about 75 percent of the most frequently represented cards showed players that the Topps people themselves considered journeymen or neophytes.

On the other hand, I hadn't exactly proved that Topps weighted its print runs. For among my duplicates were 10 Vida Blues, #110; 9 Rick Mondays, #605; 8 Joe Morgans, #20; 8 Tom Seavers, #100; 8 Lee Mazzillis, #355; 7 Steve Garveys, #50; 7 Rick Burlesons, #125; 7 Dave Lopeses, #290; 7 Catfish Hunters, #670; 7 Reggie Jacksons, #700; 6 Fred Lynns, #480; 5 Rod Carews, #300; 5 Dave Parkers, #430; and 4 Pete Roses, #650. In fact, you could field a pretty fair all-star team from among these redundancies.

What's more, I couldn't spot any pattern when I judged my collection in the light of team competence. Of my 765 most duplicated cards, 347 represented teams in the top half of their respective divisions, while 418 played for teams in the bottom half. As for the balance between extremes: my multiples included 129 players from first-place teams and 125 from last-place teams, so there was no visible trend in terms of team ability. In fact, the only pattern I could see was that I seemed to be accumulating players from the National League West Division, of which I had 287, faster than I was collecting players from any other division, and over twice as fast as I was gathering players from the National League East, of which I had 117. Since I'd bought all my cards in the East, where collectors were least likely to want Western Division players, this made small sense from a conspiracy theorist's perspective, unless perhaps the Topps company was trying to promote increased contact between the two parts of the country by flooding each with what the other most desired.

Nor was there any pattern apparent when I considered the cards I was still missing. By the middle of June, when my total collection was approaching 2,700, the group of players I lacked had shrunk to a mere thirteen. These could fairly be described as a mixture of stars and mortals. Among the stars were Don Gullett of the Yanks, #140; Carl Yastrzemski of the Red Sox, #320; Jim Palmer of the Orioles, #340; and Dave Kingman of the Cubs, #370. Among the mortals— at least up to that point in their careers—were Angel catcher Brian Downing, #71; the Tigers' Steve Kemp, #196; Bob Knepper and Jack Clark of the Giants, #'s 486 and 512; Steve Braun of the Royals, #502; Jim Slaton and Bob McClure of the Brewers, #'s 541 and 623; and Larry Milbourne of the Mariners, #199. Also missing was card #259, the team picture of the Cincinnati Reds. For me this clinched the case that the printings were not weighted. Whatever value these cards might assume in the future, it would have little to do with supply and everything to do with demand.

This didn't mean that these thirteen cards hadn't already assumed greater value for me. In fact, like so much else in life, they had begun to grow more desirable the instant I sensed their scarcity. What had started out as a diversion took on the character of an obsession. Where once I'd stooped to picking up a couple of packs whenever I had more important business at my local stationery store, now I began dropping by with no purpose other than to buy more cards. As inconspicuously as possible, I would comb the store's display case, checking the single visible card in each package to see if I could find one I was missing. Soon the two proprietors had caught the spirit of the hunt and were pulling out their backup supplies for my inspection.

By the end of June, my foraging had yielded Brian Downing, Steve Kemp, Carl Yastrzemski, Bob Knepper, Steve Braun, Jim Slaton, Bob McClure, and the team picture of the Cincinnati Reds. But the size of my collection now surpassed three-thousand cards. These had cost me over sixty dollars. With only five cards left to go, I was beginning to feel as if I were trying to swat a fly with a battleship.

So I yielded to a final loss of shame. I'd shared my project with my daughter, and she too had picked up the spirit of the hunt. She'd dropped news of her father's obsession into the network of her third-grade classmates, many of whom were traders and flippers. One thing had led to another, and on a Saturday morning early in July, I escorted two fellow collectors into my study, neither of them over four feet high. Some brief bargaining ensued, and for the price of a few duplicates, among them Steve Ontiveros of the Chicago Cubs, I acquired Don Gullett, Dave Kingman, and several vague but enthusiastic promises. Two days later, there arrived in the mail an envelope with the six names of a law partnership embossed on it. Certain that I was about to be sued for something, I anxiously tore out the letter and read the following, neatly typed on the firm's stationery:

> Enclosed please find baseball cards—Jim Palmer and Jack Clark—in full consideration for Mr. Ontiveros.
>
> Very truly yours

and there followed the signature of one of the firm's partners, whose name I now recognized from my Saturday morning trading session with his son. Things had clearly gone far enough—even if I *was* still missing Larry Milbourne of the Seattle Mariners.

But before emerging from this world, I decided to see what I could learn from the cards about reality. Since they were numbered randomly, the first thing I did was to rearrange the entire collection into teams. Then I read the biographical and statistical information printed on the back of each card. Finally, I culled the cards of the teams that were still in the race in early September and arranged their first-string players on a series of imaginary diamonds.

This got me started, at least. There were many players I'd never heard of before, mostly because they had never played against the Yankees. From the statistical summaries on the backs, I could tell the veterans from the hopefuls, the superstars from the supernumeraries. But the yield of information was limited. The stats might tell you that a team had a lot of power hitters or strikeout pitchers, but they told you nothing of game-winning hits or strikeouts with runners on base.

In fact, the clearest picture you got from the cards was one of how the teams had been built and thus of how stable they might be. At one end of this scale was the Texas Rangers, who after the Topps people had gone to press the previous winter, had wheeled and dealt so frantically that much of the team had changed. By the time I'd finished matching Ranger players to the team's media-guide roster, I had an assortment of Yankees, Indians, and a Padre, as well as a dozen Rangers who had been playing with the team only a season or so. Near the other end of the stability scale was the Cincinnati Reds, made up of eight players who'd played their entire careers with the Reds and six others who'd been with them for over five years.

But if you looked at how all the teams were doing, stability didn't seem to be much of a factor. True, the Texas Rangers were nearly out of the race in their division, while the Cincinnati Reds were close to the top of theirs. And the stable Pittsburgh Pirates were winning their division, while the labile Atlanta Braves were trailing badly in theirs. But the California Angels, a very unstable team when it came to developing its own players, was winning its division, while the Kansas City Royals, the very model of stability, with four-teen players that had started out with the team and five more that had been on board for over five years, were trailing the Angels by four games. And no one had been more unstable in recent years than the Yankees, and no one had done as well, except maybe the Los Angeles Dodgers, a stable team that was doing badly this year.

So there was only so much to be gleaned from the cards about the true characters of the teams. As therapeutic as my obsession might be proving, it wasn't telling me nearly enough about the real world of baseball. With the pennant races winding up and the World Se-ries looming on the horizon, it was time for me to pull my head out of the cards and see what was happening. I would have to follow baseball objectively and to look at the game as if it weren't played only by the New York Yankees.

By late September, the division races had been all but settled. In the American League East—the Yankees' division—the Baltimore Orioles, an extremely stable team by bubble gum–card standards, had run away from the pack and were winning the championship by a big margin. In the American League West, the California Angels—a team that could be described as a ragtag collection of superstars put together with the money of owner Gene Autry, the tycoon cowboy, and the brains of both his vice-president, E. J. "Buzzy" Bavasi, and his part-time superscout, Frank "Trader" Lane—were somehow beating out the Kansas City Royals, despite being crippled by injuries and having compiled the worst record of all four division leaders.

In the National League, two veteran teams were prevailing over two young expansion teams. In the Western Division, Cincinnati's "Big Red Machine," having undergone vital repairs just as it seemed headed for the junkheap, clanked ahead of the Houston Astros just at the finish line and won the title by a game and a half. And in the Eastern Division, the swashbuckling Pittsburgh Pirates—a team of old-timers that had been bolstered by a couple of shrewd trades—finally cut down the fledgling Montreal Expos after chasing them in circles throughout the final weeks of the season.

As I began to watch these events more closely, even going so far as to attend a couple of the games, the Baltimore Orioles beat the California Angels in the American League Championship Series three games to one and probably would have swept the series in three had not Baltimore's speedy centerfielder, Al Bumbry, run down a line drive in the ninth inning of the third game, and then let it drop for a two-base error. In the National League Championship Series, though Cincinnati had taken eight of twelve from Pittsburgh during the regular season, the Pirates, on target now, destroyed the Reds in three. So finally, it was to be Pittsburgh against Baltimore in the World Series—a satisfying enough outcome to me since, from what little I'd been able to learn about them, the Bucs and the O's appeared to be the class of the field.

Now the question arose whether or not I was going to be able to attend the World Series. Of course I wanted to go; who wouldn't? But Methuen was wondering out loud whether the expense would really be worth it. They were also growing balky over the time and energy it was taking them to arrange for my press credentials.

So I tried reconciling myself to the idea of staying home and watching the Series on television. TV might not be so bad. Indeed there had been occasions in recent weeks when TV had proved positively revelatory. For example, there was one game during the National League East pennant race that I had been strongly tempted to attend. That was the third and last game of a Houston Astro–Cincinnati Red stretch-drive series. It was played Sunday, September 23, and if the Astros had been able to win it, they would have completed a four-game sweep of the Reds and gained a half-game hold on first place with just seven games left to play. But that game was to be televised nationally by ABC TV, which had promised to keep its audience up to date on the rest of the National League race. At the same time, Channel 9 had the New York Mets against the St. Louis Cardinals in the Mets' last home game of the season, Channel 11 had the Yankees against the Toronto Blue Jays, Channel 4 had the New York Jets playing a football game against the Buffalo Bills, and Channel 2, later in the afternoon, would have the football Giants against the Philadelphia Eagles.

So instead of flying down to Houston, Texas, to watch a single baseball game from a faraway seat in the Astrodome press box, I was able, with my usual serendipitous channel-jumping, to watch the Reds beat the Astros 7–1. I also saw Pete Rose get his 199th hit in his record-breaking quest to get 200 hits in ten consecutive seasons, while his team, the Phillies, lost to eccentric Bill Lee of the Montreal Expos to keep the Expos a half-game ahead of the Pirates. I saw Lou Brock of the Cards steal his 938th base to take the all-time lead in steals over Billy Hamilton, who had stolen 937 from 1888 through 1901. I saw a close game between the Cards and the Mets until the miserable Mets fell apart in the tenth inning to lose the team's ninth straight game. I saw Tommy John of the Yankees beat Toronto for his twentieth win of the season, and heard Frank Messer, the announcer, pronounce it a "great year for Yankee baseball" when in fact, considering Thurman Munson's death, the injury to Goose Gossage, the firing of Bob Lemon, and the team's all-around dismal performance, it was probably one of the worst years in Yankee history. I saw the Buffalo Bills beat the Jets 46–31 with the Bills' rookie receiver Jerry Butler catching ten passes for 255 yards and four touchdowns. And I saw the football Giants sink to yet another hopeless defeat in the miasma of the New Jersey Meadowlands.

Sure, I knew all the arguments against the tube. It was true that it trivialized the game with its incessant chatter. How could you fantasize about larger-than-life heroes when, sometimes during the very action of the game, their tiny faces—or occasionally even the tiny faces of their wives—would appear in the corner of the screen to mumble something on the order of "Hopefully, we'll play good today and win." No wonder there were no more nicknames like the Yankee Clipper, the Splendid Splinter, Big and Little Poison, or the Georgia Peach. How could you have stuck a microphone in the face of Fredrick Francis Lear, an infielder who played briefly for the Cubs and the Giants back in the teens of the century, and said, "King Lear?"—for that's what this player was called, King Lear— "how are the hemorrhoids feeling today, King Lear?" By putting us on such intimate terms with the players and their families, television had robbed baseball of its mythic dimension.

All the same, the incessant chatter was not mere noise. Los Angeles Dodger pitcher Don Sutton, hired by NBC to provide expert commentary for the Cincinnati-Pittsburgh series, was actually informative. From what better authority could you hear that no less than 80 percent of the successful pitchers in the major leagues either dampen or scuff the ball, or that home plate probably "gets a little wider" when a batter complains to the plate umpire about called strikes, or that pitchers who seem to get "stronger" during a game don't actually do so; their rhythms simply speed up, most likely because their muscles are getting looser? It was from television that I got my first taste of the Willie Stargell legend when sportscaster Howard Cosell, his voice rumbling on like an endless freight train passing in the night, quoted Stargell's description of himself as "an old oak tree with a lot of limbs." Cosell droned on, "When you get to know Willie Stargell, you get a good feeling about the human race." And it was on television that Tony Kubek finally answered my question about how his career would have been affected if he'd played on artificial turf. On September 29, Kubek announced, sounding as cheerfully breathless as if he'd just finished helping three dozen blind old ladies win a crocheting contest, that the ball bounced truer on artificial turf "unless it hit a dent or a seam," which was to say that the incident in the 1960 World Series could also have occurred in the new era. So much for progress.

It was also true of television, as deep thinkers about the game were forever pointing out, that baseball's space was fundamentally wrong for the cool medium. Baseball was one of those rare games in which the object was not to score points with the ball, but rather to score by getting rid of the ball and making one's opponent play with it. During the game's most dramatic moments there were always at least two centers of focus to the action. Indeed, what many regarded as the most exciting play of all—the long throw from the outfield to catch a base runner trying to score—was something television could never do justice to, because it was not possible to show the outfielder, the relay man, the catcher, the base runner, and the ball all together in a single continuous shot.

Still, despite this handicap, the technicians had certainly worked marvels of compensation with their close-ups, their split-screen shots, and their multiangled, slow-motion, forward-and-backward replays. For example, there was no seat in the whole Houston Astrodome that could have matched the TV view of the single play on which the Astros might be said to have blown their entire season. This occurred in the top of the fourth inning of the third game of that final Houston-Cincinnati series—the one the Astros had to win to sweep the series and take over first place by half a game. The play put the Reds ahead, 3–1, but, more important, it kept alive a big inning that finally left the score 6–1 and served to neutralize the Astros' Punch-and-Judy hitting attack.

With the Reds leading 2–1, two outs, and runners on first and second, Frank Pastore, the Reds' pudgy rookie pitcher came to the plate, lunged at an outside pitch, and hit what used to be known, before television bleached out the game's more colorful metaphors, as a dying quail to right field. Ray Knight, the Cincinnati runner on second, took off for home, arriving there just a moment after the Astro catcher, Luis Pujols, had caught the relay from right field and turned to block the plate from the careering Knight. But Knight lowered his shoulder, plowed hard into Pujols and sent him spinning to the ground, and though it didn't appear as if the ball had left the catcher's mitt for even an instant, the plate umpire, Joe West, was suddenly waving his arms with great vigor to signal that Knight was safe.

Consternation and dismay on the Astros' bench. Even the announcers called Knight out. But through the magic of close-up slow-motion replay, we could see the whiteness of the ball rising just over the rim of the catcher's mitt, and then, with the tape playing in reverse, setting down behind the brow of the glove. Pujols had definitely bobbled the old orb. When the arguments had abated, the next hitter, right fielder Dave Collins, lined authoritatively to right. His Astro counterpart, Jeff Leonard, fell down and let the ball get by him. Hector Cruz, the Reds runner on third, scored to make it 4–1. Pastore the pitcher, who was on second, came lumbering and heaving around third, his face straining ecstatically. The relay throw from second baseman Rafael Landestoy was a little wild and got away from catcher Pujols, who charged after it, leaving home plate bare. Pastore slid triumphantly (if pointlessly) and scored. Collins, who had hit the ball in the first place, came home, arriving at the deserted plate a little ahead of both Vern Ruhle, the Astro pitcher, who was racing to cover home, and Pujols, who had belatedly retrieved the ball. It was 6–1. The Astros had finally come apart. And every detail of the farce, every muff and pratfall, every grin and grimace, had been intimately caught—and revealed—by the camera. Baseball at its best should be seen from a distance. But when the game's geometry broke down, it was entertaining to watch it up close.

But the more I thought about it the more I realized it would be out of the question not to see the World Series live. For all of television's technical dazzle, the bond between the spectator and the event remained too tenuous. It was far too easy for the observer to get caught up in events extraneous to baseball—by the need to run household errands, for instance, or get involved in office politics. During the second game of the Pittsburgh-Cincinnati League Championship Series, I'd had to leave my perch in front of the TV screen and drive downtown to pick up my wedding anniversary dinner from the family's favorite Chinese restaurant. This meant that I was reduced to listening on the car radio to the tenth inning, and to missing, because of the airwave interference in the East River Drive underpasses, half of what went on when the Pirates won the game on an Omar Moreno single, Tim Foli's sacrifice bunt, and a hit by Dave Parker. This is not to mention the difficulties of writing on a scorecard while weaving through Manhattan traffic. It was a dangerous way to take in a baseball game.

In contrast, watching the event live meant being awash in the atmosphere of the game, not just the sounds and smells and the feel on the skin of the sunshine or the soft night air, but also the little rituals and routines I'd discovered were part of being a baseball reporter—the pregame gathering around the batting cage, the postgame visit to the clubhouse and manager's office, and the camaraderie of life on the road. By comparison, it was not only monotonous to watch baseball while cooped up in a darkened room, it was probably downright unhealthy.

Anyway, I'd gotten rather to like the two teams that were going to meet in the Series. Aside from having beaten out my Yankees and therefore being worthy of the respect that the defeated owe the victorious, the Baltimore Orioles were an advertisement for how a professional baseball team should be run. What made them special? The most impressive thing about them was the team's ability to succeed with limited resources. Baltimore was not a rich organization. Though the O's were currently drawing very good crowds, attendance was normally on the skimpy side, so sparse indeed that management was threatening to move the team to Washington. It didn't choose to pay its stars enormous salaries, preferring to put its money into its farm system. Over the years, it had lost to free agency such outstanding players as Reggie Jackson, Bobby Grich, Ross Grimsley, and Don Baylor—each a star whose departure you would have thought would devastate the team. Yet season after season, the Orioles continued to be among the pennant contenders.

For this one had to credit the organization, all the way from the team's owner, Jerold C. Hoffberger, an affable beer company executive, down to its superscout, James J. Russo, whose appetite for the details of the game seemed insatiable. But the jewel in the display window of the organization was the team's manager, Earl S. Weaver—the so-called Earl of Baltimore, on whom sportswriters were forever wearing out such clichés as "feisty," "combative," "scrappy," and "pepperpot." Everybody said he was also the smartest manager around, and though I didn't really know enough to judge for myself, it stood to reason that anyone who had been working successfully for so long for such a crack outfit had to be pretty smart. One also had to credit the way the Orioles allowed the players to disagree in public with Weaver's managerial thinking, as the star pitcher, Jim Palmer, had been doing vociferously for years. Such permissiveness surely showed the confidence that management had in Weaver's brains, even if it didn't tell you all that much about those brains themselves.

Certainly Weaver was the smartest-*sounding* manager around, to judge from the stories about his prowess that one kept hearing. Frank Deford of *Sports Illustrated* wrote about one that Weaver had told him to illustrate why he insisted on making all the decisions for his team. It seems that the year Reggie Jackson played for the Orioles, he asked for permission to run the bases on his own—

which Weaver denied him. This hurt Jackson's feelings, so he decided to prove himself to Weaver. One day, with Jackson on first base and Lee May, the Orioles right-handed designated hitter, up at bat against a left-handed pitcher, Jackson took off for second without Weaver's green light and stole the base easily. Lee May was then walked intentionally, and a pinch hitter flied out to end the inning. When Jackson came back to the bench all full of himself, Weaver looked at him and growled, "Sure, you stole. That opens first base. The left-hander walks May. Then I've got to bring in a right-handed pinch hitter. I had the gun loaded with May. You take the bat out of his hands and make me waste another player. That's what the stolen base got us." Jackson never asked to run on his own again.

And Weaver was certainly entertaining to be around. By the time of the playoffs, I'd seen enough managers conducting their postgame interviews with the press to know just how dreary they could be. In the composite post-mortem, a tired old man would sit numbly staring at some object on his cluttered desktop until a member of the nervous semicircle of reporters in front of him could think of a sufficiently penetrating question to fracture for a moment the leaden silence. At this the weary strategist would heave up his eyes, grunt a cliché or two about "playing the percentages," and return to contemplating the bottle of liniment or the sodden paper cup of coffee or the baseball waiting to be autographed.

Earl Weaver was a different proposition altogether. Instead of slumping behind his desk, he perched low on a stool in an open corner of his office. Dressed only in sweatshirt, jockstrap, and a can of beer, he bristled with a mixture of humor and malevolence at the reporters who stood around watching him as if he were an illegal cockfight or a craps game in a back room of the barracks.

The first time I saw him up close his Orioles had just finished beating the California Angels 9–8 in Baltimore to go up two games to none in the best-of-five American League Championship Series. But the O's had jumped out to a 9–1 lead in the first three innings, and the Angels had nibbled away, getting one run in the sixth, one in the seventh, three in the eighth, and two in the ninth. The game had finally ended with the bases loaded and one of the Angels' best hitters, Brian Downing, grounding out to third off the Orioles' shaky relief pitcher, Don Stanhouse, who had eventually prevailed despite giving up four hits, two walks, and two earned runs in the only two innings he pitched. Now, in the clubhouse, reporters were curious to know how Weaver had felt there at the end—wasn't he just about as nervous as he could get?

WEAVER: I'm always nervous. I was nervous when we were winning nine to one. As nervous as I can get I was when the score was nine to one, so I was just as nervous as I can get when the score was nine to eight! And I hope I never lose that feeling!

REPORTER: Earl, how nervous do you get when Stanhouse does what he does?

WEAVER: As nervous as I can get!

REPORTER: You weren't more nervous than at any other time?

WEAVER: No! I'm as nervous as I can get! Look. Why do you argue? You ask me a question and argue. Just listen for the answer. I was as nervous as I could get when the score was nine to one and I'm as nervous as I can get when the score was nine to eight.

REPORTER: Okay. Now, Stanhouse walks two guys . . .

WEAVER: Now, you're going to ask me if that makes me more nervous.

REPORTER: Well, I . . .

WEAVER: I'm a son of a bitch! I'M AS NERVOUS AS I CAN GET! YOU CAN'T GET NO MORE NERVOUS THAN I WAS WHEN THE SCORE WAS NINE TO ONE!

SECOND REPORTER: Why were you nervous then?

WEAVER: Because I am! That's the type of personality I am! As nervous as ya' can get is as nervous as ya' can get. Regardless of nine to one or nine to eight.

THIRD REPORTER: You take nothing for granted?

WEAVER: Nothing! Never in this game. You can't afford to.

LEHMANN-HAUPT: Didn't you think about bringing Stoddard in for Stanhouse?

WEAVER: You can say Stoddard could have come in and got 'em out. Maybe he could and maybe he couldn't. I've been goin' through this with Stanhouse for two years. And it's been very successful and he's made me look like a genius. The minute he starts making me look like an asshole, then you gotta go to somebody else, y'know, or the minute he starts losin' games is what it boils down to. But he doesn't do that! He does it occasionally, 'cause he's human. But he doesn't do it often. And as I said before, he's in there till they tie it or go ahead.

FIRST REPORTER: Earl, do you think Stanhouse likes to get in trouble with those walks?

WEAVER: It's because he does not give in to the hitter.

FIRST REPORTER: That's the answer?

WEAVER: That's the answer. He does not give in to the hitter.

FIRST REPORTER: Then why does he . . . y'know . . .

WEAVER: Because he does not give in to the hitter!

SECOND REPORTER: Do you hear the question?

WEAVER: Yes, I do. He . . . What's the question then?

FIRST REPORTER: Well, my question is . . . y'know . . . he walked two guys and then he strikes out a couple. So many times he's done that all season long.

WEAVER: Because he will not give in to the hitter! You wanna try again?

FIRST REPORTER: I'm trying.

WEAVER: Well, that's the only thing I can say. He will not give in to the hitter.

FOURTH REPORTER: Then how come so many times he'll walk two guys and then the third one strikes out?

WEAVER: BECAUSE HE WILL NOT GIVE IN TO THE HITTER!! He doesn't give in to the third hitter. It just happens that the third hitter swings at the fuckin' pitches that the first two hitters don't.

LEHMANN-HAUPT: Isn't that a coincidence?

WEAVER: Listen, if you're going to ask me a question, just let me answer it. And that's the answer to that question. It's no coincidence. Here's the answer to your question—the only one I have. He does not give in to the hitter. That's why it happens. Now I know you don't understand it. But if you print it down there . . . those are my words . . . maybe your readers will.

At this point, Jimmy Russo, the Orioles' superscout, stuck his head in the door and called out some encouraging remarks to Weaver. When the reporters resumed asking questions, the tension had dissipated—somewhat.

THIRD REPORTER: Come on, Earl. Didn't it cross your mind to take Stanhouse out in the ninth?

WEAVER: Yes, it did. And I'll tell you, he didn't have half the stuff he had yesterday. But yet he didn't come down the middle and throw the home-run ball. Again, he did not give in to the hit-

196

ter. He'd 'a walked Downing, the tying run, in, before he'd give Downing a pitch to hit out of the ballpark. He'd 'a done that. And that's why he has success. 'Cause some of those balls hit the corner, and we thought some of them hit the corner in the eighth when he walks a guy. Y'know. We're thinkin' that we're hittin' the corners. We didn't get 'em today. Does that help answer?

FIRST AND THIRD REPORTERS: That's it! That's the answer we were looking for.

WEAVER: Well, you didn't ask the question! But you're right. I don't think he had as good stuff. But he did not give in to the hitter. And as a result we wound up with the biggest out you can get.

NEWLY ARRIVED REPORTER: Earl, how did you feel there when Stanhouse starts walking those guys . . .

Weaver and the entire crowd dissolved in hilarious laughter.

I simply had to see more of Earl Weaver.

As for the Pittsburgh Pirates: they seemed to have everything a baseball team needed: power at bat, speed on the base paths, strong pitching from both its starters and its relievers, a manager who knew just how loose a rein to hold on a group of rowdy personalities, and character, team character—most of all, team character. Among all the clubs that had fought for the various division titles, the Pirates left one with the strongest impression. Part of the reason for this was the team's physical appearance on the field. The unusually large number of tall men on the club, their partially black road uniforms, and their squared-off centennial caps with horizontal stripes—all contributed to the impression of a band of night-riding outlaws from out of the past. And part of it was the image the Pirates always managed to project of raucous compatibility. A team with a history of racial tension that had been resolved somehow during the 1970 season, Pittsburgh, like its spiritual counterpart in professional football, the Oakland Raiders, had ever since managed to accommodate all the extreme types that passed through its locker room. As the disco hit that pounded increasingly hard over the speaker system at Three Rivers Stadium kept insisting, "We Are Famil-ee." And the heads of the family were impressive too—the father figure and the prodigal son—Willie "Pops" Stargell, with his sympathetic mobile face and big dramatic home runs, and Dave "I Am the Team"

Parker, as swaggering and boastful as Muhammad Ali and probably as talented as the Great One was in his prime.

I had one other strong impression of Pittsburgh. I'd gotten it on a night I spent there after watching the Pirates beat the Montreal Expos and virtually wrap up the division championship. After the game, I was standing in the joyous Pittsburgh clubhouse next to the team's gleaming space-age quadriphonic Yamaha-Sanyo tapedeck complex. I was watching a curious little skirmish over how loudly the machine should be pounding out Bill Withers's "Boot Love." One half-naked Pirate would walk over and turn the volume low; another would go over and turn it up again; a third would lower it irritably; then the second would angrily raise it again. Finally, a stocky black player whom I recognized as a former Met named John "The Hammer" Milner stalked over and jerked the volume down, screaming over his shoulder, "You got ten minutes, and then I'm blasting this motherfucker!" When I looked to see where this ultimatum had been directed, I spotted George Kimball, the shaggy reporter from Boston I'd been running into all season. He was standing next to a smaller, dark-haired, shifty-looking man dressed in jeans and a denim jacket. Compared to the Pirate players they were talking to, they reminded me of a couple of comic-strip characters, Al Capp's Hairless Joe and Lonesome Polecat, the keepers of the powerful steaming Kickapoo Joy Juice.

Relieved as always to see even a vaguely familiar face, I walked over to find out what all the screaming had been about. "Oh, it's nothing," Kimball mumbled. "Hammer's just saying I got ten more minutes to do my interviews. He's only screaming 'cause he hasn't come down off his speed yet." Then Kimball's non-glass eye lit up in recognition, and though up until that moment he'd never done more than nod "hello" to me, he was suddenly addressing me as if I were a regular member of his entourage. "Hey, man. Come on up later and help us with a bottle of Irish." He nudged the smaller man who was fidgeting and smiling beside him. "Jack here'll be there. This is Jack McClain. And Lee and Willo are probably coming. It'll be good." Though I hadn't the faintest idea who "Lee" and "Willo" were, I accepted at once and wrote down Kimball's hotel room number.

It had not been a night to remember. "Lee"—by which Kimball meant the eccentric Expo pitcher, Bill Lee, the notorious Spaceman who had earlier in the season run afoul of Commissioner Bowie Kuhn for announcing that he sometimes sprinkled marijuana dust on his morning cereal—had not shown up. "Willo" had, with his wife, Kathy, and turned out to be Jim Willoughby, the high point of whose career had been to pitch well in relief for the Boston Red Sox in the middle of the seventh game of the storied 1975 World Series. Because the Sox eventually lost this game, and hence the Series, Willoughby became the subject of a famous anecdote reported by the *New Yorker's* Roger Angell. This concerned an old man in a Cambridge bar who was seen sadly shaking his head during a broadcast of Monday Night Football late in the fall of 1975—months after the Series had ended—and overheard muttering to himself, "We never should have taken out Willoughby." But Willoughby, now a marginal member of the Pirates, was facing the end of his career and was therefore filled with some bitterness toward past employers. The night of the Irish whiskey—as I ruefully came to think of it because of the amount of Bushmills I consumed—began with a rundown of the shortcomings of various scoundrels who had managed or owned Willoughby's teams. The Boston Red Sox were bigoted, he insisted. They had a quota for the number of blacks who could play or coach for them. As for Bill Veeck and his Chicago White Sox: the books he'd written made it sound as if it might be fun to play for his teams. The trouble was, he was more interested in drawing crowds than he was in building a winning team. In fact he didn't really want to win, Willoughby believed, because it would end up costing him in higher salaries. From here the discussion moved to one player's tightfistedness with money, to another's alcoholism, to the drug habits of a dozen others, and finally to why Gatorade wasn't really good for you.

At the low point of the night, Kimball's sidekick, Jack McClain, who was tagging along as his drinking partner cum adviser after having served time in prison for what he described as "a minor violation involving fraudulent securities," suddenly burst forth with a dazzling display of baseball trivia that he'd stored up over the years. What major-league pitcher had accumulated the most wins in his lifetime without ever winning 20 games in a season? Even Kimball didn't know that the answer was Jack Quinn, with 212, if you didn't count his two years with Baltimore of the Federal League (during one of which, 1914, he'd won 26 games), and if you did, then it would be Milt Pappas, with 209 wins. What batter played 154 games one year and batted into more triple plays than he did double plays? Augie Galan of the 1935 Chicago Cubs, who hit into one triple play and no double plays in 646 official times at bat.

Through all these dissonant exchanges, I sat slumped in an armchair in the corner of Kimball's cluttered room, my mind increasingly stupefied by both the gossip and the whiskey. I'd wanted to try out some of my impressions on this gathering of experts: Had the Yankees been hurt this season by the tension I had sensed in spring training? Was Tom Lasorda of the Dodgers as much fun to play for as he was to watch? But the talk kept drifting into subjects too scandalous to record on the miniature tape recorder I'd stuck in my pocket, let alone repeat. When I took my bleary leave, a debate had broken out over whether it had been fair of Kimball the night before to make his buddy Jack, instead of himself, sleep in the bed that Kathy Willoughby had vomited on earlier, Kimball's loudly declaimed theory being that Jack, with his recent prison experience, would be more accustomed to inferior accommodations.

After I left, the evening had gotten even wilder. As Jack McClain told me over a very late breakfast the following day, Kimball, who was beginning to feel a little ruttish, had called the switchboard, identified himself as one Father Burke, and asked for the numbers of the rooms of any of the young Christian ladies who might be staying in the hotel while attending a religious convention in town. When this stratagem failed, he had climbed up on the window sill of his room and expressed his frustration by pissing down on the city of Pittsburgh. Now, over breakfast, Kimball stared at each of us in turn as McClain delivered his report. His glass eye lent his face a permanent look of amazement, so it was hard to tell whether he was outraged or amused by his friend's account.

The three of us must have been a strange sight over that breakfast table: Kimball, with his red face and his shaggy head of hair, ordering beer after beer to wash down his eggs and potatoes; McClain, a denim-clad raccoon, reminiscing darkly about a voodoo houngan, or priest, he'd visited in Haiti in 1971, who was prepared—for a price—to bring "great harm" to any enemy of McClain's until he learned that the target would be President Nixon, whereupon he just laughed and changed the subject, as if perhaps that particular piece of business had already been taken care of (while McClain talked of these bizarre exploits, Kimball gazed at him fondly, occasionally checking to see whether I was being properly appreciative); and I, an owl in blue blazer and necktie, listening and nodding attentively, as if I were auditing a seminar.

Much later, after the World Series was over, I learned that some of the other reporters had referred to Kimball and me as "the gentleman and the bum" (McClain, lacking press credentials, would join us only before and after the games) and had wondered what we saw in each other. I never thought much about what Kimball and McClain saw in me. Both of them were interested in the world of writers. Kimball himself had published a novel, *Only Skin Deep*, and a book on professional football, *Sunday's Fools*, and McClain nursed ambitions to write books, though at the moment these didn't go much beyond a collaboration he was planning with Kimball on what he kept referring to as *The Ultimate Bar Bet Book*, obviously intended to cash in on McClain's prodigious command of trivia. Mostly, I think, they were simply fascinated by the incongruity of my invasion of their turf.

But I knew what *I* saw in *them*. For one thing, they opened up to me a side of baseball I'd never seen before, and while it might be a seedier side, it was one I felt I ought at least to be aware of. For another thing, they knew a lot. McClain's mastery of statistical detail might be quirky, but what I'd seen of it so far was impressive. Kimball's command of the scene seemed at once more practical and more irreverent. To judge from the machine-gun bursts of gossip that would spew from his lips unpredictably (the Boston Red Sox, he would suddenly announce, had been forced to hire a black coach because they were about to be sued by the Massachusetts Division of the American Civil Liberties Union), he seemed to know the inside news, where the odd body was buried, or who had it in for whom. He harbored a sufficient assortment of grudges against the establishment to amount almost to a kind of one-man counterculture. His humor was perverse: at that breakfast, to fill a lull in the conversation, he'd said, beaming at me, "You know, once on a Red Sox airplane flight Luis Tiant grabbed the stewardesses' microphone and announced, 'Too many nigger on this plane!'" Yet his view of the baseball world was original and sharp. The articles of his that I'd read in the *Boston Phoenix* were amusingly impudent. (In a piece on Luis Tiant that made friendly sport of the Cuban pitcher's Hispanic accent, Kimball concluded, "And that's why Luis Tiant is a New York Junkie. He finds it difficult to comprehend himself, actually. Tiant in pinstripes is sort of like Cheryl Tiegs with a mustache. It doesn't really fit.")

For another thing, the two of them were incredibly generous to me. I had overheard them talk the night before about certain obligations they had the next day. But when I suggested we meet for breakfast, they seemed delighted to oblige, as if they had all the time in the world. They didn't mind being interrupted at their work, or rather at Kimball's work. In fact, they seemed absolutely delighted.

Finally, there was the prospect of some poker. When I asked Kimball if he ever played, he grinned wolfishly at me and said that, hey, one of the best things about covering the World Series was the poker. So when he jabbed my shoulder and said, "Hey, come on, man. You can't miss the Series. You gotta go," I decided at once that I was definitely going to be on hand. If there wasn't enough money in my Methuen account, I would pay for it out of my own pocket. If Marion Wheeler stopped getting me press credentials, I would contrive somehow to make my own arrangements.

Many people recall the 1979 World Series as a great one. "Nineteen seventy-nine? Oh, yes!" they exclaim when I tell them which year it was that I spent immersed in baseball. "Baltimore against Pittsburgh. Seven games. You certainly picked a good one."

But it didn't seem all that great to me. First, there was the lack of a team for me to root for. Though I favored the Orioles because they'd beaten the Yankees, this Series was the first I'd ever followed closely without caring much who won.

Then there was the weather. Cold rainy evenings might be natural for mid-October, but they were so far from the brisk yet sunny afternoons I associated with the World Series of the past that I began to feel like an old man yearning for his youth. Just before Game Two it had even snowed in Baltimore, which led everyone to speculate snidely on whether Commissioner Bowie Kuhn was wearing his long johns, as well as mutter curses upon greed and the lure of television money for having turned baseball from a summer pastime into the Winter Game.

And the weather affected the playing, no question about it. For a while it even looked as if cold and dampness might be the dominant forces of the Series. The first game was rained out. When it was made up the next night, the near freezing, wet conditions helped the Orioles to a win. Still more rain interrupted Game Three, once again to Baltimore's benefit. So at the end of the first three games, it looked as if it were mostly the weather that had put the Orioles ahead two games to one.

Finally, there was the lack of dramatic tension that usually builds in a seven-game Series. Baltimore won the fourth game too, on Earl Weaver's clever use of pinch-hitters, and it gave the team a three-to-one edge over the Pirates, an insurmountable lead to judge from past history. But with several lucky breaks going their way, there seemed to be something phony about the way the Orioles had jumped out in front. They appeared to be playing over their heads, while the Pirates were performing beneath their potential. The O's also looked vulnerable, especially because they were a team built with a designated hitter in mind, and this year the Series was being played without the DH rule in effect. Lacking slugger Lee May in the batting order, Weaver was forced to go with Kiko Garcia at shortstop and Benny Ayala in left field, and while both of them had hit well so far, they were not nearly as good defensively as the regulars, Mark Belanger and John Lowenstein, were. The Orioles could very well pay for this weakness.

Sure enough, these impressions were borne out in Games Five and Six, with Pittsburgh winning 7-1 in Pittsburgh and 4-0 back in Baltimore. The Bucs' pitching turned stingy and their bats began to boom. At the same time, the Orioles' hitting went stone-cold dead, their pitching, while good, was not quite good enough, and their fielders, particularly Garcia and Ayala, began making costly mistakes.

Even Weaver seemed to lose his touch. At a critical moment in Game Five, he insisted on having Mike Flanagan pitch to Bill Madlock with first base open and weak-hitting Steve Nicosia on deck, even though Madlock had gone seven for sixteen in the Series so far and two for two in the game itself. Madlock responded by lashing his third hit and driving home the winning run. "I pitched to Madlock because we chose to pitch to him," said Weaver after the game, retreating into inscrutability.

So here we were, tied three apiece after six games—a close Series and yet not such a close Series, for the current had run one way and then turned around and run the other. And except for Game Two, no single contest had been exciting enough to raise anybody's blood pressure. Now, for the fifth time in the last ten years, the sixteenth time in thirty years, and the twenty-seventh time since the World Series began in 1903, it all came down to the seventh game.

But even if it wasn't that great a Series, it made no difference to me. I was having too much fun watching the sideshow, which I found far more entertaining than the main event. There was all that food at Memorial Stadium to eat—some ten thousand pounds of it, prepared at a cost of more than one hundred thousand dollars, to feed five thousand people over the course of the American League playoffs and the World Series by a team of Baltimore caterers that included the firm that had fed the Camp David peace talks. On a typical evening in Baltimore I would devour a dozen freshly opened chilled clams on the half shell, a bowl of crab soup, a plate of fresh green salad and sliced tomatoes with blue-cheese dressing, two hot buttered rolls, half a dozen oysters Rockefeller, a piece of rare roast beef, a golden brown crabcake, a couple of lobster tails, a scoop of potatoes au gratin, a slice of vanilla ice-cream cake with chocolate sauce, and two cups of coffee with cream and a half a grain of saccharin to help keep my weight down. Then I would barely be able to make it from the Hit-and-Run Room in Baltimore's Memorial Stadium, where this feast was laid out, to the field where batting practice was in progress.

And there was the atmosphere of the two ballparks to soak up: Pittsburgh's spanking-new Three Rivers Stadium, perched at "the confluence of the Ohio, the Allegheny, and the Monongahela" as Kimball put it (imitating W. C. Fields), yet another output of the bear that shits concrete—inside, with all the fans' signs and banners on display, it looked like a beachfront condominium with the wash hung out to dry; and Baltimore's Memorial Stadium, as down-at-the-heels as the blue-collar city that surrounded it—to spruce it up for national television, they had painted the field's bare patches a brighter green than grass and made sure that none of the cops on duty were overweight.

There were also dozens of places to explore, the various features that every ballpark has in common—grandstands, bleachers, box seats, locker rooms, managers' offices, press boxes and interview rooms. In Memorial Stadium, the point of convergence was a hall they had named the Herb Armstrong room after the team's first general manager. There, after each game played in Baltimore, when stories were filed and the day's work done, reporters, broadcasters, baseball executives, advertisers, and anyone else who could wangle a pass from the Orioles' front office would gather to drink from two well-stocked bars and sample more of the wonders those ambitious caterers had cooked up. Though you could feel the tensions of the day diminishing as all the food and drink began to recede, it was still possible to look around at the preoccupied faces of the reporters in the room—Roger Angell of the *New Yorker*, Dave Anderson of the *New York Times*, Ron Fimrite of *Sports Illustrated*, Jerry Izenberg of the *New York Post*, Alison Gordon of the *Toronto Star*, Hal Bock of the *Associated Press*, Tom Boswell of the *Washington Post*, Ken Nigro of the *Baltimore Sun*—and almost visualize word balloons filled with their descriptions of the latest game, floating above their animated heads.

In Pittsburgh, the focus of all off-field activity seemed to be the lounge just behind the press box. I first discovered it during the sixty-seven-minute rain delay that occurred during Game Three, when I fled with a crowd of reporters from the cold and dampness of the auxiliary press area out near the left-field foul pole. This big warm room was filled with tables and chairs and featured a loaded beer cooler standing against one wall, as well as a big-screen television set on a table nearby. Though there was something slightly decadent about watching a baseball game on television while sitting inside a ballpark, the embarrassing fact is that at least during the remainder of the Pittsburgh portion of the Series, I never really did leave this room. True, for honor's sake, whenever something significant seemed to be happening, I would venture just outside into the main press box and watch the action live. But for the rest of time, I lounged inside with Kimball and his other cronies (except for McClain, of course, who had to watch the games from the grandstand). After all, where else could you see a game with the former Red Sox star Rico Petrocelli sitting next to you? Petrocelli, who was starting out on a baseball broadcasting career, told us about the exercises he was doing, like practicing on a tape recorder or describing games from different vantage points in the ballpark, to make himself a better announcer. Where else could you sit and have the likes of Dodger manager Tom Lasorda or former Cincinnati skipper Sparky Anderson stop by with a word or two of gossip? I asked Lasorda if he'd ever brought his wife to New York for the long-promised visit to Scavullo's studio. He frowned and said no. Then he leaned toward me and said plaintively, "You sure would make my life easier if you could get Scavullo to send us some of those pictures he took." I explained that Scavullo wasn't working with me anymore, but that if I ever got the chance I'd ask him. "Nah, he'll never send them," he concluded sadly, then brightened up.

"Hey, fellas!" he exclaimed. "Did you hear about the restaurant owner that Jack and Jill worked for? When times got bad he couldn't figure out whether to lay Jill or Jack off."

Finally, there were the various pregame and postgame rituals to observe. The bus rides from the hotel to the ballpark and back again. The gathering at the back of the batting cage to watch the hitters take their warm-up licks, and the migration to the dugouts to hear what the rival managers had to say before the start of each game. The rush to the postgame interview room to see and hear the important players of the game talk about their performances. The final amble through the locker rooms to eavesdrop on individual interviews and maybe ask a few questions of one's own. The postgame drinks with Kimball and McClain. And whatever else might turn up in the riotous milieu of two big American cities that were taking their long-awaited turns to go crazy in the glare of national publicity.

Out of all this activity came many moments I would savor. Once again, I'd begun the whole experience with a stroke of airport luck. On my way to Baltimore for the opening game of the Series, I had spotted Joe DiMaggio waiting in the ticket line at Kennedy Airport. Convinced that he would remember me from among the thousands of strangers he'd no doubt encountered since we had met in Portland, I'd rudely broken into the line and reintroduced myself. He had tolerated this intrusion with impressive grace. He'd pretended to remember me; he'd refused to let me hold his carry-on bag when his turn came to pick up his ticket, preferring to drape it over the counter as he signed the necessary forms; he'd even invited me to join him in the waiting lounge. There, while writing a note to a friend, he had spoken to me about the demands of autograph hunters ("I've learned to get to airports early"); about the changes in the game since the days when he'd played ("I guess it's the way the fans act at the games—the language they use . . . they even smoke pot"); and about whether he'd said, "I haven't read Mailer" or "I don't read Mailer" when I'd been so clumsy as to mention *The Armies of the Night* to him in Portland ("I probably said both!"). We had separated upon boarding the plane—because I'd telephoned my wife before collecting my boarding pass and so missed my chance to get a seat next to his. But when we'd met again at the luggage carousel in Washington, DiMaggio, surrounded now by several friends who had come to pick him up, had asked where I would be staying in Baltimore. When I told him that I'd been unable to get hotel reservations and was therefore going to stay with friends in Washington, he'd responded, "Gee, that's too bad. I just gave away the couch in my hotel room. You could have used that."

Though nothing quite compensated for *that* missed opportunity, there were many notable experiences in store for me. I would re-member especially the fun of drinking and gossiping in Memorial Stadium's Herb Armstrong Room, which, for some whimsical rea-son, soon came to be called the Howard Cosell Room. It was there that I first learned that on the evening of Game One, while the teams were waiting futilely for the rain to subside, someone had gotten into Willie Stargell's hotel room at the Hilton and removed some twenty-five hundred dollars in cash, three books of personal checks, assorted jewelry and clothes, and a cassette-tape player. Stargell's misfortune had had a peculiar sequel, Roger Angell told me one evening. Howard Cosell had mentioned the robbery during the telecast of Wednesday evening's game and had added that the first person Stargell had contacted was none other than himself, Howard Cosell. When reporters asked Stargell after Wednesday's game why on earth he'd even bothered to tell Cosell about the theft, Stargell replied that that was a good question; why on earth *would* he have bothered to tell Cosell, because of course he hadn't. The incident was vintage Cosell, Angell added wryly.

It was in the Herb Armstrong Room that I finally got a chance to talk with Red Smith, the *Times*'s sports columnist, whom I'd last seen in the rickety press box at the Yankees' spring training site. When I asked if I could sit down with him for a drink, he welcomed me with a wave of his arm.

"I was just laughing to myself," he said, "at the thought of all the distinguished people, including the mother of the President of the

United States, Miz Lillian Carter, who have been the guests of a convicted felon. I mean of course George M. Steinbrenner."

We sat next to each other on the bus back to downtown Baltimore, and he told me that he was about to depart for South Africa to cover the John Tate–Gerrie Coetzee World Boxing Association heavyweight championship fight. When I saw that he was tugging at a heavy suitcase, I asked him if he would be insulted by an offer of help. He said he wouldn't mind at all. We got off the bus and walked a block or so to a taxi stand. Whatever else they might say about me, they could never accuse me of not being fit to carry Red Smith's bag.

I would remember an interview with Baltimore's star pitcher, Jim Palmer—one of the few instances in which I'd heard an active player express himself with total honesty. It was after Game Six, which Palmer had pitched extremely well—"one of the finest exhibitions of pitching I have seen in the last decade," no less an authority than Earl Weaver called Palmer's performance. But he had lost 4–0 owing to shaky defense. Four key plays had combined to do him in. The first involved a ground-ball single hit by Omar Moreno that got past Eddie Murray because he was positioned close to first base, or "playing the line," as the saying went, against the possibility of an extra-base hit down the foul line. The second happened when a bouncer over the mound was barely tipped by Palmer himself and then got past shortstop Kiko Garcia because he tried to field it with his foot on second base to get a force-out on the speedy Moreno running from first. The third occurred when a "knuckling" line drive hit by Dave Parker got by second baseman Rich Dauer. And the fourth was a line shot hit by Phil Garner to left field that Benny Ayala somehow deflected into the stands for a ground-rule double.

Now, long after the game, Palmer, still dressing slowly in front of his locker, had fallen into a mood of ironic insouciance toward the failings of the Oriole defense. A reporter from one of the Baltimore papers asked him how he felt about Benny Ayala's miscue on Garner's line drive.

PALMER: He misplayed the only ball hit to him! I'm sure he tried to catch it. He just didn't. He ran in on it and then tipped it with his glove so it bounced into the stands for a ground-rule double. That's not the first time. Don Buford! [an outfielder who played for the Orioles from 1968 to 1972] You remember the tip-ins in Cleveland? Got me four times. One was fifteen feet from the fence—an amazing tip-in. It was almost the same pitch that Garner hit, except he went running back . . . he had the red glove on, the stock glove. He had a red-and-green glove . . .

REPORTER: Sears and Roebuck . . .

PALMER: No, this is the truth. We used to have the No-Touch Award, and Buford used to get it. And he would throw it in his locker and be pissed. But finally he got it so much, he just finally relaxed. A good offensive player—on base 40, 44 percent of the time—so you could put up with his fielding. But on this day in Cleveland, Ray Fosse hit it out there, and Buford tipped it in from fifteen feet. Then Buddy Bell hit a curve ball, Buford ran in, and the ball went over his head. The next day, the way we lose is: Gaylord Perry, the Cleveland pitcher, hits one out to left and it hooks down the line. Buford takes off for left center, and the ball goes the other way!

REPORTER: Would you rather have gloves in the field than bats? I mean, would you prefer good fielding to good hitting?

PALMER: Well, I'll tell you my line on this. In 1975, the last year Jim Northrup was here, I was going for the Cy Young Award. I had Northrup in center and he would drive in two and give up three. I mean, it wasn't *balanced*. He really had a good year offensively, but he couldn't play center field. It was just that he wasn't a center fielder. Anyway, I'm going for the Cy Young Award and Hank Peters [the Orioles' general manager] had come to me in Cleveland and said, "We want to adjust your contract." So we're coming into New York and I'm pitching in Yankee Stadium, so I said to Earl, "You know I have a chance to win the Cy Young Award. You mind if I make out my own line-up?" He says, "Go ahead." So I think all day, and I get the whole line-up made up, and I come to the ballpark and Earl hands me three line-ups. "Because," he says, "if you make up your own line-up and you win, then you'll know you're smarter than me." He says, "You just pick one of the three and they'll think it's me." So anyway, two of them have Northrup in them and one has Paul Blair, who's a fantastic fielder. So I said, "Throw the other two out. I want the one with Blair. I can get a raise losing three to two, but I can't get one losing five to four." So I take that one and I win two to nothing. Blair gets ten put-outs in Yankee Stadium, and I end up winning the Cy Young Award, though I really didn't deserve it. I mean, it wasn't that great a year. But Pauly Blair was fantastic. It's like a Mark Belanger [the regular Baltimore shortstop, for whom Kiko Garcia had substituted that evening]. Kiko has had a great Series, but when you're talking about a guy like Belanger, you're talking about people that are peerless as far as defense is concerned.

REPORTER: Then you get a scoreless tie!

PALMER: Yeah, but you don't lose! What my theory on it is, until they got one more run than you, the game's not over. That's the way I pitch. If you're ahead two to one, and you got a couple of guys on and you give 'em a single, you never lose when the score is two to two. But if they get two runs—if you gamble and you try to just throw it by them and they double, you end up losing three to two. And that's the way I pitch, very conservatively. 'Til they get one more than you, you never lose. As it turned out tonight, I did. But if you pitch conservatively, and you keep the ball in the ballpark, and you don't walk a lot of guys, you're gonna win. And that's where defense comes in. Paul Blair can go oh for four for me every night, but if he makes the plays for me in center field. . . . Guys never went from first to third on Blair.

REPORTER: That does make a difference!

PALMER: When I pitch, and I have a left-handed hitter up and a man on first, I move Rich Dauer [the Orioles second baseman] in the hole [between first and second] because if the guy hits the ball to center field, the guy stops at second. He hits it to his left—in other words, between first and second—the guy goes to third base . . . and I'm not a double-play pitcher. I mean, you have to play percentages. That's like with a man on first, I throw all left-handers fastballs away. If they single to left, the guy stops at second. If you throw him a good curveball and he hits a routine hopper into right, it's first and third, and now whatta you do? So that's why I always prefer defense.

REPORTER: Do you think this club has embarrassed itself by getting away from things you do best? I mean defensively . . . ?

PALMER: Well, we gambled, that's all. You take gambles. Earl took a gamble: offense for defense. Tonight it backfired. It backfires sometimes. But I'll tell you what: if Kiko's not in the third game, we lose. If he's not in the fourth game, we might lose. So it's a calculated risk. Tonight we lost. That's what managing's all about. You can second-guess him. Like I say, you don't play the lines [meaning play close to the foul lines]. You're playing off the lines, that makes the game a lot easier.

LEHMANN-HAUPT: Why *were* they playing the lines?

PALMER: 'Cause it's nothing-nothing and you don't want a double. [Grimaces.] Which is ridiculous, if you don't throw the ball [so they hit it] down the line. I don't want to play the lines, because they don't hit the ball down the lines. I mean, when Omar Moreno hits the ball down the line off me, I deserve to lose. That means I made a bad pitch and I didn't throw the ball away [from the batter]. So what I did is I threw him a fast-ball knee-high in the middle of the plate; he hit a routine ground ball, but we're playing the lines and it goes for a single. Now it sets up the whole inning, 'cause he's gonna run, I gotta get rid of the ball quicker, Foli hits a high chopper and Kiko tried to get him [Moreno] at second, and instead of catching the ball, you lose. I mean, that's the way it goes. But you gotta give *them* credit. I mean, they can knock Moreno all they want, but I'll tell you what: I'll take anybody in baseball that gets on and can steal 77 bases and get 196 hits . . . whether he did it on Astroturf or he did it in the shower. That's a tremendous player.

REPORTER: Was there some question this season that your arm was done?

PALMER: That's always been a favorite question. My arm was done in 'sixty-seven. But I've made more comebacks than Nixon . . . or Sinatra.

REPORTER: You gonna keep laughing, Jim?

PALMER: I told you—it's funny!

I would remember the trivia showdown at the Pittsburgh Hilton's cocktail lounge, The Pub. It had begun when Jack McClain encountered four newspapermen from Ottawa sitting near him at

Game Four, the one played Saturday afternoon at Three Rivers Stadium, and invited them back to the hotel for a postgame drink. When I joined them, McClain had just accepted the Ottawans' challenge to a trivia duel, and to show what a sport he could be, was suggesting that the questions be confined to Canadian teams and players. McClain went first and, with only a moment's reflection, asked what Canadian-born pitcher, playing for a Canada-based major-league team, had defeated another Canada-based major-league team in a game played on Canadian soil? The Ottawans stared into their drinks, and McClain announced that Billy Atkinson, from Chatham, Ontario, had won in relief on June 29, 1978, in an exhibition game in which the Montreal Expos had beaten the Toronto Blue Jays 5–4. The Ottawans then put their heads together and asked which two Canadian pitchers had beaten a Canadian major-league team in both ends of a doubleheader. McClain instantly replied that the question contained an inaccuracy. On June 17 and June 18, 1978, the Toronto Blue Jays had lost consecutive games to the Texas Rangers' Ferguson Jenkins and Reggie Cleveland, both of whom were Canadians. What was more, the following day the Blue Jays had succumbed to a third Canadian pitcher, John Hiller of the Detroit Tigers. But no doubleheader was involved. The Ottawans looked crestfallen. It was McClain's turn again. In a gentle but confident voice, he asked them to name the only Canadian player ever to have had his number retired by a major-league team. Then before anyone could feel humiliated, he supplied the answer: Sherry Robertson, number forty-seven, a utility man for the Washington Senators in the 1940s. The honor, McClain pointed out, had more to do with Robertson's ties to the Griffith family, which owned the Senators, than with his lifetime .230 batting average. Then, to heal the Ottawans' wounds, McClain salved them with the names of former Montreal Royals and Toronto Maple Leafs: Babe Birrer, Lynn Lovenguth, Pat Scantlebury, Ebba St. Claire—the Ottawans gave happy little cries as each forgotten name emerged from obscurity—Angel Scull, Walt Derucki, Solly Drake, Ultus Alvarez. McClain later confided to me that he'd lived in Rochester, New York, an International League city, in the late 1950s and had rooted for the Montreal Royals because it was a farm club of the Brooklyn Dodgers.

Not all of my memories, however, were wholly happy ones. There was the telegram I received from Marion Wheeler of Methuen just before the first game in Baltimore, informing me that she could not get me press credentials for Pittsburgh. When I telephoned for an elaboration, she explained that her overtaxed staff would no longer handle such details. In fact, as far as she was concerned, I'd done enough research—I should go home now and finish writing my book based on my experience so far. If I wanted to go on to Pittsburgh, I was on my own, at least as far as making the arrangements was concerned.

Then there was the incident that occurred while I was listening in on an interview with Kent Tekulve after Game Two, which the sinkerballer had saved with a hitless ninth in which he'd struck out two batters. In squeezing into a crowd of reporters surrounding Tekulve, I'd found a path next to a row of lockers in the Pirate dressing room and was leaning to within earshot of the interview with my elbow resting on the upper shelf of the locker next to me. A shift of position to get more comfortable produced a soft clunking thump near my elbow and then an ominously familiar fizzing sound. I'd knocked over an open can of beer that someone had left there. Since the compartment defined by the shelf was otherwise empty, there didn't seem to be any damage done. Then, to my horror, I discovered that the shelf itself was perforated and the beer was streaming through. It was falling directly into one mate of a beautifully shined pair of loafers lying neatly below. The loafer was already half full. There was even a head of foam developing in it. I glanced at the name printed at the top of the locker, recalled that Jim Bibby, the occupant, was the *larger* brother of a professional basketball player, and fled. I would deal with Bibby later, after the big pitcher had recovered from the initial shock of finding his loafer brimming. But to ease my conscience a little, I confessed my mishap to Roger Angell, George Kimball, and Jack McClain when I encountered them a few minutes later at drink time in the Howard Cosell Room. Angell laughed drily and looked, as usual, inscrutable. Kimball roared, held a brief conference with McClain, and then, with mischief in his eyes, started buttonholing bystanders to tell them the story and to add that he and Jack had just awarded me the 1979 Earl Butz Award, a tasteless reference, altogether typical of Kimball and McClain, to the ex-secretary of agriculture's catastrophic remark about black men wanting nothing more out of life than a loose pair of shoes, among other things.

Another unhappy memory was the trip I made from Baltimore to

Pittsburgh later that same night. Despite my publisher's refusal to help, I'd managed at the last minute to reserve a seat on a plane chartered by the Baseball Writers Association. The flight was uneventful if wearying. But I'd waited until too late to try to get hotel reservations. So three o'clock the next morning found me steering a Hertz rental along Route 22 a dozen miles to the east of city limits, searching woozily for the only motel in the Greater Pittsburgh area able to accommodate me. I thought enviously of all the reporters on the flight who must be snugly tucked in at the Hilton by now, just a stone's throw from Three Rivers Stadium instead of where I was, to hell and gone in Monroeville, Pennsylvania.

Finally, there was the moment late the following Saturday night when I located the poker game that Kimball had been telling me about. It had been a good day. The Orioles had won that afternoon with their barrage of pinch-hits and taken a 3–1 lead in the Series. Old friends from New York, TV critic Marvin Kitman and his wife, the photographer Carol Kitman, who were in town to indulge Marvin's lifelong passion for the Pirates, had looked me up in the press box during the game and invited me out for dinner that evening. There had been the trivia showdown in The Pub. Now, a little after midnight, I'd been dropped off back at the Hilton, and through a series of well-placed inquiries had located the inner chamber where the poker game was going on. Playing poker was exactly what I felt like doing at that slightly sozzled juncture of the morning. Although I was a little short of cash, Kimball would surely be there and Kimball would surely provide.

But alas, the table was crowded with players and the room was ringed with backups waiting to get into the game. On top of that disappointment, one of the players looked up at me the moment I entered the room—it was none other than George Kimball—and called out desperately, "Hey, man, ya got a yard? For God's sake, man, gimme a yard!"

My whole life passed before my eyes. A "yard" was obviously a hundred dollars. I knew I had only about a hundred and fifteen to get me through another day of Pittsburgh and back home to New York. I doubted seriously that Kimball would use the yard to turn a bad streak to his cash advantage. And I hated under any circumstances to hand over that much money.

I looked around the room for help or reassurance of some kind and saw only the dozen pairs of averted eyes of those who'd obviously themselves just minutes earlier turned down Kimball's application for a loan. Even Jack McClain, who was there as a spectator, shrugged helplessly. But I was supposed to be Kimball's buddy. So I did what I hated to do; I handed him five twenties. I could almost feel the shock of pity that this act of prodigality sent around the room.

Of course the "yard" didn't last a dozen hands. Betting pairs against obvious straights, straights against palpable flushes, and a flush against what had to be a full house, Kimball quickly succeeded in losing the money. There being no more bankers available, he now heaved himself up with a groan, mumbled a surly good-bye to McClain and me, and went off into the night. Since I no longer had my bankroll, I decided I might as well head back to my motel in Monroeville. I took along McClain, who needed a bed for the night and happily accepted my offer of the extra one in my room. On the way, I asked him about my chances of getting back my "yard." He mulled the matter over, most of the way to the motel. Finally, he said that it really depended on whether Kimball considered it a gambling debt or a barroom loan. If he judged it to be a gambling debt, he would make it a point of honor to repay me at once. The trouble was, I hadn't been part of the game, so he could conceivably call it a barroom loan. It all depended, McClain murmured just before dropping off to sleep, but he wouldn't write off that "yard" yet if he were me.

Yet each of these mishaps had a more or less happy sequel. I got press credentials from the Pirates without any difficulty. Big Jim Bibby laughingly forgave the spilling of the beer in his loafer when I eventually admitted my guilt. The pitcher conceded that he might not have been so gracious had he caught me right after the incident. But now it was five evenings later; the Pirates had tied the Series at three wins apiece; and Bibby was not only happy, he was positively ecstatic at the prospect of pitching Game Seven the next day. It was much easier for him to forgive than it was for me to confess.

And, as it turned out, I got to bed that Friday morning of the flight to Pittsburgh long before the other reporters did. Evidently, the Pittsburgh Hilton had expected the press entourage to show up early Thursday morning, not Friday, and when it didn't (because of the rescheduled game that had to be played Thursday night in Baltimore), the hotel had for some reason canceled all its reservations. So while I was snoozing in Monroeville, the reporters were trying to get comfortable in lobby chairs at the Hilton or blearily ransacking the suburbs for motel space.

As for the hundred dollars: to my astonishment, Kimball came through with a personal check first thing the following morning—apparently he'd decided to call it a gambling debt—and only a few minutes later the check was turned into cash when, to my shame, Hal Bock of the Associated Press acted much less hesitantly about trusting Kimball than I had. And now that I'd seen Kimball's poker game with my own eyes, I made sure I wouldn't be caught short again. At home in New York the following day, I prepared myself accordingly by cashing a check for four hundred dollars. Traveler's checks would have been safer, of course. But one of the few things all poker players have in common is that, given a choice, they would rather be paid in cash.

Indeed I was prepared in a number of ways when I returned to Baltimore for the final two games of the Series. Not only did I have my poker bankroll, I had a hotel room in the center of town. This was not to be taken for granted. While the Series was playing out its middle act in Pittsburgh, something called the American Planning Convention had moved into Baltimore and taken almost every hotel room in town. As Kimball quipped, "Whatever they were planning, it sure wasn't for the Series to come back to Baltimore." So the Pirate team, having earlier been ensconced in Baltimore's Hilton, now had to settle for a Holiday Inn, which immediately announced on its marquee, THE BUCS STOP HERE. And the press was evicted from the stately Lord Baltimore and dispersed to motels as far away as Pikesville and Annapolis.

Meanwhile, I'd gotten inexplicably lucky. Maybe because I lacked any press affiliation and had thus been mistaken for a planning conventioneer when I made my reservation, I wasn't only given a room at the Hilton, I was even greeted there by an Oriole cap and (synthetically) autographed baseball lying neatly at the foot of my bed.

I also had myself a proper set of clothes at last. The matter of dress had been an irritating little problem right from the start of my baseball adventure. I'd never been able to achieve that formally rumpled look that was one stamp of the good sports reporter. (The alternative, double-knit polyester pastels, was definitely not for me.) Somehow, no matter what I wore, I felt either overdressed or underdressed. Now, someone had warned me that no matter which team won the World Series, the boisterous Pirates or the more subdued Orioles, there would be a champagne-soaked celebration hazardous to decent clothes. Better wear something you didn't care about. So I'd gone out and bought myself a cheap pair of dark blue corduroys, a heavy navy blue sweatshirt, and a denim jacket. It seemed to strike just the right note of casual formality. It made me feel streamlined, mobile, loose, "together."

In the early afternoon of the seventh game, I'd taken a taxi alone to the outskirts of the city to see the film *Apocalypse Now*. When I came out of the theater in the late afternoon, there were no taxis around to take me back. Asking at a gas station about the best way to the center of town, I was given a skeptical look and a shake of the head by the attendant and told that a bus that had just passed the station was probably my *only* way, "though I don't think you're going to feel too comfortable on it, man, and obviously [chuckle] you won't be riding on that particular one."

But I would. Taking off with a sudden burst of exhilaration, I found myself running, running fast, positively sprinting. The bus was already slowing at its stop about 150 yards away—I knew I would catch it. I floated effortlessly at a speed I hadn't run for years and years, and I glided up to the door just as the last passenger was stepping aboard. I hadn't broken a sweat. I wasn't even winded. I felt a surge of euphoria. It was a sign that inside my head something was right. As the bus chugged along the thoroughfare, stopping frequently to pick up and disgorge passengers, I realized why the gas station man had answered me that way. The bus was rapidly emptying itself of white people and filling up with blacks. Soon mine was the only white face in a considerable crowd. Yet contrary to what he'd said, I felt nothing but euphoria. It was the clothes. I could go anywhere in them, do anything in them. But no, it was a place I'd arrived at inside my head. My sense of liberation made me laugh with sheer delight.

The feeling of freedom and mobility continued to bubble up inside me as the bus moved from one of the largest and poorest ghettos in America into the more gentrified precincts of downtown

Baltimore. I soon realized that I was now only a few blocks from my hotel. I could go anywhere I wanted to in America—up, down, or sideways, I thought to myself as I left the bus and bounded into the street.

Back in my hotel room, a pretty young maid was gathering up her cleaning equipment. Still euphoric, I engaged her in casual talk while I waited at the door for her to leave. I'd just gotten back from the Reistertown Plaza shopping center, I told her. Did she know that area? "Oh, yeah." It was sure a long bus ride back, I said. "Oh, yeah. I know."

Now at last it was time to go out to Memorial Stadium for the final game of the 1979 World Series. Do a few last things: load the camera and the tape recorder; hide the four hundred dollars in the pocket of a suit hanging in my closet (no point tempting pick-pockets in the postgame celebration crush); make sure I have pencil and pad.

Shortly I was finishing my final sumptuous meal in the Hit-and-Run Room, drinking a last beer with Kimball, and heading out to the field for the ritual hangout behind the batting cage. I felt so much like an old hand by now that when a fouled-off ball bounced under the cage's bottom rung and came to rest within a few inches of my feet, I sensed that it might be uncool to pick it up, much as I wanted to. "A person could take that ball," I mumbled to the reporter standing next to me, Henry Hecht of the *New York Post*, to test what his reaction would be were I to pocket it. "Are you kidding?" he exclaimed, a little loudly for my comfort. "Do you have any idea how many hundreds of baseballs I could get a year if I wanted them? Every day, I . . ." "Where's the poker game tonight?" I asked him, to stop his tirade. "Poker?" he shouted even more loudly. "With stories to file and a one A.M. deadline? No poker tonight, man!" At this point, a uniformed attendant told us that President Carter was on his way to the stadium. A leashed dog, sniffing for bombs presumably, was patrolling the area where the President and his entourage would sit. Good thing the mutt's not trained to sniff dope, observed Kimball; he'd be clawing at the doors of the Pirate clubhouse. Harty, har har!

Then Kimball and I were locating our seats in the grandstand press section behind home plate. The ballpark was throbbing with anticipation. The Oriole mascot, a man dressed up as an orange-and-black bird, was cavorting along the third-base foul line. President Carter arrived at his fieldside box. Cheers and a few boos. The mascot danced over and threw his arms around the President. Wild Bill Hagy, the bearded taxi driver who had become the Orioles' true mascot with his season-long cheerleading pantomime of the letters O-R-I-O-L-E-S, led his crowd up in Section 34 in a loud cheer. The national anthem was half-sung, half-chanted: "OOOOOOOOOOH," shouted the fans at the start of the final line, "Oh, say does that star-spangled banner yet wave," as if the "Oh" was meant to stand for "Orioles." The rest of the song was drowned in an ovation as the first Pirate hitter, Omar Moreno, approached the plate, and the game began.

It was almost too perfect a climax—tense, close, dramatic. Scott McGregor, the Orioles' left-handed ace, gave the Pirates little to chew on for the first half of the game, while Rich Dauer, one of Game Six's goats, put Baltimore one run up with a line-drive home run to left in the third inning. But the Fates had long since written a script favoring the Pirates, and everyone in the park seemed to sense it. In the sixth inning, Bill Robinson hit a hard grounder that bounced over shortstop Kiko Garcia's groping glove. Though it was scored a hit and not an error, everybody was certain that Mark Belanger, had he been playing, would have fielded the ball and thrown Robinson out. Then up stepped Willie Stargell and mashed McGregor's first pitch, an inside fastball too close to the center of the plate, on a towering arc that ended in the Pirates' bullpen in right field. You knew that that was it—that if not the Fates, then everyone's unconscious sense of a fitting climax to the season had designated the popular Pirate leader the ultimate hero of the game. And that indeed *was* it, although the Fates further dramatized their mastery by making Eddie Murray fly out high and deep to right with the bases loaded in the eighth. A couple of sloppy Pirate runs in the ninth, and the Bucs were in their locker room smashing high fives, hugging one another, crying out "Aww-RIGHT!" and spraying champagne and mocking Wild Bill Hagy's pantomime with gleeful giggles. World champions of baseball and bedlam.

I was there in the Pirate locker room to witness and record the frenzy. I was also there when President Carter arrived a few minutes later with Commissioner Bowie Kuhn, and in a sunburst of floodlights proceeded to talk with and congratulate Manager Chuck Tanner, Willie Stargell, and others. In fact I was close enough to the President to photograph him, which gave me pause, since no one had checked my right even to be present in the room, and the place was now jammed with similar intruders. (As it later turned out, the situation had given pause to members of the President's Secret Service detail as well: they had been led to expect that they would be facing only a pool of five approved reporters, not the crush of five hundred assorted writers and hangers-on that was now shoehorning itself into the room.)

Still, despite my being only ten feet from the President of the United States, I had the uneasy sense that I was missing out on something. Perhaps because of all the years of watching victory celebrations on the tiny space of the television screen, I had the instinct that somewhere in Memorial Stadium there must have been a more significant focal point to all this emotion and activity. It was not here in the Pirate locker room, where the players were now settling down, dressing, and talking about their performances. It was not in the Oriole clubhouse, where sadder post-mortems were being held. It was not in Earl Weaver's office, where he and his sidekick, Oriole superscout Jim Russo, were softly discussing the "ifs" and "if onlys" and "might have beens"—the heartbreak of Jim Palmer's beautifully pitched game, the lack of the designated hitter, and the price of having had to use Kiko Garcia and Benny Ayala in the field. It was not even when Oriole owner Jerold Hoffberger, who had recently sold the team to Washington lawyer Edward Bennett Williams, came in to tell his manager to "forget this year now" and "go get 'em next year." For a moment I wished I were not on my own. I envied all the newspeople around me. They had whole staffs working alongside them to locate wherever the essence of a story might reveal itself. Then, on a whim, I wandered back into the formal interviewing room.

It didn't seem as jammed as it had been before. In fact, though there were at least a hundred reporters there, the crowd seemed almost sparse. Perhaps it was just the unusual quiet that prevailed—a nearly pious attentiveness. This was immediately explained by the presence at the microphone of Willie Stargell, the hero of the game, the hero of the series, the hero of the entire season. Indeed the only thing Stargell had done wrong was to get robbed the previous week in Baltimore. Fittingly enough, he'd just been voted most valuable player of the Series, the news of which—and of the Chevrolet Corvette that came with the honor—had just prompted him to clap his hand against his chest, mimicking a backward swoon. Now he was standing close to the microphone again, still dressed in his black-and-gold uniform, with a towel around his neck and a wine bottle in his left hand, speaking in the soft and measured tones of a man who possesses greater power than he feels he needs to exercise.

I hadn't so far been much taken by the Stargell mystique. I couldn't help admiring him as a ballplayer, of course, but his qualities as father-figure and leader had eluded me. On several occasions I'd watched him from a distance and glimpsed signs of his inner force and idiosyncratic nature, whether revealed in his habit of swinging the bat in rhythmically syncopated arcs and circles while waiting for a pitch, or in his postgame ritual of reclining in front of his locker in an overstuffed armchair and consuming a bottle of wine, or in the peculiar routine he had of putting on his clothes—socks first, then shirt and vest, then finger rings, then pants (no underwear), and finally boots, which made me distinctly uncomfortable and also forced me to wonder why *I* did it just the other way around (underwear, shirt, pants, socks, shoes—no rings).

But like many unpolished men who have worked their way up from oblivion, Stargell had a tendency when he talked to the press of hiding his true character behind a squid spray of clichés, which made him sound like nothing so much as a sales manager or an infantry basic-training instructor. In fact, he was displaying that tendency right now, in response to the question, did he feel he'd be able to "take charge of the game" when teammates yelled from the dugout during his sixth inning time at bat, "Come on, Pops, get us out of here!"

STARGELL: Uh, when I'm at the plate, worrying about what McGregor was going to throw me, I certainly didn't hear what the guys on the bench were saying. But I just feel that any time I'm in a situation—and Howard Cosell is telling me how many guys that I've been leaving on base—well . . . [laughter in the audience] . . . I told Howard on a very serious note that when I go up to the plate and there's men in scoring position, I put out an all-out effort, that sometimes I do and sometimes I don't [drive in the runs], and when I don't it's not because I'm not trying, it's because I gotta give that pitcher credit because he's certainly trying to get me out. But I wish like hell that I could drive in every runner that's in scoring position each time I go to the plate, and when that particular time come up, only thing I was concentrating on was basically eliminating some of the problems that I was having the first two times up, so that I could do the things that I felt that I was capable of doing, and I certainly enjoyed that particular moment and I wanted to rise to the occasion because our ballclub really thrives on everybody giving an all-out effort in these types of situations and, fortunately enough, I was able to hit the ball . . . and get the score.

But there were also signs here of the spontaneous Stargell, and in the next few minutes we reporters would be seeing more of them.

REPORTER: Willie, can you imagine any moment being higher than this at any time in your career?

STARGELL: Well, I . . . I just looked in the audience and saw my sister . . . [He smiles and gives her the thumbs-up sign] . . . and . . . and I think the only other time [there is the hint of a break in his voice] that I been so elated, and she [nodding at his sister] can probably tell you about this, is when in 1959, when I got a contract with the Pittsburgh Pirates to play professional baseball, they give me fifteen hundred dollars and a hundred and seventy-five a month and, boy, I'm telling you, you talk about a proud individual. So that particular moment and now is something that again I'm having trouble finding the words appropriate to put it together.

ANOTHER REPORTER: Two questions. One: Is that wine or champagne? And second, how does this rate with 'seventy-one, when you scored the winning run in that World Series against the Orioles?

STARGELL: This is a Robert Mondavi Chardonnay 1977. I do enjoy a good California white. The second question was, How does this rate with 1971 by me scoring the winning run? Uh, it never really dawned on me until somebody asked me in the clubhouse about doing that and we won that game two to one. But in 1971, it was Roberto Clemente's moment of glory [a reference to the Pirate star who was killed in a plane crash in 1972], and his presence was felt throughout the Series and because he traditionally started something years before I got here with the winning, driving attitude and it's carried on to this point. And we just feel good about the Pirates in so many ways, and whatever contribution I can make to this outstanding unit, I'm only pleased to put forth the effort. . . .

As Stargell was talking, his sister picked her way through the audience up onto the stage. He greeted her with a long embrace. When they broke apart, they were both visibly moved. Stargell turned back to the audience and, wiping his eyes with the back of his hand, tried to catch the next question.

REPORTER: The business of saying that the important thing is to have fun: Is that a thing that you say to young players to relax them—this is a long-winded question—or is it something you decided for yourself, and if so, at what point in your career did you decide it?

STARGELL: [Still wiping his face and trying to get control of his voice] Big ol' dummy . . . up here!

REPORTER: Introduce your sister, Willie!

STARGELL: Yeah, let me introduce my sister, 'cause we do go back a long way. [Laughter in the audience.] And it's been hell, but, y'know, we both come a long way.

They embraced again. Both were weeping openly now. Stargell took the towel from around his neck and buried his face in it, his shoulders heaving. After a few moments of stunned silence on the audience's part, another reporter called out, his own voice cracking, "You had a hell of a Series, man!" Everyone burst into prolonged applause. There were probably very few dry eyes in the room.

STARGELL: [Finally getting his voice under control.] We . . . we do go out to . . . to have fun, because it's important that we only have a few years to play this game. We have so much to learn and to enjoy and we can't be tied up in knots and keep a loose attitude too. This game will continue to roll on long after I'm gone and I think each moment should be cherished. And to be part of this, gentlemen, I guess the good Man above has given us the right to shed tears in moments like this.

The rest of the evening seemed anticlimactic. I stopped by Earl Weaver's office once more, but the Oriole manager was uncharacteristically mild and philosophical in defeat. He was cleaning out his locker, shrugging and patiently answering a few inconsequential questions from reporters who straggled by. In the Pirate locker room, the celebratory atmosphere had begun to seem forced. Even the Howard Cosell Room was a letdown. The place was jammed, but the food had begun to run out at last, and the few writers I knew had retreated into the stories they had just filed or would have to file in a matter of hours or days. Now I could not only imagine the word balloons floating out of their heads, I could almost visualize the stories that would shortly be published under their bylines. There was Ron Fimrite of *Sports Illustrated* ("Baltimore right fielder Ken Singleton had backed up as far as possible in his futile pursuit of the soaring fly hit by Willie Stargell, and as it passed overhead he made a last desperate leap"). With him was the *New Yorker*'s Roger Angell ("Baseball, so various and voluminous are its possibilities, often gives the impression that it will always arrange the thrilling complexity, the obligatory challenge and response, at the summit of every important game or series"). And there was Dave Anderson of the *Times* ("In the sixth inning, Willie Stargell was swinging his big brown bat in the on-deck circle when Bill Robinson bounced a single off Kiko Garcia's glove into left field"). And Joe Durso ("The great shootout of the seventy-sixth World Series came to an end at 11:30 tonight when Pat Kelly of the Baltimore Orioles pinch-hit a fly ball to Omar Moreno of the Pittsburgh Pirates in center field. On the pitcher's mound, Kent Tekulve turned to watch"). And Murray Chass ("Willie Stargell, who is Pops to Pittsburgh's most-famous family, helped the Pirates win their fifth World Series championship tonight"). And Malcolm Moran ("Everyone and everything was in place. The television camera was mounted in the center of the Orioles' clubhouse, the champagne was nearby, and the President of the United States was there to offer congratulations. Except there was no celebration to record, no bottles to pour, and the President's only words to the Orioles were of consolation"). There was Jerry Izenberg of the *New York Post* ("The first time Earl Weaver saw him, he was a big monster of a kid who had just finished a season in A ball at Asheville and the Pirates had sent him out to the Arizona Instructional League to hasten his graduation day"). And

Phil Pepe of the *New York Daily News* ("Wonderful Willie did it for the Pirates. Super Stargell did it"). Even George Kimball seemed to have tunneled back into that part of his head where the prose came from ("Late last Wednesday afternoon, the word began to filter through the downtown press headquarters that the President of the United States had it in mind to attend the seventh game of the World Series. It seemed only logical. While placing President Carter in full view of 53,000 plus somewhat demented baseball fans did pose some obvious security problems, it could be expected that the more violence-prone crazies were a lot more likely to take a shot at Howard Cosell or Dave Parker than Jimmy Carter").

I decided to head back to my hotel room. The bus ride was subdued. When I got into bed I tossed restlessly, trying to make some order out of the day's events. I felt satisfied but overstimulated. Drifting into sleep, I envisioned Willie Stargell standing in the front of that bus from Reistertown Plaza, his sister embracing him, all the passengers cheering and waving their raised fists. A young man, ill-clad and hardly out of adolescence, knelt in the aisle, unslung a duffel bag from his shoulder, set it down on the floor, reached inside, and started handing Stargell its contents—books of personal checks, handfuls of gold rings, necklaces and watches, a brushed-aluminum cassette tape recorder, and finally piles and piles of hundred-dollar bills. At the vision of the money, I snapped wide awake. I clambered anxiously out of bed, struggling for a moment to remember where I was, then stumbled across the room to the closet, and groped my hand into the side pocket of my suit-pants. I thrust so hard that I pulled both pants and jacket loose from the hanger.

My money was gone.

DEALING

NATURALLY, I REPORTED the theft of my cash to the Hilton's management. But I got just what I expected, and their routine promise to investigate—although of course they were not responsible for any valuables left in the rooms—did little to relieve my pain. All I could do to rid myself of the sick feeling in my stomach was to rationalize that I probably would have blown the money playing poker. Easy come, easy go, I kept whispering to myself as I crawled back to New York and tried to forget the world of baseball.

I had plenty of time to recover from my loss. It wasn't until the beginning of November that baseball began to interest me again. On the first day of that month, the Yankees began a blitzkrieg that was positively panzerlike in its speed and suddenness. It was launched at Manhattan's Tavern on the Green restaurant, where the team had called a press conference to introduce its new manager, Dick Howser; its old one, the ever-combative Billy Martin, had gotten himself fired by boss Steinbrenner for punching out a marshmallow salesman in the bar of L'Hotel de France in Bloomington, Minnesota, and then pretending that he hadn't.

In the buzzing Terrace Room, as seventy-five reporters began to digest their curried chicken, rice, and salad, Yankee publicist Mickey Morabito introduced Dick Howser, who seemed so agitated by his appointment that he had to be asked by the *Daily News*'s Dick Young to speak a little more slowly. After fielding a few inconsequential questions, such as what number would he wear and what did he think of his center fielder ("Who is he? Just joking," he replied), Howser turned the mike back to Morabito. He in turn presented Gene Michael, the newly designated general manager. Michael seemed less surprised than Howser about the various sudden changes in the team's organization; still, the best he seemed able to do was mumble. First he mumbled praise for Dick Howser. Then he mumbled, "We have an announcement here, talking about center field. We've just acquired Ruppert Jones in a trade with the Seattle Mariners. We get Ruppert Jones and a player named Lewis—he's a pitcher—for Jim Beattie, Juan Beniquez, Jerry Narron, and Rick Anderson."

The gathering seemed puzzled for a moment, more by the throwaway style of Michael's announcement than by the significance of the move. "Is the key to this trade to get a center fielder?" one reporter finally asked. To this Michael responded without mumbling, "I'll let you know in a couple of years about that," and got a round of laughter. But the upshot seemed to be that by giving up a collection of prospects, the Yanks had gotten a young center fielder, who, having just completed a season of twenty-one home runs and thirty-three stolen bases, seemed to be able to hit like lightning and run like the wind. That certainly plugged the big hole in the Yankee lineup that had been created by the trade of Mickey Rivers to Texas. And as nearly as one could make out from Michael's murmurings, the Yankees had only begun to maneuver.

Five hours later, the team moved again. I learned of this from a radio interview with the *Daily News*'s Phil Pepe that evening, but apparently late in the afternoon Mickey Morabito and his assistant had telephoned all the sportwriters covering the team to say that a trade with the Toronto Blue Jays had just been completed. The Yankees were giving the Jays Chris Chambliss, the star first baseman; Damaso Garcia, the hard-hitting but inexperienced young second baseman; and Paul Mirabella, a promising but so far erratic left-handed pitcher. In exchange they were getting Rick Cerone, a good young catcher thought to be improving steadily; Tom Underwood, a left-hander considered the best pitcher on a bad team; and Ted Wilborn, a minor-league outfielder. It was too bad about Chambliss, whom Yankee fans still worshipped for winning the 1977 playoff series against Kansas City with his final-inning home run. But the gaping hole behind the plate that had been left by Thurman Munson's death might at least be partially filled, and another starter might be added to a shaky pitching staff.

The next day the free-agent reentry draft was held at the Plaza Hotel. I couldn't be there, but I followed the news all day on Sportsphone and learned that the Yankees had selected, among others, Bob Watson, a slugging right-handed first baseman who had spent years with the Astros before going to the Red Sox back in June; Bruce Kison, the great September pitcher of the Pittsburgh Pirates; and Rudy May, the veteran lefty, lately with Montreal, whom the Yankees had relinquished in that disastrous 1973 trade with Baltimore. Within a week, they had signed both Watson and May and were rumored to be close to making a deal with Kison.

I loved all this activity. Not only had the bickering and backbiting stopped, but the Yankees seemed quickly to have improved themselves. As George Steinbrenner was reported to have crowed at yet another news conference at the flossy Tavern on the Green, held exactly one week after the unveiling of Michael and Howser: "We've solved four problems in ten days. We got a center fielder, a catcher, a right-handed hitter, and a pitcher. It's probably never been done before in baseball so fast, and that doesn't count getting a new manager and general manager. We took a team with holes and made it strong again." Though his rivals in Detroit, Milwaukee, and Baltimore quickly announced that they weren't quite ready to concede the Eastern Division championship, it did look as if the Yankees would be back in the thick of the race next year.

I too was convinced that the Yankees had sewn up the championship with these moves. Of course, I hadn't any idea what kind of players Ruppert Jones or Rick Cerone might be, nor could I remember much about Rudy May. But the sports pages were saying hopeful things about the new acquisitions. And the Yankees had always been master dealers. How else had they gotten Babe Ruth? And Waite Hoyt, Herb Pennock, and Urban Shocker, the foundation of the pitching staff of those great 1920s teams? And before them, at the dawn of Yankee history, the great spitballer, Jack Chesbro? Then, years later, they had dealt for Eddie Lopat and Allie Reynolds, two key pitchers of the forties and fifties. And after them came Bob Turley, a big winner in the late fifties, and Don Larsen, the only man ever to pitch a perfect World Series game. And what about all those shrewd late-season pickups from the National League—Johnny Mize in 1949, Johnny Hopp in 1950, and Johnny Sain in 1951? So what did it matter if I'd never heard of Ruppert Jones or Rick Cerone? What did I know of Roger Maris when he first came over from Kansas City in 1960? Or of Graig Nettles or Chris Chambliss when they were acquired from Cleveland in the seventies?

All right, so the Yanks had dealt away Lew Burdette in 1950. And the year before that they had bought Fred Sanford, "the hundred-thousand-dollar lemon," from the St. Louis Browns. And yes, there was that terrible deal with Baltimore in 1973. But looked at from another angle, that trade just went to show what you could achieve with a shrewd exchange, because the players that the Orioles had gotten now formed the backbone of the American League champions. Yes, the 1980 Yankees were bound to be a better team thanks to Steinbrenner's stunning blitzkrieg. Cerone would probably develop into the spark plug that Rick Dempsey now was for Baltimore. Ruppert Jones would turn out to be a version of Mickey Rivers lacking Rivers's problems with women, horses, and money. And Tommy Underwood would most likely be another Eddie Lopat. Why, the Yanks were loaded now! The more I thought about it, the more they looked unbeatable.

This is just what I'd always loved about the winter baseball season, or what used to be known as the Hot Stove League when there were still such things as stoves to sit around and chew the fat by. Well, one was always free to dream. But so far this season, there had not been much to dream about. True, the usual rumors had been floating around. Even during the World Series there was talk of Ron Davis, the Yankees' bright new relief pitcher, going to the Dodgers for catcher Steve Yeager. Reggie Jackson was supposed to be traded to San Francisco for Jack Clark, its promising outfielder. And the Cubs were said to be offering a whole bunch of players to San Diego for their discontented superstar, Dave Winfield. And true, there had been the commotion that the era of free agency habitually provoked. For instance, the Yankees had signed Bucky Dent and Jim Spencer to new contracts, while various minor players like Don Hood and Jim Kaat had opted for the open market. Around the leagues, bigger fish, like California pitcher Nolan Ryan and Montreal first baseman Tony Perez, had taken the plunge and were being pursued with sweet talk and money. And Billy Martin had been fired amid histrionics and headlines. But I needed much more to stoke the fires of my imagination. Now the Yankees had stirred things up. George Steinbrenner had once again shown himself to be a man of military decisiveness as well as Prussian authoritarianism. The season of dealing was finally underway.

And further excitement lay dead ahead. There would be more free-agent signings. Already the Yankees were vying with the Houston Astros and their new general manager, Al Rosen, who had signed on with John McMullen's team soon after leaving the Yankees, for the services of the flame-throwing Nolan Ryan, though in my opinion Ryan was more of a gate attraction than a stopper who could win the games that mattered. There were bound to be more trades; the interval between the last day of the World Series and the second week in December constituted one of the two times during the year when any team in the two major leagues could deal with any other, the second being the last two weeks of spring training.

And to climax the season of dealing, the baseball winter meetings were about to begin. That was when the best and biggest deals were made, like the one in 1959 that I'd always thought of as the Roger-Maris-for-Marvin-Throneberry trade. Actually, along with "Marvelous Marv" Throneberry, the Yanks had sent to the Kansas City A's two aging but still able stars, Hank Bauer and Don Larsen, as well as Norm Siebern, a player thought at the time to have as much potential as Maris. And along with Maris, the Yanks had gotten the veteran infielder Joe DeMaestri and a rookie first baseman named Kent Hadley. But I still liked to think of it as the Maris-for-Throneberry deal—the swap of baseball's future home run king for a husky young first baseman only a few years away from becoming the symbol incarnate of the New York Mets' ineptitude.

It was at the winter meetings of 1947 that the Brooklyn Dodgers had sent Dixie Walker, Vic Lombardi, and Hal Gregg to the Pittsburgh Pirates in a straight trade for Billy Cox, Preacher Roe, and Gene Mauch, a deal they wouldn't regret, considering that Cox and Roe became vital to the championship Dodger teams of the early fifties. In 1949, the New York Giants had gotten Alvin Dark and Eddie Stanky from the Boston Braves for Sid Gordon, Willard Marshall, Buddy Kerr, and Sam Webb—a trade that had solidified the middle of the Giants' infield and led to a pennant in 1951. So if the Yankees hadn't sewn up the 1980 World Championship, the coming winter meetings would help them put in the final stitches.

Many felt it was fitting that in the year when snow had fallen during the World Series, the seventy-eighth annual convention of the National Association of Professional Baseball Leagues and Major Leagues should be held in arctic Toronto, Ontario, Canada. Why loll in sunny Hawaii, Florida, southern California, or some island in the Caribbean when you could be shivering in what was presumably the fourth most frigid playing site in major-league baseball, the three more northerly ones being, in descending order, and many people would be surprised by the order of these locations—Seattle, Montreal, and Minneapolis–St. Paul? Granted, Canada with two big-league teams was due for a turn at hosting the meetings, and Toronto, with its theater, ballet, museums, symphony orchestra and the biggest film festival on the North American continent, was the cultural center of Canada. Moreover, the city and baseball were old friends. At the banquet that would climax the convention, the Honorable William G. Davis, Q.C., premier and president of the Province of Ontario, would read aloud a description of a game played on August 25, 1873, in which the celebrated Redstockings of Boston, champions of the world, defeated the Dauntlesses of Toronto by a score of 68–0. Years later, Babe Ruth, during the single month he played in the minor leagues, hit his first professional home run in Toronto—or so it was said. And then for years the Toronto Maple Leafs had served as a farm team for various major-league clubs, including the Boston Red Sox. But it was cold up there in Toronto, so cold that one thought twice about straying outside the precincts of the Sheraton Centre, where everyone had a heated room and all the events were scheduled. As Tommy Lasorda was to announce at the beginning of the meetings—he'd already made plans to return to Toronto the following winter . . . to pay a visit to his toes.

On Sunday evening, December 2, I arrived at the Sheraton Centre in a state of high anticipation, convinced that the interior of a hotel was bound to prove a better setting than a ballpark for getting close to the people who ran the game. But the lobby of the hotel with its high-tech light fixtures and ornaments suggested an airplane hangar designed by a disciple of Brancusi. A cocktail party seemed to be in progress, and though I recognized a couple of friends in the crowd, it was filled with so many faces that were only vaguely familiar that I could have used one of those numbered silhouettes to help me identify them. Still, in no time at all I was part of it myself. After registering at the desk and tossing my luggage into my room, I was back downstairs and listening to Alison Gordon of the *Toronto Star* confide how Early Wynn, the Hall of Fame pitcher who was now part of the Toronto Blue Jays' radio broadcast team, had told her that all she had to do to become a baseball writer was learn how to buy everybody drinks and stand up at a urinal. ("But I buy drinks all the time," she'd protested. He'd shot back, "What about the other? Are you practicing?") On the other hand, Earl Weaver, during the World Series, had pronounced Gordon a serious baseball reporter, unlike the women who he knew were in the locker rooms mainly to ogle the players. ("You're not a peckerchecker," he'd avowed. "You're for real.") In another part of the lobby I found Joe Durso, who proposed that we have dinner some time during the coming week. Except for the absence of Kimball and McClain, I felt as if we'd never left the Howard Cosell Room in Baltimore's Memorial Stadium.

And once again, all sorts of diversions offered themselves. There was one's goody bag to collect along with one's press credentials. This time it was a plastic airline bag with the Blue Jay logo on the side, containing the usual assortment of candy, pens, insignia, toilet articles, balloons, and restaurant advertisements; and while I'd grown blasé about such perks of the sports-reporting trade (though not as blasé as the reporter who, when told that the supply of bags had run out, asked heatedly, "How'm I gonna shave?"), I still made a point of being one of the first on line for my prize. There were press conferences and banquets to attend, speeches to hear, and exhibitions to see. There were parties to go to and gossip to catch up on. And while I was finally growing accustomed to what was evidently routine in the baseball reporter's life, there was still enough novelty to it all to keep me happily entertained for awhile.

At the major-league managers' reception and lunch in the Civic Ballroom, I sat next to Tommy Lasorda, who launched into a routine about the book he was planning to write called *How to Get Your Money's Worth at a Smorgasbord.* "There are a couple of things in it that are gonna really help people," Lasorda deadpanned. "First, you have to wear a truss so you don't get a hernia. Then, a lot of times, you know, people won't go back through the line a second time 'cause they're embarrassed. But I say in my book that the second time through the line when you get to your table, say 'hello' to everybody so it looks like you just arrived. And don't go to the salads, go straight to the big stuff. And how to stack a plate is important because when you go through a smorgasbord, the guy serving it always puts it in the middle of the plate because he doesn't want you to put a whole lot on it. Don't drink before you eat; it fills you up. Don't talk because air gets in your lungs. Always bend at the wrist—there were a lot of times I quit eating not because I was full but because my arms were tired—so I teach how to bend at the wrist rather than the elbow."

Once Lasorda had the floor, there was no stopping him. "This group was traveling out West by covered wagon and got caught in this terrible blizzard in the Rockies. One old guy got sick and summoned his best friend to hear his dying words. 'I ain't gonna make it, Joe!' 'Sure, you are, Al!' 'No, Joe. I ain'ta gonna make it. So I want you to promise me something, Joe.' 'Anything, Al, anything, but you're gonna make it.' 'No, Joe, I ain't. So promise me when you and little Joe there get out West, you'll name a town after me.' 'Sure, Al. Of course we will.' 'Don't forget, Joe. Name a town after me. Little Joe, will you promise to remind your father to name a town after me?' 'Sure I will. I promise, Mr. Buquerque.'"

Lasorda went on to reminisce about the last game he'd ever pitched in professional baseball. "It was 1960. I was pitching against the Montreal Royals. I think it was the first or second inning. I'd gotten wild and walked three guys in a row. Bases loaded; the guy's warming up in the bullpen; the manager has his foot up on the top of the dugout step. I saw that, so I turned my back to the hitter, and I looked up at the heavens, and I said to the Big Dodger in the Sky . . . I said, 'Lord, I have never asked You to get me out of a jam. All I have asked is to know You'll always give me the strength to do the best I can. Now this is the last game I'll ever pitch in organized baseball. So I want to be out of this mess. I'm not asking You, I'm begging You to get me out of this jam.' Billy Williams was the umpire

233

and he turned around and he said, 'Hey, Lasorda, throw the god-damn ball!' I said, 'Wait a minute, man, I'm talking to God!' He said, 'To who?' I said, 'God!' He said, 'Oh.' I said, 'God, please, get me out of this jam.'

"So I turned around and threw the ball, and the guy hit a jackrabbit line drive toward left field. I felt it was a base hit. But we had a tall third baseman—his name was George Risley—he leaped up as high as he could; he looked like he run up two steps on a ladder—and the ball hit the top of his glove and caromed directly behind him . . . alive . . . it kinda like looped . . . so the shortstop, Jerry Snyder, came running over, and he turned his glove—on the ground—and the ball fell into it before it touched the ground. He threw to second for two outs, and the second baseman threw to first base for three outs. Triple play! And I walk off the mound and say, 'Thank You, Lord, but why did You have to scare me like that?' And that was the last time I pitched in baseball. I pitched seventeen summers and thirteen winters—that's a lot of baseball—and that was the only time I was ever involved in a triple play. That was the last game I pitched. But you could say I went out a winner."

As the managers' lunch broke up, a reporter told me that the New York Mets were about to trade their top pitcher, Craig Swan, to the Detroit Tigers for slugging first baseman Jason Thompson.

Then there was the press conference and lunch sponsored by The Gillette Company, Safety Razor Division, to introduce the Gillete/Baseball Hall of Fame Exhibit. This turned out to be a portable selection of artifacts from the Cooperstown Hall of Fame that would soon begin touring various shopping malls around America. Any shopper who had never been to Cooperstown, New York, would get a taste of the Hall of Fame, as well as be offered a chance to give money to both the United States Olympic Committee and the Baseball Hall of Fame Building Fund. At the lunch, Edward W. Stack, the president of the Hall of Fame, was introduced. Bob Feller, the fireballing Hall of Fame pitcher, was introduced. Samuel N. Schell, the president of Gillette's Safety Razor Division, was introduced. Some of the artifacts in the exhibit were even introduced—Bob Feller's uniform top from 1956, his last year of active play, the ball he threw when he pitched his record twelfth one-hit game, a Joe DiMaggio glove, the bat used by Stan Musial to collect his then National League–record 3,431st hit, Ernie Banks's five hundredth home run ball, and a bat used by Babe Ruth notched to record the twenty-eight home runs he had hit with it.

At the press conference, a film was shown—historic baseball moments narrated by Mel Allen—then questions were asked: Was there any reason that in the official logo of the exhibit, which was the outline of a baseball diamond, home plate was turned the wrong way round? [Laughter] ("I think someone goofed. The proper adjustments will be made on everything before January, when the exhibit starts traveling.")

After the lunch, I stared at the artifacts, trying to coax from them an image of another, younger Bob Feller to displace the middle-aged businessman who had just been droning on from the dais. While I was thus preoccupied, a reporter next to me leaned over and whispered that Jim Palmer, the Baltimore pitcher, was about to be traded to Kansas City for outfielder Al Cowens and a minor-league pitcher to be named later.

Then there was the Annual National Association Banquet held in the Grand Ballroom, where bagpipers skirled, swizzle sticks twirled, long speeches were unfurled, and more trade rumors swirled. Finally a major deal had been made, I was told by someone at my table. The Mets were sending Craig Swan to the California Angels for slugger Willie Mays Aikens.

There was the lavish cocktail reception presided over by a Japanese businessman, who soberly greeted several hundred guests and then, as the last few were trickling out of his suite, collapsed in an alcoholic stupor. And there were the promotional exhibits of baseball products and accessories in a lower-floor hall of the Sheraton—balls, bats, gloves, caps, bags, jackets, shorts, warm-up jackets, T-shirts, buttons, banners, pennants, trophies, scoreboards, fireworks displays, soft-drink dispensers, even computer programs for compiling statistics (including biorhythms).

At the Topps Chewing Gum booth, I introduced myself to a man with a nametag that identified him as "Vice-President, Sports and Licensing," and asked him if it was true, as I'd sometimes heard it said, that the print runs of baseball cards were weighted against the star players. "No way. We don't stack!" he insisted.

But I was not to be so easily put off. Back in November, I had discovered a baseball card catalogue that listed the values of each year's issues going back to the nineteenth century. I had at once browsed through it and when I got to the end, I found, under the heading of "1979 Topps (726)," a statement that "the 66 double printed cards are noted in the checklist by (dp)." Double printed? Presumably, that meant that 66 out of the 726 cards in 1979's collection had been printed in twice the quantity of the remaining 660 cards. So the printings *were* weighted after all. But if there was a pattern to the double printings, it eluded me. Predictably enough, the ten most redundant items in my collection were dp's. And just as predictably, none of my singletons were.

Otherwise, I could see no rhyme or reason to the cards selected for redundancy. There were superstars and journeymen. There were promising youngsters and there were old-timers nearing the ends of their careers. There were blacks and Caucasians, small-town boys and big-city men, American Leaguers and National Leaguers, northerners, southerners, easterners, and westerners, players from championship teams and players from cellar-dwellers. There was an ex-con (#660, Ron Leflore of the Detroit Tigers). There was a player born in the Dominican Republic (#107, Jesus Alou). There were cards representing the holders of the all-time strikeout and earned-run average records, as well as three of the pink checklist cards. Not even a paranoid could detect a conspiratorial pattern in the selection. But now I had a chance to clear up the mystery.

"So what about the cards that are double printed," I shot back at the man aggressively.

He gave me a look of forebearance. It was really very simple, he explained. The cards were printed on sheets containing 132 players per side, 11 across and 12 down. To include the full series of cards, they had to print at least three sheets, or six sides. That was 2 times 132 times 3, or 792. Take away the 726 cards that were in the 1979 series, and you had 66 spaces left over, which were filled with duplicate impressions. What they did was to stick whole rows in and whoever happened to be on those rows, well, they got double printings. If there was any criterion for picking which rows were to be duplicated, he had never been able to figure it out. Why, just look at the 1979 duplicates.

"I know, I know," I succumbed.

So much for a conspiracy theory. I thanked him humbly and said that if he ever came across a spare copy of #199, Larry Milbourne, I could use it.

Even though it had misfired, my small discharge of skepticism reflected the progress I was making as a baseball reporter, which was really no more than to say that I was getting almost as good as the next person at passing along rumors, waiting around for something to happen, and doubting that any news source could be telling the whole truth. Still, it did take certain skills to get a story, such as having the nerve to interrupt a monologue or recognizing the right moment to ask a certain question; and the rudiments of such weapons were beginning to collect in my hitherto empty arsenal.

That was how I'd gotten my interview with Bobby Valentine. A group of reporters, including Joe Durso and me, had been idling in the Sheraton lobby late one afternoon when Valentine, a much-traveled but bright and articulate utility player who had spent the past season with the Seattle Mariners but was now all but finished with his playing career, arrived at the front desk to check into the hotel. Greetings were exchanged and introductions made. Valentine let it drop that he'd come to Toronto almost straight from a two-day union meeting in New York. The shop stewards of the Baseball Players Association had gathered there to review the prospects of rewriting the industry's labor code, which was due to expire December 31, and of avoiding a shutdown similar to or worse than the one that had closed down spring training camps four years earlier. As I shook Valentine's hand, something prompted me to ask if we might get together and talk about the mood at the players' meeting, which he had already indicated was tense. Sure, said Valentine—he was free for breakfast on Friday, the last day of the meetings.

And finally, there was the poker game. By buttonholing such reporters as Phil Pepe of the *Daily News* and Henry Hecht of the *New York Post*, I finally got into a poker game. Beginning late each night in a conference room on the hotel's mezzanine, it was a somewhat disorderly affair by the standards I was used to. Instead of chips, the players threw Canadian dollars into the pot, which gave the giddy illusion that it was play money that was being tossed around. The regulars seemed to be Pepe, Hecht, Moss Klein and Stan Capitano of the *Newark Star Ledger*, and Jerry Holtzman of the *Chicago Sun-Times*, but players of varying styles and abilities, not to mention degrees of sobriety, would wander in and out, some of them too drunk or too unknowing to be bluffed, which meant you had to hold strong cards to win. Despite the late hours, shoptalk would occasionally disrupt the smooth flow of the play. At one point in the middle of a game, discussion erupted among the New York area reporters about what for them was the big story of the day—the canceling by Mets chairman Lorinda de Roulet of a trade the club had just made. This prompted Jerry Holtzman, who affected an old-timer's exaggerated apathy toward his duties as a beat reporter, to lay down his hand, dig out a pencil and a scrap of paper from his pocket, scribble a few notes, and then excuse himself, pausing only to ask, "How do you spell 'Deeroolay'?"

But the games were clean and classic: mostly familiar varieties of high-low stud and draw; no wild cards, no passing to the right or left, no crosses or circles laid out in the center of the table. To my surprise, I found myself winning; maybe I had overestimated the gambling ability of sportswriters. And one of the games produced the most amazing set of hands I'd ever seen, a single deal of high-low draw in which a full house and a flush were topped by four of a kind for high, and for low a 6-5-3-2-1 was beaten by a 6-4-3-2-1. Had the deck been stacked? It wasn't likely, considering the level of play and the lack of a consistent winner.

But the winter meetings were basically tedious. The daily routine was humdrum, at least from this reporter's point of view. While the team owners and their executives conferred upstairs in their private suites—which were said to consist of bedrooms adjoining well-appointed lounges—the sportswriters were left with little to do. They could either hang around the pressroom, located at a corner of the mezzanine, and wait for a press conference to be called or some galvanizing announcement to be posted on the bulletin board, or they could wander down to the lobby to see if they could buttonhole any insider who might have descended from his lair to stretch his legs, mix and mingle with his peers, and even leak an item or two.

It was a setup designed to play on my most atavistic fears of exclusion. Here were all these meetings and plannings and plottings going on in the secret rooms of the hotel. I would even have been willing to settle for a seat of my own at such unpromising-sounding events as the major league public relations directors meeting, held Thursday afternoon in the Oxford Room, or the physicians meeting, held Tuesday morning in the Kent Room, or the Mexican League meeting, held Sunday morning in the Dufferin Room. But of course the point of the P.R. directors' meeting was probably to discuss strategies for handling the press; the doctors were most likely confronting the growing problem of drugs; and who knew that the Mexican League might not be planning yet another raid on big-time baseball, as it had in the 1940s. So the closest one could get to baseball's elusive insiders was watching such lobby loungers as Roy Hartsfield, recently fired as manager of the Toronto Blue Jays, who had positioned himself in a spot near the bar felicitously named the Trader Lounge in the hope that some stray morsel of a job might drift his way, or seeing an occasional owner pass by, like Lorinda de Roulet, who could be observed upon her arrival slowly crossing the Sheraton lobby behind her luggage like a yacht being pulled by a tugboat.

What everyone kept waiting for was a blockbuster of a trade. As the days passed, a couple of modest deals were disclosed. Toronto sent Chris Chambliss and shortstop Luis Gomez to the Atlanta Braves for outfielder Barry Bonnell, right-handed pitcher Joey McLaughlin, and infielder Pat Rockett. The Tigers sent Ron Le-Flore, their speedy center fielder, to the Montreal Expos for left-handed pitcher Dan Schatzeder. The Atlanta Braves, after failing to get Jeff Burroughs's permission to trade him to Texas, dealt Pepe Frias, Adrian Devine, and a player to be named later to the Rangers for Doyle Alexander and Larvell Blanks. Exactly a minute before the midnight trading deadline Friday night, the St. Louis Cardinals sent outfielder Jerry Mumphrey and pitcher John Denny to the Cleveland Indians for outfielder Bobby Bonds, one of baseball's most talented players, who, for reasons never made clear to the public, was also one of its most frequently traded. And Texas tried to send relief pitcher Sparky Lyle and outfielder Johnny Grubb to the Phillies for Bake McBride, an outfielder, Larry Christenson, a starting pitcher, and Tug McGraw, a reliever, but couldn't close the deal because of certain deferred payments required by Lyle's contract, under the terms of which he was to be paid fifty thousand dollars a year for ten years as a radio broadcaster of Ranger games.

But there was no transaction even a third of the size or significance of the great Yankee-Oriole trade of 1954—one of the more memorable of winter-meeting history. At the core of this huge deal, the Yanks got pitchers Bob Turley and Don Larsen in exchange for veteran outfielder Gene Woodling and a couple of promising young catchers named Hal Smith and Gus Triandos. But eventually the deal involved no fewer than eighteen players. Nor was there anything approaching the activity of the 1971 winter meetings in Phoenix, where eighteen of the twenty-four teams closed a total of fifteen trades involving fifty-four players, including such notables as Frank Robinson, Richie Allen, Lee May, Sam McDowell, Gaylord Perry, Ken Holtzman, Rick Monday, and Dave Roberts. What with long-term contracts containing no-trade clauses and the new rules granting veteran players the right to veto deals they didn't approve of—in other words, what with the players having won their rights and thereby having turned themselves from inanimate playthings into insistently complicated beings—the game of dealing had been transformed. As Jim Campbell, the president and general manager of Detroit, was heard to mutter about a minor deal the Tigers had just completed with the San Diego Padres, "In thirty-one years in baseball, this is the first time I've traded a player who has to give his permission for a player to be named later."

Indeed, the most exciting deal of the entire winter meetings was the one that didn't get made. I'd heard vague rumors of it all day Tuesday, but it wasn't until I'd taken my seat at the banquet that evening that a neighbor at my table confirmed that the Mets were definitely trading Craig Swan, their ace right-hander and only true quality pitcher, along with catcher Ron Hodges and veteran outfielder Elliott Maddox, to the California Angels for slugging first baseman Willie Mays Aikens and a promising young second baseman named Dickie Thon. Finally, it looked as if the serious stuff had begun.

The trading of Swan seemed plausible enough to me. As a rule, I didn't like to waste time thinking about the New York Mets, my favorite example of a gold-plated bone for underdogs. But as the 1979 season had progressed, the ownership of the Mets itself had become a kind of underdog. Ever since the death in 1975 of the club's original owner, Joan Whitney Payson, the exuberant sportswoman and racing stable owner who along with her brother John Hay Whitney had inherited one of the largest fortunes ever probated in America, the ballclub had gone into a decline. The era of miracles that produced the 1969 World Championship and the 1973 National League title had faded into the hazy past. Management had dealt away enough good players to form an all-star team. Shea Stadium had deteriorated. Attendance had dwindled. And the club was now rumored to be losing around $3 million a year. Weary of this erosion, Joan Payson's widower, Charles Shipman Payson, had a year before made up his mind to sell the club. But his daughter, Lorinda de Roulet, had prevailed on him to let her take charge to see if she could reverse the team's fortunes. She had tried. With the help of her two daughters, Whitney and Bebe, she had set to work enthusiastically and even made the rounds of the radio call-in shows to promote and revivify the team's image, assuring her listeners that all her players were "darned good." ("Richie Hebner is darned good! Alex Trevino? He's darned good too!")

But the team had finished last in its division with the worst record in the National League and the third worst in both leagues (surpassed in futility only by two expansion teams, Seattle and Toronto). Attendance had continued to slump, falling below eight hundred thousand for the season. Now the team was definitely on the block, with its price estimated to be in the $25 million range, the highest ever paid for a baseball team, and its dozens of rumored buyers ranging all the way from Robert Abplanalp, the Yonkers aerosol-valve king and buddy of Richard Nixon, to Eddie Kranepool, one of the original Mets players, who was claiming to represent a syndicate willing to pay $22 million.

Still, the team's normal business had to go on, especially at such a crucial interval as the winter meetings. It was vital that something worthwhile be gotten for Craig Swan, whose contract had only a year to run and who looked as though he was going to be difficult to re-sign. The people who were running the team had given every indication that they were doing business as usual. I myself had heard Joe McDonald, the Mets' general manager, say that his mission at the meetings was to field the best team possible, come spring training time. Well, did that mean he was free to make any trades he wanted? Yessir, it did, if they would really help the team. So the news of the Swan-Aikens trade seemed entirely logical.

But hardly had the trade begun to be digested by the banqueters—along with their Alberta Roast Prime Rib of Beef, Prince Edward Island Potatoes, and Baked Yukon "Flambé"—when Joe Durso returned to the table after a brief absence and announced that the deal had been called off. Apparently, only minutes after Joe McDonald and Buzzy Bavasi, the Angels' general manager, had ironed out the last wrinkles and shaken hands, Lorinda de Roulet had decided to renege. Gee, someone at the table asked, had anything like that ever happened before? Not in Bavasi's experience, said Durso. "He's mad as a hornet and swearing that it's the first time in his forty years in baseball he's ever heard of such a thing."

In the hours and days that followed, everyone gossiped about what had really happened to the "Dying Swan" deal. Was it fair of Mrs. de Roulet to exercise her rights as the Mets' sole owner? Had Buzzy Bavasi really called her a nasty name? Next morning's *New York Times* was objective. A story under Murray Chass's byline quoted Mrs. de Roulet, "the lame-duck chairman of the Mets' board," as saying, "I thought it over and I decided to try and leave the team in place as much as possible in fairness to the new owners. We don't think it would be fair to a new owner to trade a pitcher of his [Swan's] quality." But when Buzzy Bavasi was told of Mrs. de Roulet's decision, he "unleashed a tirade at the Mets' boss for keeping the Angels hanging for two days during what is a precious time of year for baseball teams." "I'm not going to tell you why it fell through," Chass quoted Bavasi as saying. "Let the Mets tell you why it fell through."

But the New York tabloids were outraged. "METS VETO SWAN DEAL" blazed the back-page headline of the *Daily News* over a story by Phil Pepe that went so far as to speculate "that there had been a new development regarding the sale of the Mets. Perhaps she had discussed the deal with a prospective buyer, who turned thumbs down and that caused her to renege on her agreement with Bavasai. However, she acted improperly in stringing the Angels along on the deal." In the following day's edition of the *News*, Bill Gallo ran a cartoon, captioned "A Woman's Prerogative," comparing Mrs. de Roulet's behavior to that of a woman unable to make up her mind about choosing a hat. And Dick Young took her furiously to task for violating the most sacred rules of a men's club. "I'm afraid 'Linda' de Roulet is giving equal rights a bad name," he blustered in a column headlined "Mets' Lorinda Is Playing Way Out of Her League."

> In the male chauvinist world of baseball, where a man is as good as his word, a woman is expected to live by the same rules. Apparently, Lady Linda did not? . . . The point is, the trade was made. Both sides said okay, you have a deal, over the phone. That is the code of honor. You don't change your mind. The woman's prerogative is no excuse. You play with the men, you play with their rules. Equal rights means equal responsibility, and all that balderdash.

But it remained for a session of lobby gossip to unfold the intimate details of how the Swan deal had sunk, or one man's version of those details, at any rate.

"Is it true you called the Met owner a cunt?" Jerry Holtzman asked Buzzy Bavasi as a gathering of reporters and general managers formed spontaneously on Wednesday afternoon.

BAVASI: [Laughing.] Oh, you've been talking to Dick Young. He asked me, "You called her a cunt?" I said, "Don't give me that. I wouldn't use that kind of language. She has a right to do anything she wants to. It's her ballclub, her money, right?" I didn't call her anything like that . . . to her face.

HOLTZMAN: To her face!

BAVASI: [Smiling.] But I am pissed off. I'm really mad. We had a deal! They called me out of my room. Joe McDonald calls me up and says, "Come on up. We got a deal."

DURSO: Willie Aikens and Dickie Thon for Craig Swan and . . . ?

BAVASI: At that point it was to be some minor-league infielder not yet named. So I went up there and we settled it and shook hands on it, Joe and me and Bob Scheffing [the Mets' super-scout], and then *she* walks in and calls it off.

LEHMANN-HAUPT: Just like that?

BAVASI: Yeah. And the funny thing is, now I get on the elevator, and who's there but Gene and Mrs. Autry [the owners of the Angels]. And Gene asks me, "What's the matter?" because I'm muttering to myself about rich women in baseball, because last year I quit the San Diego Padres because of a rich woman, right? So I said, "Gene, come on off the elevator and I'll tell you about it." And Mrs. Autry—she's very sedate and quiet, y'know—she comes too. So I said, "I don't like rich women in baseball. You're excluded, Mrs. Autry." So then I tell him what happened with the Mets, and he's laughing . . . see, he thinks it's funny. But I'm mad. I say, "It happened to me last year too. I quit the best job in baseball with one of the nicest guys in baseball because of another rich woman." I told Gene I quit because I wouldn't take that from a broad. He said, "What do you mean?" I said, "Last year . . . two years ago, the woman was in the box watching the ball game . . . she'd had a couple of drinks . . . and she said . . . she's rather obscene . . .

and she said, uh 'Buzzy, you're full of . . .' " —I didn't want to say it in front of Mrs. Autry, so I said, "You're full of S. H. I. T.!" And Mrs. Autry looked at me sweetly and said, "You mean *shit*, Buzzy?" [Laughter.]

But I felt sorry for Joe and Bob. We worked for three days on this. Then I said, "All right, don't do anything now." I said, "You've gotta take the best offer. Wait until just before the trading season ends. If you don't come up with something better, fine. You fellows are in a spot. You've gotta make a good deal. Right?"

DURSO: Well, when they told you on the phone to come up to their room, was that a deal?

BAVASI: Yes!

LEHMANN-HAUPT: Did they say you had a deal?

BAVASI: Hell, yes!

HOLTZMAN: Did you really shake hands on it?

BAVASI: Oh, you don't shake hands anymore; you take a guy's word for it. If I can't take Joe McDonald's word, we've lost everything. We might as well go out of business.

DURSO: But she was in the room when he told you about it!

BAVASI: No, she wasn't. She was not in the room when I walked in. She came in later and said, "That fellow, Thon, how old is he?" I said, "He's twenty-one." She said, "My goodness, he's just a baby." I said, "I'll give you a thirty-nine-year-old if that's what you want. I'll give you Bert Campaneris." [Everybody laughs, because Bert Campaneris is thought to be at the end of his long career.] Okay, so everything's fine. It's Aikens and Thon for Swan and whoever. But now they can't come up with. . . . We got a deal, but they can't come up with the infielder that's part of the deal. I said, "I told Gene Autry it's two-for-two, and that's all it has to be, right? Fine. So give me somebody to make it right." So they said, "What about Elliott Maddox?" I said, "What the hell difference does it make. Fine, if you want." I didn't need him, but what the heck? So they said, "No, we can't do that." Now we go in the bedroom.

LEHMANN-HAUPT: Why in the bedroom?

BAVASI: Joe Torre's there now, with Mrs. de Roulet. And I said, "Are you seriously telling me you're not going to make this deal after we've been talking for three days?" She said, "Not for Swan. I'd do it two for one, but not two for two." I said, "Then why are you paying this fine gentleman?" meaning Joe Mac. She said, "Well, I'm running this club." I said, "Fine. You're telling me that you're not going to make it." Never happened to me in forty years of baseball, somebody's going back on a deal. I said, "Tell me . . ." There's the three of them standing there, Joe McDonald, Bob Scheffing, and Joe Torre. I said, "Joe, do you want this guy Maddox?" He said, "Hell, no. I don't want him. That's why I gave him to you." I said, "Bob"—that's Scheffing—"do you want him?" "Hell, no. That's why we gave him to you to settle the deal." But when I ask Torre, the newcomer, if he wants him, he says, "Oh, he's GREAT! He's my center fielder."

DURSO: Why did he do that?

BAVASI: I have no idea! I guess he felt Mrs. de Roulet wanted him to say it.

LEHMANN-HAUPT: He must have been trying to please her, because he couldn't possibly have really believed it.

BAVASI: That's what he said, so help me. So I walked out of the room. And now I'm gonna see. I'm coming to the Mets' opening day to make sure Maddox is playing center field.

DURSO AND LEHMANN-HAUPT: He won't be.

BAVASI: I'm gonna still wait and see if he's as great as Torre says he is.

DURSO: Well, I thought the reason they turned it down was that they didn't think the new owner oughta be saddled with it.

BAVASI: That's what she told you fellas, right? Now let me tell you. She said, quote, she would make the deal, Thon and Aikens, for Swanny. She called him Swanny. Two for one. That's the deal she would make. Yep. She wanted to cut it down. She'd sell Swan for two but not for one. That doesn't make sense. She said, "Oh, the owners would be mad if I sold him two for two." See what I mean? She had a deal. I could have made the deal right then and there if I'd have given her the two players for the one.

DURSO: But you had the other deal . . .

BAVASI: I thought so. We had a deal. Even with her. You ask all the Mets if she did not agree to the deal if it was only two for one. You ask them. They were embarrassed about it.

DURSO: The *Daily News* even went so far as to suggest today that she may have spoken to a new owner, in fact that they've identified a new owner, which they haven't done. They haven't come close to it.

BAVASI: It's all very strange.

The next day Bavasi finally found someone to take Willie Mays Aikens off his hands. He dealt the slugging first baseman, along with shortstop Rance Mulliniks, to Kansas City for outfielder Al Cowens, shortstop Todd Cruz, and the inevitable "player to be named later."

At such straws as these were reporters left to grasp. Otherwise there was little to do that was much more exciting than waiting for grass to come up. On Monday, the first official day of the meetings, the big event was the annual major-league selection meeting, technically known as the Rule Five Draft, in which nine clubs paid $25,000 a man, or a total of $225,000, for such players as Michael W. Macha, Bruce E. Kimm, Guy P. Sularz, Esteban M. Castillo, and Douglas M. Corbett, among others, none of whom had yet become household names exactly.

On Wednesday, Commissioner Bowie Kuhn called a press conference to report the business that had been transacted so far by both major leagues. He started off by announcing that it would come as no surprise that he had no surprises. The meetings had been largely devoted to such economic matters as the implications of collective bargaining and everything "entailed in that." Otherwise, he told us, there had been some minor legislation, such as doubling the contract payments made to minor-league clubs (Triple A from five thousand to ten thousand dollars per club, Double A from three thousand to six thousand dollars, and so forth), and the "usual housekeeping," which he did not go into.

The commissioner then turned the microphone over to American League President Lee MacPhail, who started off by saying, "Well, I don't really have that much to talk about either. There's not too much that's happened at our league meeting that's newsworthy or represents any final action taken on anything." In a weary tone of voice, he then reviewed such matters as new committee appointments; the efforts to standardize umpiring procedures in the two leagues, including the design of a common uniform; the possible pending move of the Oakland A's to Denver, and the efforts the league was making to facilitate that transfer; the possibility of instituting automatic fines for the throwing of equipment during a game, "which would enable us *not* to eject the player from the game"; and the problems involved with making up schedules for the following season.

After fielding a few spirited questions on how much the league might be exerting itself to *force* Charles O. Finley to sell his Oakland A's to Denver oil magnate Marvin Davis—Finley having established himself over the years as something of a burr under Commissioner Kuhn's saddle—MacPhail turned the microphone over to his National League counterpart, Chub Feeney. Feeney assured the gathering that almost nothing had been happening in his bailiwick either. "Things have been going so well in the National League that we've probably had the lightest agenda that I can ever remember in history." He then mentioned housekeeping chores, committee reports, the reelection of certain league officers, and ended up by saying, in response to a question about the new design of the umpires' uniforms, "I think it'll be a nice surprise for the fans of America on opening day next year when those 'men in blue' run out on the field."

Later that same afternoon, the Pittsburgh Pirates held a press conference to announce that they had extended the contract of their manager, Chuck Tanner, for an additional four years. Tanner, after carrying on at length about his good fortune and the pride he took in working for the Pirates, suddenly began to heap elaborate praise on relief pitcher Joey McLaughlin and outfielder Barry Bonnell, the two players that the Toronto Blue Jays had gotten in their deal with the Atlanta Braves. This was evidently Tanner's response to an item that had appeared in the *Toronto Star* that morning. Headlined "Jays Made a Bad Deal, Cleveland Scout Says," the story, written by Alison Gordon, began, "One Cleveland scout, who had watched the Jays pull off coups like the Alfredo Griffin–Victor Cruz deal last year, just shook his head. 'This time,' he said, 'Toronto got the bad end of the deal.'" The trouble was, unknown to Alison Gordon, the "one Cleveland scout" she had referred to in the story turned out to be the *only* Cleveland scout attending the meetings. So everybody at the convention knew that it had to be Danny Carnevale she was referring to. Carnevale was now rushing around to undo the insult he had inadvertently inflicted upon his host, the city of Toronto. Chuck Tanner was simply trying to lend Carnevale a hand. (When Tanner was finished, Alison Gordon stood up and promised the gathering that if she were ever given the opportunity to mention him in a story, she would be sure to refer to him as an "unknown Pittsburgh Pirate manager.") Such was the exquisite etiquette practiced among the members of baseball's fraternity. Such also were the doldrums in which the profession's annual convention now lay becalmed.

Whatever conclusions these events might have implied, I was finally learning not to jump to them. Most of the time, anyway. One exception was the last evening of the meetings, while I was waiting for a friend in the Sheraton's Trader Lounge. With nothing else to do, I decided to try guessing the professions of the people in the lobby. I knew from a bulletin board that many of the women there were attending a convention of the National Foundation of Temple Sisterhoods. I was determined not to make the mistake that the Coca-Cola Company was rumored to have made a day or so earlier. According to a story that was making the rounds, their people had gone around the lobby of the Sheraton handing out invitations to a promotional party about to get underway in the company's hospitality suite. Some of these impromptu invitees, who arrived at the suite in droves, had turned out to be prostitutes and proceeded to solicit the men who were present. One of the stories even had the Coca-Cola man in charge being offered a freebie. I was not about to put myself to the test of seeing if I could tell a Temple Sister from a hooker.

Looking at the baseball people in the lobby and noticing how unnatural they looked in civilian clothes, I was reminded of my army days. The managers stood around stiffly "at ease," like NCOs attending a barbecue thrown by their company commander. The executives looked a bit more comfortable, but even the ones who had never played the game appeared as if they had only recently put their uniforms aside. Even the owners, in their blazers and flannels, seemed like generals on leave. And the few women present looked completely out of their element, eyeing each other for support like wives who had gone out with their husbands to watch field maneuvers. Except of course for Lorinda de Roulet.

So baseball, like the army, was a tribe, a sect, a subculture, a totemic group, as an anthropologist might say. It had its own code of dress and deportment. It initiated its members into a system of body signals, locked them in a semiological embrace, and left them marked men for life. You could spot a baseball man in any crowd.

The validity of this insight held up for about ten minutes. When Alison Gordon showed up at the cocktail lounge, she had in tow a slight young man, dressed in a sober but expensive business suit, who reminded me a little of Walt Disney's Jiminy Cricket. He must be an accountant, or a rabbi on his way to address the Temple Sisterhood, perhaps. Certainly not a reporter or a baseball man. But when the three of us got to drinking and talking, it turned out that Charles, as he insisted on being called, had recently redesigned the uniform of the Montreal Expos, adding an inch-wide blue-and-red slash down the shoulder on the outside of the sleeve and down the entire length of the body portion of the jersey and pants. He seemed delighted with his accomplishment. I asked him politely, "How does one get to redesign the uniform of a major-league baseball team?" for this quietly self-assured young man was surely not in the uniform business. "I'm with the Expos," he said offhandedly. "What do you do with them?" I asked, becoming aware that Alison Gordon was tugging my sleeve. "I thought you knew," she moaned. "This is the chairman of the board—Charles Bronfman."

The combined presence of a club owner and an attractive female reporter seemed to act like a magnet on the baseball people near the cocktail lounge. Soon a party was in progress, which had about it an air of the valedictory. Joe Durso was there with Jerry Holtzman, who told me he'd heard that the only reason the umpire Lou DiMuro was still angry at Cliff Johnson for crashing into him at home plate back on Memorial Day was that the resulting period of idleness had led to DiMuro's wife becoming pregnant. Bobby Valentine was there, assuring me he'd have a lot to tell me over our breakfast the following day. There was Spec Richardson, general manager of the San Francisco Giants, shaking his head over the impossibility of swinging deals anymore. There was a blond woman in a green cocktail dress who, Alison Gordon insisted, was a campaigner from the Coca-Cola party.

The evening began to lose its sharp edges. Charles Bronfman described how he'd searched out a place to be alone in Olympic Stadium and had quietly wept after his Expos had been eliminated on the last day of the season. A man materialized wearing a double-breasted camel hair overcoat and a white leather touring cap. I told him he looked as if he'd stepped out of the pages of either *The Great Gatsby* or *The Wind in the Willows*—it was hard to tell which. He pretended to ponder his preference. He turned out to be John McNamara, manager of the Cincinnati Reds. I got so tipsy I ended up the evening telling Bronfman how much I admired the design of New York City's Seagram Building, which his family had built and owned. Would it be possible for me to buy a square inch or centimeter of it so that I could think of the building as partly mine? Bronfman assured me with exaggerated graveness that he would be looking into the matter first thing in the morning.

On the last day of the meetings, I woke up early with a pounding hangover. I didn't feel at all like joining Bobby Valentine for breakfast in the hotel's clattery cafeteria, absurdly named Le Pavillon. But this appointment had begun to look like the high point of my time in Toronto. By now it was clear that no monster deal was going to climax the meetings; the new power of the players had not only killed the trading market, it had even snuffed out the fantasy of such an event occurring. And with the fantasy gone, my whole outlook on the game had changed.

In the war between the players and the owners, I had always sided with the owners. After all, they financed the game, at least in my simpleminded view, so they were the keepers of my fantasies. But with their loss of power over the players, they had begun to look a little different. The way they acted seemed suspect. They kept complaining that the players were going to break them. Commissioner Bowie Kuhn, the owners' man, had sounded the warning once again in his keynote address to the current meetings: as a result of free agency and the inequality it was inevitably creating among the various teams, there was "a time bomb ticking away in our operation." The gap between the top and bottom teams was growing wider. The bottom eight clubs in baseball had lost on the average of a million dollars a club in 1978—the last year for which financial figures were available—and over half the teams in baseball had "lost position." Presumably, when this "time bomb" went off, no one would be able to afford to own a baseball team any more. That would truly be the end of the game.

Yet despite the alarms that Commissioner Kuhn was sounding, dozens of people were vying to pay at least $15 million for the New York Mets. During the season just past, the Baltimore Orioles and

Houston Astros had been sold for about $12 million. And two years earlier, the Boston Red Sox had gone for $15 million. Though some owners weren't willing to spend as much on players as others were, nobody was declaring bankruptcy. Thirty years ago, they were griping about paying their stars one hundred thousand dollars. Today, that was the salary of a utility infielder, and the stars were pulling down ten times as much. Yet the number of baseball franchises in the land had nearly doubled. Baseball was busting out all over, but the owners hadn't changed their tune. They were still complaining about going broke.

It was therefore a little hard to take seriously the owners' stance in their negotiations to rewrite the industry's basic labor code, which was due to expire December 31. On the premise that they were headed for the poorhouse, they were asking the players to give up some of their gains, which had been won not only at the bargaining table but also through legal arbitration. In fact, this seemed so outrageous to me that I could feel stirrings of vestigial sympathies for the underdog—something I would frankly never have expected of myself. I was now actually ready to hear the players' side of the story. And what better source would there be than Bobby Valentine, a former player representative himself who was a veteran of labor negotiations and who had come to the Toronto convention straight from the union meeting in New York? So after getting out of bed cautiously and dressing with the utmost care so as not to jar my furiously pounding head unduly, I left my room and steered a gentle course for Le Pavillon.

But what Valentine had to say did not inspire sympathy for the players; it served only to confuse me more. We had a good talk at our tiny table, even with all the waitresses and cigarette smoke swirling around us. Valentine was friendly, relaxed, articulate. He didn't seem to have any ax to grind. He appeared to understand both the owners and the players, and described their respective positions with an amusement shot through with irony.

I began by asking about the financial stability of the game. Baseball's imminent demise had been a theme from the very start of my season-long odyssey. Al Rosen, then still president of the Yankees, had told me on the flight down to Florida that what with the escalating price of free agents, the owners were "rushing headlong toward suicide." Commissioner Kuhn had echoed that prediction with his talk of a time bomb ticking away. Some of the clubs were rumored to be committed to salary payments as far ahead as the twenty-first century. As someone by nature uncomfortable with huge outlays of money, I couldn't help feeling worried.

But when I aired my concern to Bobby Valentine, he looked at me hard and spoke with measured diction. It was the law, he said, tapping his fingers on the tabletop, that at the start of any contract negotiations between a business and a labor union, if the business was suffering from financial hardship, a public statement had to be made to that effect and the business's books opened to the union. During every negotiation that had occurred so far between the Player Relations Committee and the Players' Association, the first comment made by whoever had presided at the meeting—the commissioner, Ray Grebey, John J. Gaherin [the latter two having been successive chief negotiators for the club owners]—had been that the clubs were not pleading financial hardship. One had to suspect that the reason they weren't doing so was simply that they didn't want the players or the public looking into their books.

But, I protested, what about those eight teams of Bowie Kuhn's that had lost $2 million each last year? Valentine replied that there might be losses on paper but that he tended to doubt it—after depreciation allowances and other tax write-offs, the teams all made money. Don't forget that each of them got an equal share of the national TV contracts, he pointed out. That by itself provided an enormous cushion.

But there had to be some limit to the spending, I insisted. Sure, said Valentine. And that limit would be reached when all the owners realized that you couldn't just go out and *buy* a championship. Everyone talked about the Yankees being the best team money could buy. But no one seemed to remember that they won the 1976 pennant—their first in over a decade—*before* they entered the free-agent market for Reggie Jackson. The point was that at best the free-agent market would do nothing more than supplement a team that was already good. And it could just as easily hurt a team that was already good if the guy you bought turned out to be a lemon. But it was a "free-agent market" in the most literal sense of the phrase: if you didn't have the most money, it didn't mean you weren't going to get the best buy; and the highest-priced player wasn't necessarily the one who was going to contribute the most to your team. It was simply wrong on the face of it to say that free agency had created an imbalance of competitiveness. It depended on the organization. It was possible to build a team out of home-grown talent. If money wasn't the ultimate standard of excellence, then baseball would survive the free-agent revolution. Salaries would go up as teams decided to bind their key players with long-term contracts, but brains and organizational skill would prevail. That, after all, explained the success of the Baltimore Orioles and the Pittsburgh Pirates.

But what an unpleasant picture Valentine drew of the contestants in the struggle for power. It made you wonder for a moment if it ultimately mattered whether baseball even survived. Particularly appalling was Valentine's account of the Ken Griffey case. One of the issues in the current negotiations was whether the time a player spent in the minor leagues after being sent down fom the parent club should count toward the six years it took to become a free agent. What brought this issue to light, said Valentine, was the incident that arose when Griffey, an outfielder with Cincinnati, was sent down to the minors during his second year with the Reds. As the contract now stood, it was the rule that if you were assigned to a minor-league team, you were to be credited with major-league service up to the day you signed your reassignment papers. You were to date them and sign them; that's what the contract said.

Well, Ken Griffey had been sent down to Indianapolis on May 15, but the team had been on the road at the time, and it hadn't gotten back to Indianapolis until the evening of the eighteenth. So Griffey hadn't signed his reassignment papers until he'd gotten to the ballpark the next day, the nineteenth. Then, four years later, when Griffey thought he was going to be a free agent, Cincinnati pulled out his records and said, "Sorry, Ken, but you're a few days shy of having six full years of service. You were sent down to Indianapolis on the fourteenth of May. It says it right here, the fourteenth. And you signed it, right here, on the fourteenth." Well, Griffey's mind was blown. It might have looked like a four to them, but it wasn't one of his fours, which are very distinctive. The case went to arbitration, but Griffey was afraid of losing, so he accepted Cincinnati's offer for a longer-term contract, just in case. But the fact of the matter is he would have gotten a better deal as a free agent. The clubs shouldn't be allowed to do that, the players and Valentine felt—and they did it all the time with first- and second-

253

year players: sent them down long enough to cost them credit for a full year. The next contract was not going to allow that, Valentine was certain.

But the owners had no monopoly on selfishness. Valentine also described how he'd sat at the most recent union meeting and counted sixteen millionaires. These were player representatives! They were supposed to be together, strong and united, but really all they had in common was that they made their living the same way. Benefits and improved working conditions were no longer their primary concern. It was what their apartment houses were going to net for the first quarter!

It was a whole other ballgame now, Valentine said. During past meetings, Marvin Miller's role had never exceeded that of mediator. His position had always been that he was at the players' service; he'd always made it clear before every negotiation that if at any time during the talks the Players' Association felt that he was getting in the way of reaching an agreement, he would willingly step aside. But at these latest meetings, he'd felt the need to remind the players that, in so many words, united they stood, divided they fell. And then, at the end of the meetings, there was a fifteen-minute discussion among the player reps. And the main issue they talked about was whether the Players' Association could arrange for a certain player to *incorporate*. Apparently, this player wanted to be able to set up a corporation, to which his salary would be paid and of which he would be an employee. He wanted the tax benefits and a more favorable retirement plan than his present contract allowed. Essentially he was asking, "Why doesn't the association dissolve itself so I don't have to pay dues and be part of an inferior pension plan?" That, as far as Valentine could see, was what all the talk had come down to: sixteen millionaires looking out for themselves!

Did the other players understand this? I asked Valentine. Would the rank and file tolerate such an attitude in their plutocratic representatives? Valentine shrugged. What did the players care? The only time a player representative ever did anything that touched his constituents' lives was when it came down to the votes and the question of whether to act during the negotiations over the basic agreement. Bill Buckner, the Cubs' infielder, had said to Valentine point-blank that the only reason he volunteered for the job was to make sure his interests were protected when it came time to vote.

What did the players care? Look, said Valentine, the most heroic performance by a player rep that he'd ever witnessed took place in 1972. He was then with the Los Angeles Dodgers. There was a strike vote. Wes Parker was the Dodger player rep. Jim Brewer was the alternate. All the reps and their alternates were directed to fly to Florida, convene an executive meeting, and vote yea or nay on whether or not to strike. Well, the Dodgers, led by Maury Wills, formed a group that gathered the day before Wes and Jim left for Florida and directed them not to vote on anything without consulting them first. Fair enough, right? So both players flew to Florida; Marvin Miller presented the case; the vote was taken. But Wes Parker, the Dodger rep, abstained during the roll-call vote because he hadn't gotten back to the Dodger group, as he'd been directed to do. When it was his turn to vote, the count stood at thirty-six in favor and none against, but he still felt obliged to consult, so he abstained and called the group back in California. After Valentine and the other members of the group got the word from him, they voted in favor of a strike and told him to do the same. But the voting had been completed by this time, and it was forty-seven in favor, none against, and one abstention. Wes was the abstention. So of course he got all the attention and publicity after the meeting. Why had he been the lone abstainer? Maybe he had a point? No one wanted to hear his real reason for abstaining, which was simply that he wanted to represent his team. So stories were written about his independent attitude and whatnot, and when he got back to California he was impeached! The one player who had truly represented his group! To Bobby Valentine, that story was symbolic. That was how much the players looked out for one another.

As I left my breakfast meeting with Bobby Valentine, I asked myself if it wasn't time for a break from baseball. I headed back to my room wondering how to kill the remaining few hours until my plane took off for New York.

A friend at home familiar with Toronto had recommended a highly innovative technology museum that had recently opened, full of machines that visitors could actually work for themselves. This sounded like a perfect remedy for the feeling of helplessness I had been fighting all week. I consulted the woman at the information desk in the lobby who was puzzled at first, but then, after checking with a colleague, wrote down the address of the Royal Ontario Museum. In the taxi I hailed just outside the hotel, I was still so perplexed by what Valentine had told me that I hardly noticed where the driver was taking me. As I climbed the steps in front of a monumental limestone facade and pushed open its heavy oaken door, I found myself still worrying if the game of baseball could survive.

Bobby Valentine's summing up had not been hopeful. "This is my third round of negotiations," he said. "I began as a young player representative in 1972. And this time it's different. This year is really different."

On the one hand, the owners were "out of touch with reality. They feel they can get things back the players have already won, but I think that's impossible, mainly because they're out of their depth negotiating with Marvin Miller. He's much too good for them." On the other hand, "the players have come so far that they really don't need the association anymore. They do not have the common bond that they had in 1975." It was pure conjecture on Valentine's part, but things might have gotten to the point where in order to hold the players together, Marvin Miller might be secretly preparing to merge the Players' Association with the A.F.L.– C.I.O. That would mean if the peanut vendors had a problem, the players wouldn't be able to cross their picket line. One big union! Gone would be the fantasy of baseball's being anything other than a way to make a living.

So what did I care about either the players or the owners? Or the game itself, for that matter? Inside the museum now, I found myself standing in a room full of geologic exhibits. I must be in the wrong museum. It was not the gleaming technological future that surrounded me, but the dusty past—deep time, as the geologists liked to call it. Geology. Cenozoic, Mesozoic, Paleozoic, Precambrian. Folds and faults. Sedimentary and metamorphic rock. Glacial firns, bergschrunds, cirques, arêtes, moraines, eskers, kettleholes. Primitive men in caves mining early metal. The very idea of geology had always made me uneasy. I found it hard to imagine the enormous forces that made time flow into centuries and magma harden into rock. I could not conceive of mountains being tossed up by the grinding of the earth's crustal plates. I couldn't even understand how glaciers moved.

Still, I might as well make the most of where I was. It was too late to find the other museum, and being here was no worse than hanging around the Sheraton lobby for the rest of the afternoon. Maybe I'd even learn something.

But as always when confronted with boring subjects, my mind began to wander. It wandered back to baseball. In front of an exhibit of early man unearthing flint and copper, I found myself thinking of a book called *On Human Nature,* by the controversial Harvard sociobiologist Edward O. Wilson, in which the author argued that the need to root for sports teams was tied to a fundamental biological instinct. Deep within all creatures, Wilson speculated in a chapter on altruism, there was a genetic urge to sacrifice oneself to the fellow members of one's species. This urge Wilson called "identification with the in-group." The rules that governed the urge were strong: they called for teamwork, bravery, and aggression against the external threat, or "out-group." But the object of allegiance had always remained weak, particularly among human beings. Social units were flexible; the "in-group" could easily become the "out-group." According to Wilson, professional sports thrived on these instincts. Few athletes were identified with where they came from anymore, and most of them were sold or traded without much thought of the fans' attachment to them. The teams themselves moved from city to city. But it didn't matter; the fan identified with an aggressive in-group, admired teamwork, bravery, and sacrifice, and shared the exaltation of victory. For an hour or so the spectator could reduce his world to an elemental physical struggle between tribal surrogates.

And so it was that by rooting for the New York Yankees I'd fulfilled my biological destiny.

In the hallway outside the geology room an enormous carved and painted totem pole thrust up through the museum's stairwell from the basement to a height of several stories.

What Edward Wilson didn't say was that rooting for a player or a team also led to my kind of magic thinking. I always felt secure when the Yankees won and threatened when they lost. That sort of thinking, however silly, pervaded my life, tempting me to make improbable connections and defy impossible odds. Step on a crack, break your mother's back. If I can spot ten out-of-state license plates in the next twenty minutes, it means the Yanks are going to win tonight. Why, just look at that incredible hand of poker the other night. In a game of five-card draw, I'd picked up my cards and found myself looking at three kings, a three, and a ten. Now, the sensible thing to have done would be to throw away the three and ten and draw two new cards in the hope of getting the fourth king, which would have given me an all but unbeatable hand. But because I'd been on a winning streak, I'd gone with an inexplicable hunch to toss the ten and keep the three, and, sure enough, I'd pulled another three to give myself three kings and two threes, a full house. It was a dumb play—magic thinking at its worst—because the odds against filling the full house were astronomical, and at the same time I'd cut in half my chances of getting the fourth king. It was almost as bad as the early days of my poker playing, when everything I did depended on my mood and had little or nothing to do with what the other players were up to. This time, happily, my delusion had not been reinforced. With a huge pot on the table, my kings and threes beat out the heart flush drawn by the player to my right, but they were beaten in turn by four of a kind across the table, held by a player who had made the correct move of drawing *two* cards to his three jacks. Reality, as well as the weather, had laid a chilly hand on me in Toronto.

Upstairs in the Royal Ontario Museum, I walked into a room that was literally filled with bones. In one corner a display case contained skeletons of both a bear and a man. The bear looked like a catcher risen from his crouch to throw out a runner trying to steal second. What, I wondered, would remain of baseball when the present had receded into deep time? Bats? Balls? Gloves? The monuments and plaques in center field of Yankee Stadium? Stadiums themselves? They had better pack the contents of that Gillette Hall of Fame exhibit into a space capsule and shoot it into orbit around our star of stars, the sun. But what would some future space traveler make of Bob Feller's uniform shirt or Stan Musial's bat? Would he be able to construe the game from Joe DiMaggio's glove? They had better throw a rule book into the capsule too. But would future civilizations catch the subtleties of the game—the sacrifice bunt, the pick-off play, and the knuckleball? And would the scale of the game be right for the human animal of the future? Would the speed of future base runners gain at the same rate as the power of future catchers' arms? Would future bats be as quick as future fastballs?

In the display case, the human skull seemed to grimace inscrutably into that unknown future. It was time to head home.

REPORTING

BY THE END OF 1979, I could see that there wasn't going to be any natural conclusion to the baseball year. One season blended into the next like a Möbius strip looping around forever. The last game of the World Series might be the official end, but already many players were looking ahead to the winter season in the tropics or a special-team tour of Japan. Baseball never stopped; it only slowed. Now, even in the freeze of winter, the summer game was still hot news. Sparky Anderson had just been hired to manage the Tigers. The sale of the New York Mets was on the front burner. Strike talk was boiling. And Billy Martin, still angry at George Steinbrenner for giving him the sack, was erupting almost daily with insults and imprecations.

So as far as my baseball season was concerned, I myself would have to end it, and the stopping point would be arbitrary. Midnight, New Year's Eve, 1979. That would mark the finish of whatever story I had to tell. So when my wristwatch beeped the hour, I drank a special toast to my experience and pronounced my career as a sports reporter officially at an end.

Partly to celebrate my return to the old life, the following afternoon I attended a large New Year's Day party given by a couple of writer friends, Hugh and Marilyn Nissenson. There, quite unexpectedly, I found in the crowd of literary people a man named Michael Tree, whom I liked to think of as my distant brother-in-law; he was actually the husband of my father's third wife's daughter by a previous marriage. A professional violist with the distinguished Guarneri String Quartet, Tree spent much of his time on concert tour, so I saw him only occasionally and hadn't run into him at all for a couple of years.

"What've you been up to, Michael?"

"The usual. What about you?"

"The usual. Except this past year, I've been working on a book about baseball."

"Baseball? Say, have I got a baseball story for you."

"As of last night, my ears are officially closed to baseball stories."

"It's about Joe DiMaggio. . ."

"I'm still not interested."

". . . and a game long ago where he hit three home runs. I heard it just the other day from a friend in Cleveland. Unbelievable! In fact, why don't you give my friend a call. It's a great story."

The following evening, I telephoned Tree's friend in Cleveland. I couldn't keep my ears closed after all.

"Many years ago," Tree's friend began, "I got to know a very well-known individual in town—kind of a notorious fellow. He was actually—how can I put it to you?—he was really a godfather. Well, he had a kind of get-together one night in which I was included, and for several hours he held us spellbound with stories. And the best of them was about how years and years ago the New York Yankees were coming to town to play a series with the Cleveland Indians. And Joe DiMaggio—who, being Italian, was a friend of this fellow's—called ahead from wherever the team was, and said, 'I'm coming to town. I'll be free Saturday night. I want some fun. I really want to have a ball.'

"So the man, this godfather, picked Joe up at his hotel—it was called the Hotel Cleveland then; it's now called the Stouffer Inn on the Square. He picked him up early in the afternoon after DiMaggio got in by train—the teams didn't fly in those days, obviously—and he wined him and dined him. He took him first to Little Italy—our Little Italy in Cleveland, which is called Murray

Hill—where they obviously ate and drank a great deal. Then, in the evening, he took him out to an infamous gambling place called the Mounds Club, which was then illegal. There they ate and drank some more, and they gambled. After that, they went to—all the people involved with the Mounds Club had these country retreats—and they went to one of those, for what purpose I can only guess.

"Anyway, they stayed out all night, and somewhere approaching dawn, at about five-thirty, six o'clock in the morning, this man brought DiMaggio back to his room at the Hotel Cleveland—literally carried him back in a state that could only be described by this man as 'impossible.' He put Joe to bed. He went home. He called his bookie and told him, 'I want to put a big bet on the Indians in tomorrow's game because there is no way DiMaggio is going to be able to play.' And then he went out to the ballpark, and, to his amazement, there was DiMaggio in uniform taking batting practice. And what does he do but hit three home runs—two of them off the great Bobby Feller—and drive in all his team's runs as the Yankees beat the Indians 6–5. And I can promise you this is an authentic story, because if there's one thing I can vouch for, it's that the man in question never told a fib. I can't tell you his name, but I can guarantee he was a straight shooter until the day he died."

So there it was again, the game that had made a fan of me on that sultry afternoon in adolescence. It had seemed to be following me around all season. First, way back in June, Mel Allen, the broadcaster, had told me that story, straight from the pages of a boys' magazine, about how the night before the game, on the sleeper from Chicago, he'd tipped DiMaggio off to why he'd been slumping at bat, and how the next day DiMadge had broken out with those three homers against the Indians.

Then there was Portland in July, where I'd happened on DiMaggio and Feller together and had repeated Allen's slump story, only to learn that in the series up in Chicago preceding the one in Cleveland, DiMaggio had gotten half a dozen hits or so, including three home runs.

Then, in September, Bill Veeck, who owned and ran the Indians at the time of DiMaggio's unusual feat, had reminisced about the game during the evening I'd spent with him at Comiskey Park in Chicago.

"It was a hot, hot day," Veeck had recalled when I mentioned

DiMaggio's three home runs. "I'd been in the hospital, recuperating from more leg surgery, but I snuck out to the ballpark because I knew we were going to break our attendance record, which we did. Over seventy-eight thousand people came out to see that double-header—the second-biggest crowd ever to see a game. The first ball that DiMaggio hit was a line drive right over the center-field fence. It was never more than ten feet off the ground."

And now this very different version of how DiMaggio had spent the night before the day of his famous exploit. Was it pure coincidence that that game kept coming back to haunt me?

It would be one thing if I could just believe the story and leave it at that. But if it was true, it meant two things not widely known about DiMaggio's career that reflected on it somewhat ambiguously, to say the least. One was that he broke training now and then—no big deal, though it might not suit his image as a television salesman, on which he now depended for his livelihood. The other was that he fraternized with gangsters, at least during his playing days. This too might be no big deal; to hang around with criminals didn't mean you were corrupted by them, especially if you happened to be America's leading sports hero.

But it did make him appear a little tainted in retrospect, and appearances were everything in the modern sports era. After all, Willie Mays had just been banned from baseball by Commissioner Bowie Kuhn for simply having taken an aboveboard job as a public-relations man with a legitimate gambling casino. How would Commissioner Kuhn react to the news that one of his most transcendent superstars had been a friend of a powerful mobster and had spent at least one evening carousing in an illegal gambling joint?

When I telephoned the commissioner for his reaction, he said that to comment at all on such a story would be to give a mere rumor "credibility," but that of course I was welcome to draw my own conclusions from his handling of the Mays situation.

Since the story couldn't be accepted at face value, DiMaggio himself would have to be confronted. This was something I did not look forward to. It presented an intimidating array of problems. For one thing, I couldn't simply go to DiMaggio and repeat what amounted to a fourth-hand rumor. I'd have to dig up a few supporting details, not least among them the identity of the storyteller. This was not going to be easy. I hadn't the foggiest notion of how to go about finding a dead mafioso who was active in the city of Cleveland over thirty years ago, let alone how to go about linking him to Joe DiMaggio on the night of May 23, 1948.

And even if I succeeded, it wasn't going to be much fun confronting DiMaggio. He'd been friendly to me. He had literally taken me under his wing when we'd first met in Portland. He'd talked to me as if we were all alone while the crowd surging around us badgered him for autographs and interviews.

Three months later, on my way to Baltimore for the opening game of the World Series, he'd patiently put up with my puppyish assault and was even sorry he couldn't let me use the couch in his hotel room.

And now I was going to repay him for his kindnesses with a story that would not only taint his splendid image but bring to light behavior that, were he playing in the present baseball era, could conceivably cost him a fine or, worse, suspension. In the end, his association with me might only serve to confirm the wisdom of the reticence he was famous for practicing with the press. Of course, this all depended on whether I'd even be able to reach him, which was not the least of the problems that following up the story presented. When I'd said good-bye in Portland, I'd asked if it would be okay to call him sometime for an interview. He'd said, "Sure!" but he hadn't volunteered a telephone number. And I hadn't had the presence of mind to ask.

Still, the effort had to be made; the spadework had to be done. The first person I thought of was my friend Sidney Zion. Among Zion's many passions was the subject of gangsters. Although he was obsessed with the belief that it was really the Jews who had run the American underworld and that the role of the Italians had been exaggerated retroactively by testimony before the Senate Subcommittee on Crimes and Rackets from the publicity-seeking Joseph Valachi, he would probably know who the major Italian mobsters were in Cleveland during the late 1940s.

Zion was also an expert at uncovering hidden identities. He had, somewhat controversially, been the first to discover and reveal that Daniel Ellsberg was the man who had given the Pentagon Papers to the *New York Times*. In his book, *Read All about It*, he'd described how simple it had all been. He suspected that people in the peace movement knew who had done it but would not volunteer the name, so he got several insiders to promise that they would confirm the name if he could come up with it himself. Then he found in the *Washington Post* the list of people who had access to the papers. All that he had to do then was to choose some of the more obscure names and try them out on his sources. On the second call he made, he said "Daniel Ellsberg," and scored. When he called two of his other people, they confirmed.

I telephoned Sidney Zion.

"I've got to come up with a list of Italian mobsters who were prominent in Cleveland in the late 1940s," I said.

"Why Italian?" Zion shot back predictably.

"Because I'm trying to come up with the names of some guys who could have spent a night on the town with Joe DiMaggio."

"Why do they have to be Italian?"

"Who else would a shy Italian kid hang out with?"

"By the late forties, DiMaggio wasn't such a shy kid anymore. In 1948, no mafioso in Cleveland was big enough to take DiMaggio out drinking."

"Look, Sidney, the one thing I'm sure of about this story is that it was told by an Italian. He claims to have taken DiMaggio to an illegal joint called the Mounds Club."

"Well, just check out the ownership of the Mounds Club! It was Jewish. Major Jewish guys owned the Mounds. If you don't believe me, read a book about them called *The Silent Syndicate*, by Hank Messick."

So I consulted Hank Messick's *The Silent Syndicate*. According to Messick, an investigative reporter for the *Miami Herald*, the most notorious Italian gangsters in Cleveland during the late 1940s were the members of the Mayfield Road Mob, so named for a suburb where Cleveland's Italian community was concentrated. Prominent in the Mayfield Mob at that time were Alfred "Big Al" Polizzi, big in bootlegging, gambling, and real estate, and the three Angersola brothers—Fred, John, and George—who went by the name of King and invested their bootleg profits in Miami real estate.

There was a catch, though. The Mayfield Road Mob might have been big within the Mafia—big enough to convince Estes Kefauver and his Senate subcommittee, at least for a time, that it was the only gang in town. But in the larger scheme of the Cleveland underworld it played a strictly subordinate role. In fact, its members often served as a front for the real power in the city, the men who ran the organization known as the Cleveland or Ohio Syndicate, which the Kefauver Committee eventually came to recognize as one of the chief "financial sources of gangsterdom."

It was the Cleveland Boys, as they were also called, who had owned the boats during rum-running days, who had engineered the giant underground stills when "home brew" came into style, and who had taken over the numbers racket and set up illegal gambling joints when Prohibition ended and the Casino Era began. They had been handed much of Midwest America—though not Chicago, of course—when the country was divided up into "territories" in 1934.

The syndicate was led by four men, according to Messick. There was Moe Dalitz, "the first among equals." Then there was Morris Kleinman, who was the contact with the Mayfield gang except for the time he served in prison for income tax evasion. There was Louis Rothkopf—a.k.a. Lou Rhody or "Uncle Louie" to the showgirls he liked having around him—who'd paved the way for the syndicate to set up business in Las Vegas. And there was Samuel Tucker, who specialized in laundering the syndicate's gambling profits from its Cuban operation. The four of them remained equal partners in whatever business they got into. From their early rum-running days to their time of glory as owners of the Las Vegas Desert Inn and the Nacional in Havana, it was one for all and all for one.

They liked to work behind the scenes. They would set you up and invest in you, but they preferred to keep their names and faces out of the picture. That in fact was how the Mounds Club had come into being. A Cleveland operator named Thomas J. McGinty had found the syndicate repeatedly encroaching on his various businesses. As Messick wrote, "It had muscled in on his bookie-protection racket after first taking the local wire service away from a McGinty lieutenant. . . . The syndicate-owned Thistle Downs Race Track was cutting into his track revenue, and syndicate casinos, such as the Thomas Club, were competing as well. Being a realist, McGinty offered a compromise. Always willing to use local talent, even in Cleveland, the syndicate accepted. In return for pieces of some McGinty properties," the syndicate "helped him finance a new and plush casino over in Lake County—the Mounds Club. It was for Cleveland and Ohio what the Beverly Hills Club became for Cincinnati and Kentucky—a 'rug' joint [as opposed to a joint with sawdust on the floor] offering 'big-name' entertainment and the best in food and drink. McGinty was also rewarded with a piece of the Beverly Hills and, later, the Desert Inn at Las Vegas. In time he achieved a special relationship—not so much a junior partner in the syndicate as an associate member."

That was in 1930. The Mounds Club went on to become a spot well known to Cleveland residents not least of all because of a robbery there. During a midnight performance by Mary Healy and Peter Lind Hayes, a gang of armed masked men had made off with some three hundred thousand dollars in cash and jewelry. An official investigation got nowhere tracking the culprits down. But the owners of the club took care of the matter. Federal agents learned through the grapevine that all the men involved in the holdup were dead within six months.

So the Mounds Club was a vital part of the Cleveland underworld. That made the DiMaggio story at least partly plausible. But its owners, except for T. J. McGinty, weren't Italian, but Jewish—or "preferably Jewish," as Moe Dalitz had designated his religion when he joined the army in 1942. They were so "preferably Jewish" that when Morris Kleinman went to prison in 1933 and someone was needed to fill in for him as the contact with the Mayfield Road Mob, the only Italian the syndicate would trust was a Jewish Italian, Charles A. "Chuck" Polizzi, whose refugee parents had died when he was a child and who'd been adopted by the family of Big Al Polizzi and taken its name.

The Italian, whoever he was, who'd taken DiMaggio to the Mounds Club would therefore have had to have close ties to the Jews of the syndicate. Maybe it was even Chuck Polizzi, who, Messick writes, had retained his standing with the syndicate after Morris Kleinman returned to active duty. Maybe it was Big Al Polizzi or John "King" Angersola, both of whom had clout with the syndicate because of their high standing in the Mayfield gang. Or maybe it was someone not even mentioned by Messick.

It was obviously time to get away from *The Silent Syndicate*, which, after all, was only one man's view of things. It was time to talk to someone who knew the Cleveland scene firsthand, someone who'd been there in the 1940s and was old enough to remember. I'd heard that Bob Fishel, the former New York Yankee publicist who was now the secretary of the American League, had grown up in

Cleveland, gotten his start in a public-relations firm there, and was working for the Cleveland Indians in 1948. I called him.

"Sure, I remember the Mounds Club," he said. "My parents used to go there. My father hated it, but my mother loved it. The guy to talk to though is Bill Veeck, who knew everybody in the city. He'll tell you about the Mounds Club."

That was just fine by me. Bill Veeck was probably the most approachable man in all America, as I'd learned from my visit back in September. It would be easy to telephone him again.

LEHMANN-HAUPT: I'm trying to track down some information on a place in Cleveland called the Mounds Club.

VEECK: Oh, ah . . . McGinty's!

LEHMANN-HAUPT: Right!

VEECK: Tommy McGinty's! What do you want to know about it?

LEHMANN-HAUPT: I need some names who were connected with it.

VEECK: Well, let's see if you've got these. Ah, Morris Kleinman?

LEHMANN-HAUPT: Yeah, I got him.

VEECK: Aaah, Moe . . . no, not Moe Dalitz. He wasn't involved.

LEHMANN-HAUPT: He wasn't?

VEECK: Uuuuumm, ah, Louie Rothkopf.

LEHMANN-HAUPT: I have Uncle Louis Rothkopf.

VEECK: He was called Lou Rhody.

LEHMANN-HAUPT: And Lou Rhoda.

VEECK: Ah, Morris Kleinman. Ah, Johnny King?

LEHMANN-HAUPT: Yeah, I've got that name.

VEECK: Well, that's an alias. A.k.a. What do you wanta do with the Mounds Club? It's a very interesting place.

LEHMANN-HAUPT: [Laughs.] I gather. Were there any Italians connected with it?

VEECK: No, not really . . . other than John King. That wasn't his real name. That was his alias.

LEHMANN-HAUPT: For John "King" Angersola.

VEECK: But the Mounds Club was basically Irish and Jewish. McGinty was the guiding light.

LEHMANN-HAUPT: What about a guy named Chuck Polizzi?

VEECK: Chuck Polizzi is right! Very much. But he was not really Italian. The family was, but they adopted a Jewish boy who became Chuck Polizzi.

LEHMANN-HAUPT: So I understand. Well, here's what I wanta know. I think I mentioned to you when I last saw you that the game that made me a baseball fan occurred in May of 1948. It was a game against the Indians in which Joe DiMaggio hit three home runs?

VEECK: Yes, he did. One of them was a line drive right over the center-field fence; it was about ten feet high. Everybody jumped for it.

LEHMANN-HAUPT: Right. And you remembered that game because you snuck out of the hospital to see it.

VEECK: I remember it very well. Right up there at the Cleveland Clinic. They had operated on my leg again.

LEHMANN-HAUPT: Everybody seems to remember that game. Mel Allen told me a story about helping Joe to break out of a slump.

VEECK: I don't know about that. I don't think he broke out of any slump. I don't think I ever saw him in a slump. If he ever was, all he needed to do was to play us to break out of it.

LEHMANN-HAUPT: That's what Bob Feller said: "He was never in a slump against me."

VEECK: As a matter of fact, DiMaggio . . . I remember, when I had the St. Louis Browns, the Yankees asked waivers for the purpose of giving him his unconditional release. I was the only claimant.

LEHMANN-HAUPT: No kidding!

VEECK: So, he called me up and I. . . . You see, I had claimed Henry Greenberg, under similar circumstances. So I claimed Joe. And he called me up and he said, "What do you want?" I said, "I don't care what you do. You can do anything you want. You can play. You can coach. Whatever. I don't care. Just I think you belong in baseball." "Well," he said, "I don't know. But I don't want to play." He says, "The reason I don't want to play is the ball I used to hit over the left-field wall I now hit a line drive into right field." He said, "The next step is I don't hit it . . . and I'm going before that happens." Which is what you might call leaving the premises with class instead of playing out the last seven years of a ninety-two-year contract.

LEHMANN-HAUPT: That's right. Well, anyway, just when I thought I'd finished researching this book I'm writing, I was told this story about DiMaggio coming into Cleveland one Saturday night before a doubleheader, and staying up all night drinking and gambling at the Mounds Club.

VEECK: That's not the night it was knocked off, was it?

LEHMANN-HAUPT: No no. It was the night before he hit those three home runs.

VEECK: Oh, ho!

LEHMANN-HAUPT: And before I repeat the story to DiMaggio, I've got to figure out who it was who told that it—that is, who took him out that night.

VEECK: I would guess it would be Tommy McGinty.

LEHMANN-HAUPT: Okay. Do you believe the story?

VEECK: Well, I have no reason to disbelieve it. Ah, Mary Frances and I one night went over to Early Wynn's. It was one of the times when I was unemployed, and we were running a P.R. firm in Cleveland. And we met Early at about six o'clock, maybe it was a little later, maybe seven o'clock. We had brought with us about half a gallon of five gallons of grasshoppers that we had mixed up for another occasion, and Early finished up the greater part of that half-gallon of grasshoppers. We went home, and I went to sleep and woke up the next day. Early pitched the first game of a doubleheader that afternoon—shut 'em out with two hits, struck out nine.

LEHMANN-HAUPT: [Laughs.]

VEECK: I asked him how he did it. He said, "I had to!" He said, "I couldn't have gone that much longer. I couldn't fool with 'em . . . go to three balls and two strikes. I had to get 'em out in three strikes or on the first pitch or I wouldn't have made it." So he pitched a two-hitter.

LEHMANN-HAUPT: Oh, that's wonderful.

VEECK: So I can't disbelieve anything. And I've seen Satchel Paige in action too often to have any doubt at all that your DiMaggio story isn't possible.

LEHMANN-HAUPT: Right!

VEECK: Well, it could have been Johnny King. It could have been Chuck Polizzi. Oh, wait a minute, wait a minute. It probably was Mushy Wexler.

LEHMANN-HAUPT: Mushy Wexler?

VEECK: Mush Wexler owned the Theatrical Grill. That was right behind the Highlander, the best place in the city to eat. He and a fella by the name of, ah, of, ah [long silence] . . . Shander Burns! But Joe would not have gone with Shander, but he might've gone with Mushy Wexler.

LEHMANN-HAUPT: Wexler, huh? But the guy who told the story is Italian.

VEECK: Among other things Wexler had the Theatrical Grill, an after-hours place called the Ten-Eleven—he and Shander Burns—and a stable of horses, and they lived out in the country. And then . . . Ed Strong, it coulda been Ed Strong.

LEHMANN-HAUPT: Your memory is something.

VEECK: Ed Strong is a fella that was extremely wealthy. When he died, out in the country, there was one of the great all-time gold rushes to his deposit box. There were eight keys out. Nobody will ever know who got there first, but somebody cleaned it out.

LEHMANN-HAUPT: How many of these guys are alive today?

VEECK: Well, let's see. Morris Kleinman is alive. He's in Florida. McGinty's dead. King is dead. Chuck Polizzi is dead. Mushy Wexler is dead. Shander Burns was blown up into about 4,892 pieces—I should have said 5,280 because it covered about a square mile—when he started his car one morning. But I would guess it was one of four fellas. Strong, Polizzi, Morris Kleinman, or McGinty. With an outside chance of Johnny King. Try Joe on all of them.

LEHMANN-HAUPT: Okay. How do you think he's gonna take the story?

VEECK: Well, I dunno. Ask him and find out. There weren't very many people would be invited like that, so he can't take much exception to it. It is an accolade in its way.

LEHMANN-HAUPT: Okay. Thank you very much.

VEECK: Say hello to Joe. He was one of my all-time favorite people.

LEHMANN-HAUPT: Okay, I'll tell him.

The next step was to go back to the original source in Cleveland.

LEHMANN-HAUPT: I have a couple of questions about that story you told me about Joe DiMaggio and the Mounds Club.

THE SOURCE: Yes. That was a very high-class operation. It was run by the Mafia.

LEHMANN-HAUPT: Well, that's a complicated issue. But I have some names of people who might have told you that story, and I wonder if I could run them by you. I'm going to confront Di-Maggio with them, and I want your advice on the order in which I should present them.

THE SOURCE: Okay.

LEHMANN-HAUPT: I talked to Bill Veeck, who of course ran the Cleveland Indians in those days and knew everyone in town. I told him your story, which he enjoyed. When I asked him who he thought it might have been, he said, after giving the matter much thought, "It had to be T. J. McGinty . . ."

THE SOURCE: . . . a notorious Irishman who was head of the rackets in town . . .

LEHMANN-HAUPT: . . . and who owned the Mounds Club.

THE SOURCE: That's correct.

LEHMANN-HAUPT: "Or it was Chuckie Polizzi," Veeck speculated.

THE SOURCE: A notorious Mafia figure in the late thirties, early forties . . .

LEHMANN-HAUPT: Although Jewish.

THE SOURCE: Really?

LEHMANN-HAUPT: Yes, he was adopted by Big Al Polizzi's family. "Or it was a very rich guy"—this is Veeck again— "named Ed Strong."

THE SOURCE: That name isn't familiar to me.

LEHMANN-HAUPT: "Or it was Morris Kleinman."

THE SOURCE: Another well-known figure.

LEHMANN-HAUPT: And then Veeck paused for a long time, and said, "Although I would give an outside chance to a guy named Johnny King."

THE SOURCE: [Silence] Well, it *was* Johnny King.

LEHMANN-HAUPT: Really!

THE SOURCE: But that's not his name.

LEHMANN-HAUPT: It was Angersola.

THE SOURCE: The Johnny King refers to the fact that he was the king. And when I say he was the king, he was the *king!*

LEHMANN-HAUPT: He was the king.

THE SOURCE: He was the king. He really was.

LEHMANN-HAUPT: Er, I thought Moe Dalitz was the king.

THE SOURCE: He was above Moe Dalitz.

LEHMANN-HAUPT: He was above Moe Dalitz. Okay.

THE SOURCE: There is a book in which that conference in New York is discussed. What was that?

LEHMANN-HAUPT: The Apalachin?

THE SOURCE: The Apalachin conference. He is mentioned prominently in that book, page after page after page. An interesting sidelight is he once came into the office of a friend of mine the morning after *The Godfather* made its debut in Cleveland. And one of the girls said, "Did you see that movie last night? Do you believe it?" And he said, "Believe it? I *am* it!"

So it was John "King" Angersola who had told the story of taking DiMaggio to the Mounds Club that night. It certainly figured, since King was both Italian and, according to Hank Messick at least, close to the people who owned the Mounds Club, even if he wasn't quite as "big" as the source claimed he was. Now the hardest part remained—the job of asking DiMaggio himself about the story.

I'd been working on tracking him down all the while I'd been reading Hank Messick's book and talking to my various informants. With the aid of my ever-helpful colleague Joe Durso, I'd finally pinned down DiMaggio at the Sheraton Heights Hotel in Hasbrouck Heights, New Jersey, where he regularly stayed during visits to New York City.

"What is it exactly that you want, Chris?" DiMaggio asked after I'd gotten him on the phone and rattled on about our previous meetings and my interest in that famous Cleveland game in 1948. "I don't know what details I can give you on that which you probably don't already have," he added, sounding a little gloomy—or was it my imagination? Still, he finally agreed to meet me for a cup of coffee in the motel's cafeteria early the following morning. He even seemed cheery as I launched into a stuttering and overdetailed recapitulation of what that 1948 game had meant to me, how it had kept coming back to haunt me, and the way I'd run into Michael Tree on New Year's Day.

LEHMANN-HAUPT: And I ran into, if you can believe it, my own brother-in-law, who's married to my father's third wife, and he is a viola . . . I never see him, 'cause he's a . . .

DiMaggio: A viola?

LEHMANN-HAUPT: . . . a violist . . .

DiMaggio: Oh, a violist . . .

LEHMANN-HAUPT: . . . who plays for . . .

DiMaggio: I thought you meant the fellow who's the pitcher . . .

LEHMANN-HAUPT: [Laughing.] No, no, not Frank Viola!

DiMaggio: Okay. Not a pitching-for-Minnesota Viola.

LEHMANN-HAUPT: No, he plays for a string quartet. Anyway we got to talking and I told him that I was working on a baseball book. When he heard this, he said, "That's incredible because yesterday in Cleveland I heard the greatest baseball story I've heard in my life." He said, "I was having lunch with a very dear friend of mine, and he began to reminisce about how he had once gotten involved with a family in Cleveland . . . a major hitter, a, ah, a heavyweight . . ."

As I continued, DiMaggio's mood began to change. It wasn't anger or irritation he expressed, which was what I'd been expecting. Instead he seemed to stiffen and duck his head imperceptibly. He began to regard me out of the corners of his widening eyes, which gave him a look of injured wariness. I found it hard to go on. I couldn't find the right language as I stumbled on into my account of what the Cleveland source had told me. In particular I couldn't bring myself to utter the word *mafioso*.

LEHMANN-HAUPT: And so this guy I talked to in Cleveland told me he had become involved with a family there, the head of which was a . . . a major hitter—a, ah, a heavyweight—and he said—my source did— "Long ago, many years ago, when the Yankees were coming into town for a series, I got a call from Di-Maggio, saying 'I'm going to be free on Saturday night, and I want to . . . I want to have a night out on the town.' And I made all the arrangements. I took him to a place called the Mounds Club."

DiMAGGIO: Now, I remember that!

LEHMANN-HAUPT: "We were out very very late. It was a very active evening."

DiMAGGIO: You mean your brother-in-law took me out?

LEHMANN-HAUPT: No, no, this was the guy that . . . this was the friend of the friend.

DiMAGGIO: The heavy hitter.

LEHMANN-HAUPT: The heavy hitter.

DiMAGGIO: Whatever . . . Heavy hitting in what?

LEHMANN-HAUPT: Whatever heavy hitting it was. He said, "I took him home . . ."

DiMAGGIO: [Placing his thumb on the tip of his nose and bending it, presumably to make himself look like a mafioso.] Who was one of these *kind* of heavy hitters. Okay, whatever it might have been. Okay.

LEHMANN-HAUPT: "I put him to bed. I physically put him to bed at 6:30 in the morning. Then I went home." This is the heavy hitter talking. "I called my bookie. I bet a very heavy bundle on the Indians, 'cause I said there is no way DiMaggio is playing."

DiMAGGIO: Ah, ah. I wasn't a drinking man, I can tell you that.

Now he seemed vulnerable and hurt. The effect on me was unnerving. I'd expected more resistance and had charged myself to fight it by forging ahead. Instead, I was now beginning to feel like a bully. It was as if I'd cornered a magnificent animal that I'd been searching for all my life—a mountain ram perhaps, or an eagle—except that instead of holding a camera in my hands I seemed to be aiming a high-powered rifle.

DiMaggio continued to regard me with injured calm. I stumbled ahead.

LEHMANN-HAUPT: "I showered . . ." I'm just telling you the story he told. "I showered. I took a nap. I had my chauffeur take me out to the ballpark and lo and behold, there's DiMaggio in uniform taking warm-ups. And what does he do? He proceeds to hit three home runs and win the game."

DiMAGGIO: Hmmm.

LEHMANN-HAUPT: And I asked my source if it could possibly have been in 1948 that this happened. And he said that he was sure it must have been.

DiMAGGIO: You know, you hear a lot of those stories about the fellow staying up all night. I guess if you've heard one, you must have heard dozens. But you never hear about the ones that stay up all night and they go for a horse collar and maybe make an error or two. You only hear the positive ones, not the negative ones. But in my case—I remember the Mounds . . . I remember there was a Mounds and an Arrow Club. And they were clubs that had nothing to do with me, but I used to . . . ah, but I enjoyed the fellow I went with.

LEHMANN-HAUPT: Who was . . . ?

DiMAGGIO: But I just went out there, and, as I said, I don't drink. So I don't know what kind of a night I could have had that might have been too bad. It might have been one of those mornings you get in two o'clock or so. Course we had a deadline of twelve. And, ah, I was in pretty good shape.

LEHMANN-HAUPT: [Laughing.] Apparently.

DiMAGGIO: I didn't do a hell of a lot of . . . I wasn't *that* kind of a heavy hitter.

LEHMANN-HAUPT: I asked Bill Veeck about it. I wanted to find out who it was.

DiMAGGIO: The ones that I went out with?

LEHMANN-HAUPT: Yeah.

DiMAGGIO: I went out with . . . I had a very dear friend of mine, I guess I met him through Toots Shor and Eddie Duchin, and when the World Series was going on, we all went out to the Mounds Club. There were about four or five of us—I forget the names—but that's how I was first introduced to that particular place. And the second time I went is the one that you're talking about, no doubt. The first time was during the World Series. But I was never a frequent guy that went out to this place because it's a long distance away to begin with. And it really had not that much interest for me outside of just that I was a young kid looking around, and, you know, that's about it. I wasn't a gambler. I hate to put holes in your story, but I mean this is the way it was.

LEHMANN-HAUPT: Anyway, I finally figured out that the guy who took you there must have been . . .

DiMaggio: His name was Lou Rhoda.

LEHMANN-HAUPT: Oh. Lou Rhoda. Lou Rhoda.

DiMaggio: You didn't mention the name. He's of course passed away.

LEHMANN-HAUPT: Louis Rothkopf was his real name. They also called him "Uncle Louie."

DiMaggio: Oh, then I was right!

LEHMANN-HAUPT: Well, that's not the person that I figured out you were with.

DiMaggio: How did you know about Lou Rhoda . . . Rothkopf?

LEHMANN-HAUPT: Well, I did some research.

DiMaggio: Then I hit you with a good name.

He actually seemed pleased to have been able to help.

LEHMANN-HAUPT: Well, you hit me with one of many names I had, but the name it finally came down to was a guy named Johnnie King.

DiMaggio: I don't know. That name doesn't ring a bell with me. Lou Rhoda . . .

LEHMANN-HAUPT: Which was an a.k.a. for John Angersola.

DiMaggio: That still doesn't mean anything to me.

LEHMANN-HAUPT: And he's the one who told the story. Or so I was told.

DiMaggio: Lou Rhoda was connected . . .

Lehmann-Haupt: He sure was.

DiMaggio: . . . with the Mounds or the Arrow Club . . .

Lehmann-Haupt: Right.

DiMaggio: . . . far as my memory goes. But that's about all. I mean I didn't know the other fellow that you just got through mentioning.

Lehmann-Haupt: What about Morris Kleinman?

DiMaggio: Well, Morris Kleinman wasn't there at the time, but Morris . . . I knew the name, Morris Kleinman. Course we met all those fellows at one time or another at . . . they were all part owners of the Desert Inn, and, ah, they may have started around Cleveland, but they wound up in Las Vegas far as I know. I don't believe I met Morris Kleinman. I might have. I know the name out of Las Vegas.

Lehmann-Haupt: I have to tell you: I'm not an investigative reporter. This story is for my book, and the story is about the wonderful irony of it all coming around to . . .

DiMaggio: Well, I don't know what you would be investigating anyhow.

Lehmann-Haupt: No, no.

DiMaggio: If you were, I wouldn't . . .

Lehmann-Haupt: I mean I don't mean to be cross-examining you as if I were investigating you, but I had to get your reaction. I asked Bill Veeck, "What do you think Joe will think of this story?" And he said, "He can only be honored. There were not many people they would ask to an evening like that." He said, "It's an accolade!"

DiMaggio: You mean, honored because of having that mythical night?

Lehmann-Haupt: He knew all those guys very well, and he said there weren't many people that they would include in a night out on the town.

DiMaggio: Well, I didn't know those two . . . that other fella that you mentioned. Morris I had met at the Desert Inn in Las Vegas—ah—it's a very possible thing that. . . . I know he was from Cleveland; it might have been that I met him there, but I don't remember that. But I know of him from—I say "know of him"—he's a very dear friend . . . Morris Kleinman is a very dear friend of Bob Hope's. They were dear friends . . . and, eh, as far as I know . . . he loved to play golf and he used to spend his time . . . he was in the gambling business. That I knew because he was part owner, or one of the members of D.I. But the other fellow, King, I don't—that is, when I say I didn't know him, I don't know if I ever met him. I might've met him, but the name means nothing.

LEHMANN-HAUPT: But Lou Rhoda was the guy who was your host.

DiMAGGIO: Lou Rhoda I remember. I remember him. He was very nice, very prominent . . .

LEHMANN-HAUPT: It sounds to me like—I know it was King that told the story—it sounds to me like he adopted it for his own, and maybe embroidered it a little bit?

DiMAGGIO: Yeah. You know, that's known to happen. But I can tell you that I, we were playing a doubleheader that day, and I wasn't the kind of a guy that was going to go out and raise a lot of hell if I had known I was gonna play a doubleheader the next day. I never raised a hell of a lot of hell. I mean, we had rules on our ballclub and we had a manager that was pretty strict in those days. Twelve o'clock was "all in." I mean we had to be in. Sorry to throw a hole in your story.

LEHMANN-HAUPT: It's all right.

A silence now began to yawn. DiMaggio continued to regard me with a look of polite, if pained, anticipation. He seemed ready to field more questions, but I felt uncomfortable about pushing the subject further. Moreover, I was confused. I believed DiMaggio's denial of the carousing part of the story. His protest was too simple and straightforward to be taken for anything but fact. It was also obvious that he'd never met or heard of John "King" Angersola. Why should he admit to knowing Lou Rhoda-Rothkopf and Morris Kleinman, yet deny acquaintance with someone who by all acounts except King's own was smaller potatoes in the Cleveland underworld?

Johnny King was a blowhard, which should have been obvious at once from his boast about being the equal of Don Corleone in the film version of *The Godfather*. King might even be a prime example of Sidney Zion's theory of the overinflated Italian criminal. In any case, what probably happened was that King, having somehow learned of DiMaggio's presence at the Mounds Club on the evening before his phenomenal game, had started dining out on the story and over the years embroidered it even to the point of assuming Louis Rothkopf's role as DiMaggio's host. This was simple enough to accept.

What puzzled me was DiMaggio's moral priorities. Here he was, denying that he'd been drinking or gambling or breaking the team curfew. Yet he seemed blithely willing to admit that he'd spent the evening at an illegal gambling club with a man reputed to have been one of America's foremost racketeers. Did DiMaggio have any idea who Louis Rothkopf really was? Because he'd appeared in Hank Messick's book as a lover of the good life who'd ended up committing suicide, I'd found Rothkopf the most interesting of the Cleveland Boys and could therefore recall most of the highlights of his colorful career.

Sure, Louis Rothkopf was supposed to have been an appealing character, generous and gregarious and fun-loving. His showgirl friends called him "Uncle Louie" in imitation of a nephew named Bernard who worked for him in several of his gambling joints. He liked to entertain, and for that purpose bought a six-bedroom "cottage" on a lake island in Ontario, Canada, where he held business meetings and put up such guests as Frank Costello and the boxer Billy Conn, recovering from his 1947 fight with Joe Louis. He was said to have been so considerate of other people's feelings that he would cross the street to avoid meeting men who owed him money.

But Uncle Louie also had his serious side—deadly serious, one might say, since he was the principal suspect in several murder cases. He was also a good man with a distillery, so good that in 1937 he was convicted for bootlegging by the Alcohol Tax Unit of the Internal Revenue Service. He served six months, but the conviction didn't stick because the evidence against him was acquired by wiretapping. But the incident bothered the Nevada Gaming Commission enough to bar Rothkopf from ownership of the Desert Inn. So his was a silent partnership in that lucrative venture—an irony considering it was Uncle Louie who had apparently ended the war that followed the murder of Bugsy Siegel and allowed Bugsy's dream of a gambling empire to materialize in the Nevada desert. This didn't trouble Rothkopf at first, since he knew the Cleveland syndicate would always protect his interests. But Hank Messick thought it preyed on Louis's wife, Blanche Rothkopf, and that this explained in part why she went into a depression and ended up taking her own life in 1955. A year later Rothkopf himself was found dead in his Ohio home. The official verdict was accidental carbon monoxide poisoning, but everyone seemed to agree that Uncle Louie too had committed suicide.

This was the man that DiMaggio had called a "very dear friend of mine," if I'd understood him correctly. I was now so confused by DiMaggio's attitude that I was beginning to doubt my ears. Maybe that was why I couldn't bring myself to press him further. Maybe things would become clearer when I listened to the recording of our conversation that I'd made with his reluctant permission.

But my puzzlement only deepened when I got home, transcribed the tape, and came upon a statement that I hadn't properly understood when I first heard DiMaggio utter it.

DiMaggio: I went out with . . . I had a very dear friend of mine, I guess I met him through Toots Shor and Eddie Duchin, and when the World Series was going on, we all went out to the Mounds Club. There were about four or five of us—I forget the names—but that's how I was first introduced to that particular place. And the second time I went is the one that you're talking about, no doubt. The first time was during the World Series.

That made no sense at all. The only World Series that DiMaggio could have been talking about was played between the Cleveland Indians and the Boston Braves in October of 1948, whereas the game in which he'd hit those three home runs was played the previous May. So the May visit to the Mounds Club would have had to be the first one, unless there were others—all of which made it look a little as if there were more to the story than DiMaggio was telling.

Of course he could be confused. After all, this had happened over thirty years ago. There had been other signs of his memory being confused during the interview. I'd brought up another memorable achievement of his—a Fourth of July series played in Boston in 1949, in which he'd come back from a season-long injury and hit well enough to help the Yankees win three crucial games. He had talked at some length about his decision to play in that series, and concluded with a surprising statement.

DiMaggio: But y'know, a man that's been out as long as I was—sixty-seven games or more—you just don't throw him in for three days. They weren't going to play me until I got in shape. I mean *pay* me, not play. They weren't going to pay me until I got in shape. [Laughs.]

Lehmann-Haupt: [Astonished.] What do you mean: they weren't going to *pay* you?

DiMaggio: [Frowning and shaking his head.] Oh, no, that was another time, when I was a holdout. I'm sorry. I got it all mixed up.

Embarrassed that he'd mixed up 1949, the year of his injury, with 1938, the year he'd held out for a better contract all the way through spring training and into the beginning of the season, he'd literally buried his face in his hands for a moment, a gesture completely at odds with his grave and dignified bearing.

And then, a couple of weeks after the Sheraton Heights interview, there had appeared in the *New York Post*, as part of a regular feature by Pete Coutros headlined "The Best Day They Ever Had," an interview with DiMaggio in which he put the date of the Cleveland game in September 1950. As I learned when I telephoned Coutros, the interview for the piece had occurred nearly a month *before* I'd talked to DiMaggio. So DiMaggio had already been shaky about his dates when I assaulted him with the Mounds Club story.

On the other hand, there were details of the game that DiMaggio had no trouble at all remembering. When the conversation had begun to drift, he'd pulled it back to his famous game.

DiMaggio: Those three that I hit—I kind of powered those three.

Lehmann-Haupt: You told me when we met at Kennedy Airport that there was a fourth pitch that you should have hit out.

DiMaggio: That was I think in the following game of the doubleheader. Joe Black pitched the next game, and he showed me a ball I couldn't believe. As that thing was coming across the plate, it looked that big! [He holds his hands apart.] And I took a real good healthy swing, and I fouled it off. But the thing that I do . . . I don't remember all the details about the game, but I do remember that besides hitting two off Bobby [Feller] and one off Muncrief, the papers came out the following afternoon and evening that, ah, made mention of "DiMaggio 6, Cleveland 5," because I drove in all six runs.

Whether it was confusion or evasion that lay behind DiMaggio's mix-up over the Mounds Club, it was time for another probe to clear up the matter. But he'd apparently had enough of me. Despite my asking several friends of his to have him telephone me and my addressing a letter to his home in San Francisco, he remained silent and unavailable.

I had all but decided to let the matter stand and maybe hang Di-Maggio with his own words, when I received a telephone call from Edward Bennett Williams, the Washington, D.C., attorney who had recently bought the Baltimore Orioles and who was known to be a close friend of DiMaggio's. He told me that he'd gotten a telephone call from Bowie Kuhn—who had said he was concerned about a story I was spreading about DiMaggio—and that he'd checked the whole thing out with Joe.

"I'm not sure precisely what Joe said to you," Williams went on, "but he tells me that the story is not true. He conceded to me that he did go to the Mounds Club; he apparently went there with people whose reputations were not of the best—probably the kind of people Kuhn would not like him associating with if he'd been commissioner at the time. But he denies quite vigorously that he got drunk, passed out. He denies that whole portion of the story. Y'know, I've known Joe I think for thirty-three years now, and I've spent many, many, *many* hours with him. I've never seen him drunk. In fact, he's a very light drinker. Ah, I am *sure* he wasn't drinking when he was playing ball, y'know? I don't mean he wasn't drinking at all, but I mean . . . he didn't *drink*. And I thought I'd ask you about it."

I explained that I no longer took seriously the part about DiMaggio's drinking and gambling and generally carousing all night. What interested me now was how the incident had developed into mythology.

"Listen," said Williams, "in my profession, they put out stories that you flunked the bar six times before you made it. They love to give a Horatio Alger twist to a story, y'know—lying down drunk at six o'clock in the morning and hitting four home runs at night. I'm sure half the mythology around Babe Ruth is of the same character."

Still, I explained, there was one contradiction in DiMaggio's account of the incident that it would be best to clear up. Well, said Williams, why didn't I just telephone DiMaggio about it? Here was his home number in San Francisco.

So I dialed the number and DiMaggio himself answered. After reintroducing myself and explaining a little defensively that I'd gotten his number from Edward Bennett Williams, I put to him the purpose of my call.

"In the transcript of our conversation—I sent you a copy of it—you say that the *first* time you went to the Mounds Club was with a friend you met through Toots Shor and Eddie Duchin . . ."

"Well, I hope I did the right thing in mentioning Eddie Duchin, because Eddie went around with us quite a few times. I know I went out there with Toots Shor, and it *might* have been Eddie Duchin."

"Well, that doesn't really matter," I reassured him. "That's not important. The thing is that you said that you first went out there during the World Series . . ."

"I don't know," he cut in. "Yeah, I guess it might have been. It might have been sometime else."

". . . because that would have been . . . the only time that the World Series was in Cleveland was in 'forty-eight, of course."

He hesitated. "Well, we're talking about . . ."

"We're talking about the previous May," I said.

"Previous?"

"Yes."

"I don't know," he said. "I don't know if I was out there at the Mounds Club at that time, and I don't know . . . it might have been."

"But you do remember going out there during the 'forty-eight World Series."

"Well, that's true, yes."

"Right," I echoed weakly.

"That I do remember very well. But the May before that, I don't recall it."

"You don't?" I protested. "But . . ."

"I'm under the impression that the first time and the *only* time that I've been there was with Toots."

"During the 'forty-eight Series."

"That's it," he said, sounding relieved, "During the 'forty-eight . . . Well now, was it the 'forty-eight Series or was it in May? I think it was. . . ." He laughed with embarrassment. "I'm totally confused about the whole thing."

"Right," I said, feeling a little embarrassed too by now. "I understand."

"Now, ah, of course they played the Giants, and Toots was a Giant fan. It *had* to be the 'forty-eight Series! The World Series between the Giants and the Cleveland ballclub!"

"But that was the year Cleveland played the Boston Braves, wasn't it?" I was beginning to get confused myself.

"Was it the Braves?" he asked plaintively.

"Yeah."

"Oh, I went out with Toots with the Braves, yeah. Aaah, we went to . . . no, that was in Boston. That's when I was with George Raft. We were with . . . with people, and we all had come up to see the Braves and the Boston Red Sox."

"The Braves were playing the Indians that year, I think."

"Oh, they were playing the Indians? Well, we did go up for that one, that I do know."

"Up?" I said. "But you were out in Cleveland too."

"Looks like . . . When was that?"

"That was 1948!" We were going around in circles.

" 'Forty-eight. Okay. I went to that one in 'forty-eight. But I do . . . The Giants played the Indians too."

"That was in 'fifty-four."

"Well, then that was the one."

"Oh," I said weakly.

"I had no reason to be going out there," he pressed on, "because why would ballplayers be going to the Arrow Club and the Mounds? But I did know about it and did go out there . . ."

"Right." We were back at the beginning now.

". . . because I knew some people who hung around there."

"Well," I said, deciding to change the subject, "how many times had you seen Lou Rhoda?"

"Oh," he said, then sighed audibly. "What? Half a dozen times?"

"Right. Did you know that he was Jewish?"

He paused for a moment, then said sharply, "Didn't matter."

"I know that. I meant . . ."

"I didn't think about it one way or the other."

"Well, I didn't mean to imply that it did matter. It's just that some people thought that he was Italian. They didn't know his name was really Louis Rothkopf."

"Well, I don't know about his real name, but I do know he has a nephew in Las Vegas, who I met many years ago, by the name of Bernie."

"Right. It was apparently because of that nephew that he came to be known as 'Uncle Louie.' "

"Well, if he happens to be Jewish, I . . ."

"Right," I put in quickly. "Well, listen, I'm sorry if this has caused you any distress."

"Well, it *has* in a way because, I mean, you know, it really upset me because I'm trying to do a favor and I know the whole thing is not reality. Believe me when I tell you this. And I'm only trying to give you what I thought might have happened. But I'm talking about . . . years ago, and I tell you, it's a little complicated."

"Yeah, I understand, but I wasn't trying to dig up dirt about you," I said defensively. "I'm more interested in how these myths grow up."

"How what?" he asked.

"How these *myths* grow . . ."

"Yeah, they do grow up. But see, I was just trying to do Joe Durso a favor, and if I had thought it was something like this, I would have just walked away from it."

"Well, I do appreciate your talking to me."

DiMaggio said nothing. There was silence.

"That's all the questions I have," I finally put in.

"Okay, Chris," he replied with surprising cheerfulness.

"Thanks a lot," I said.

"Thank *you*," he said, sounding genuinely grateful, and hung up.

But as it soon turned out, the conversation hadn't satisfied him any more than it had me, for within a matter of days Edward Bennett Williams was on the phone again apologizing for DiMaggio's inability to articulate his memories. But Joe was still vaguely troubled, Williams explained, if only because Bowie Kuhn had considered the matter worthy of his intervention. How exactly did I intend to use the story?

Not really knowing how I felt, I began to grope for an assessment of where I stood. Williams seemed to be listening sympathetically. In a way, I mused, DiMaggio's confusion had dispelled whatever doubt remained in my mind. For unless DiMaggio was a master of obfuscation, his inability to get his story straight probably meant that he really didn't recall what had happened. This in turn meant that it was routine business, from which one would have to conclude that he wasn't hiding anything. So the matter was cleared up, as far as I was concerned. It had just been a different era. In those days, baseball had been part of show business—it was the *only* big-business sport, Williams interjected in agreement—and show business then was part of a borderland world where all kinds of people mixed—actors, athletes, gamblers, prostitutes, maybe a gangster or two. It didn't mean that they were involved in each other's business. They simply liked to relax together, and those people had happened to include Joe DiMaggio and Louis Rothkopf. What had changed things since those days, I concluded—still thinking out loud—was probably television. Television had made everything more visible. Television had made sports big business. And the gambling industry had grown, thanks ironically to Louis Rothkopf and his friends. Gambling and sports now had to be separated in appearance as well as in fact.

Right, said Williams, warming to the subject. Why, whenever Babe Ruth used to come to Washington, D.C., he would meet for dinner with a guy named Sam Beard, a major bookmaker. They would eat at an open casino named the La Fontaine Club. It didn't mean anything. It just so happened that wherever you went in those days, the illegal clubs happened to be the best eating places—they served the best meat, the best steak, the best wine. "You're on the right track," Williams concluded. "Let's stay in touch."

But why, I wondered after hanging up, did DiMaggio continue to be half-blind to appearances? Why couldn't he see how damaging his association with Lou Rhoda appeared in retrospect? Well, maybe he could see it now, and maybe that was why he'd waffled so much in his last conversation with me. Yet even then he'd almost innocently dropped the name of the actor George Raft, whose reputation was nearly as controversial as Louis Rothkopf's.

DiMaggio seemed to have a kind of divided awareness of himself.

On the one hand, he was completely honest. Yes, he'd been at the Mounds Club. Yes, he'd been with an unsavory character. Yet on the other hand, he was proud, particularly of his reputation. So he'd told the truth about that evening at the Mounds Club and only afterward bothered to ask how it might have reflected on him. It was as if he looked at himself from two perspectives at once—one committed to the simple truth, the other conscious of appearances. Come to think of it, this trait of his could be seen in another story he'd told over coffee that morning in Hasbrouck Heights. I'd brought up a later exploit of his, that 1949 comeback series in Boston. As he'd warmed to his reply, he'd begun to speak as if he were as much of a hero to himself as he was to everybody else.

LEHMANN-HAUPT: Another unforgettable thing for me was 1949, the following season, when I think you'd been out until July with a bone spur in your heel.

DiMAGGIO: Right.

LEHMANN-HAUPT: And you came back for that series in Boston.

DiMAGGIO: Uh-huh.

LEHMANN-HAUPT: And I think you won all three games.

DiMAGGIO: Yes, I did.

LEHMANN-HAUPT: That was . . .

DiMAGGIO: Well, I didn't win all three, but what I did . . . You know, we were in a slump until that point and that's when I decided I was going to play because I didn't want to miss playing at Fenway Park in Boston. Because of that short left-field wall, of course. I'd missed playing there twice already that season, and I think if I'd missed this series, then I would have had only one more shot at it. So having that friendly fence had resolved it, not to stay away from the plate. That would have been a terrible thing. So under any conditions, I had to take a shot at it. So I did play, and I got lucky, as you know.

LEHMANN-HAUPT: I don't remember luck having much to do with it. What was amazing was how you got your batting eye back so quickly after being out for over 60 games.

DiMAGGIO: I had taken batting practice at Yankee Stadium while the team was on the road. I had a bunch of pick-up kids—

maybe six—ranging from the age of maybe 10 to 15, and all they were doing was retrieving the ball. And I had two guys pitch batting practice. One was Gus Niarhos, who was a catcher. And the other one was Al Schacht, the Clown Prince of Baseball?

LEHMANN-HAUPT: I remember both of them. Niarhos was part of that stockpile of good catchers the Yankees had who never got to play because of Yogi Berra.

DiMAGGIO: Niarhos was injured. That's why he didn't make the trip. He was a good player for that ballclub. Schacht was quite old, but still was able to throw as hard as he could, and he would throw the ball, not knowing what was coming, and that's how I got myself in shape.

LEHMANN-HAUPT: Who caught for them?

DiMAGGIO: Oh, they had kids, they had kids. One of the young boys. Today they have to take insurance out on these kids. At that time they didn't. Things have changed.

LEHMANN-HAUPT: Right. Well, where was the team at the time?

DiMAGGIO: I don't know where. On the road, but on the way to Boston. So that's why I met them in Boston. I took a plane. And I had a very good friend of mine on the airplane, and he lived in Boston. He happened to be on the same flight—we didn't plan it—and he said, "What are you going to do up in Boston? Are you playing?" And I sez, "I don't know. I haven't made up my mind." I had in my mind that I *was* going to play, but I didn't want to say nothing. As a matter of fact, even when I got into the clubhouse—this is an interesting story—there were about ten writers, and I came in and put a uniform on, and, not knowing if I was going to play or not, they kept asking Stengel about making up the line-up, you know? "What line-up you going to be using? Is Joe going to play?" And I got my back to him, and he's on the other side of the room, but I could hear all the conversation. And I'm kind of smiling to myself. And he says, "Well I can't do it," he says, "without, ah . . . I'm just waiting around to see, ah, thinking about my line-up." [Laughs.] So finally I looked over there, and he's looking at me. And maybe two minutes more—I've got my shoes on— and I sez, "I'll be able to play." And he said, "All right, fellows, here's my line-up."

At this point, DiMaggio had paused and smiled to himself and gently shaken his head, as if he were savoring the memory.

DiMaggio: He was just waiting for me to say "Yes."

Then he'd frowned, as if he suddenly realized he might be sounding egotistical.

DiMaggio: So the team was not doing that well. I guess maybe any kind of a shot in the arm to come, whatever it might have been, would have helped. I don't think I was responsible, but just the fact that you *do* get lucky, and that was a lucky three-game series I got to play.

DiMaggio was human after all. He'd told a story honestly, then looked at it from a different perspective and felt embarrassed by it. The same thing seemed to have happened with the Mounds Club story. He'd told it straight, reflected on its implications (with a little help from Bowie Kuhn and Edward Bennett Williams), and then grown vaguely embarrassed. That was really about all there was to it.

Yet it bothered me that he felt that he'd been sandbagged while doing Joe Durso a favor. After all, an interview was an interview. Durso hadn't made any promises. When I called Durso up to describe DiMaggio's reaction, he laughed and said that if Joe had really been mad at me he would have hung up. It was just Joe's way, he said. It was that honesty of his.

Still, it nettled me to be thought ill of by the man who had been my childhood hero. After all, I wasn't the one who had made up that story of his night on the town. It wasn't I who had tainted his reputation. It had all happened because he had been at the Mounds Club that night, which wasn't *my* doing. That was why if you were going to be a hero in America you had to live like a hero. If you were going to be the Yankee Clipper, you had to keep your sheets straight. And now DiMaggio would always blame me for bringing him the news that his image had been sullied. As time went by and the 1979 season receded into the past, it was one of the things I would think about late at night, and it would make me unhappy.

But I felt a measure of satisfaction too. After all, I had gotten the story—I was a reporter.

10

DREAMING

LATE IN JANUARY, 1980, I once again broke the rule I had made that I would do no more baseball research. I bought myself a ticket to the New York Baseball Writers Association banquet, which was held in one of the ballrooms at the Hotel Americana. Before hundreds of cheering sportswriters and sundry members of the baseball establishment, Commissioner Bowie Kuhn presented Willie Stargell with the Babe Ruth Award, and Stargell, accepting the prize, delivered a speech that reflected the hambone artist rather than the inner man.

> You know, in one's lifetime, you see and experience and you associate and you have the privilege of rubbing shoulders with so many fine people and this is a privilege that I've had since the World Series. And I can honestly say that around this country there are an awful lot of positive things being done. I saw this past year in baseball competition at its finest. The unfortunate thing is that being in the National League the years that I've been here I haven't had the great pleasure of seeing greatness like Al Kaline, Carl Yastrzemski, Rod Carew, all these fine in-

dividuals, but we know that they're fine talents, and it's good to be associated because this is a gathering that brings us all together and we can give a handshake and we know that it's a meanable thing, and you people come out to see us, and in turn we get a chance to see and exhibit what you fine people are all about. So I guess what I'm saying this evening, thanks to you and being associated with so many fine men in the game of sports that it's because of this you people give, New York writers, and allow me to come here and receive, the Babe Ruth Award, who to me is a man that stood for something he does for this sport, and forever will be. An awful lot of things come out of this city of New York, and it's a tremendous tradition, and to be part of it, I can't tell you, I don't think there's a word to describe the feeling that I feel at this particular time. But I just want to say that as long as baseball and the integrity that the ballplayers represent, if this continues, then we're gonna have you people screaming again next year in 1980. The Bucs, well, we're getting ready to go again. Thank you.

Later in the evening, the writers put on a musical skit. Murray Chass of the *New York Times* introduced the proceedings.

Once upon a time there was an Ayatollah named Bowie. Ayatollah Bowie Kuhn. Ayatollah Bowie practiced a religion that rivaled Islam in its zeal to preserve baseball's purity. When his subjects spoke or acted offensively, he mutilated their pocketbooks. Bowie better not throw the book at Nelson Doubleday [the head of the giant book publishing firm that had just bought the New York Mets from the Payson family for $21 million]; Doubleday will throw a whole building of books back at him. Overall, Ayatollah Bowie has been good to the owners. One of his commandments says, "Thou owners shalt make money." Another says, "Thou players shalt not make money." Willie Mays wasn't allowed to make money with the Mets if he also was making money with Al Rosen in Atlantic City. The Ayatollah Bowie didn't approve of gambling. Nevertheless tonight we open a giant casino, and we dedicate it to Bowie because he made it all possible.

To the tunes of familiar show songs, the skit poked sledgehammer fun at Bowie Kuhn's unevenhanded attitude toward gambling ("For It's Good Old Reliable Baseball"), at Billy Martin's pugnacity ("Take Me Out to the Brawlgame"), at Willie Mays's excommunication ("Say, Hey, I was the greatest of stars/Last year I made the Hall of Fame, this year I'm shuffling cards"), and at the decline and sale of the Mets under Lorinda de Roulet's mismanagement ("I Won't Sell, Don't Ask Me"; " 'Bye 'Bye, Metsies"; and "Not in Time"). In the middle of that last number, the two de Roulet daughters, Whitney and Bebe, got up from their places in the ballroom and made their way slowly to the exit. They appeared to be in tears.

A few weeks later, George Kimball asked me down to Greenwich Village's Lion's Head tavern for drinks with him and the zany Montreal Expo pitcher, Bill Lee. When the noise at our crowded table subsided for a moment, I turned to Lee and asked, "How do you find the sportswriters around the league?" Lee looked thoughtful for a moment and then said, "Just by standing in front of my locker."

Late in February, Cliff Johnson, the accident-prone catcher, finally turned on himself. On February 29, a spokesman for the Cleveland Indians, the team to which Johnson had been traded following his scuffle with Gossage, announced that Johnson had checked into a San Antonio hospital and was recovering from exploratory surgery on the middle finger of his right hand. He'd fractured the knuckle while moving storage barrels at his house the previous day, and nearly severed the bone. It would take him about five weeks to recover, the report said.

Several months later, I got a phone call from a man named Fred Jordan, who explained that he was now in charge at Methuen. I happened to know Jordan through some of his previous roles in the publishing industry; for many years he'd been editor in chief of Grove Press, the pioneering publisher that had brought out the first American edition of D. H. Lawrence's *Lady Chatterley's Lover*, among other controversial projects. I thought of Jordan as a humane man. He'd told me a story once about how, partly because of his German background, he'd been offered the editorship of a major West German publishing house and flown over to Germany to meet the staff and inspect the plant. As he was being shown around, he'd asked how many people were employed in the trade department.

"There are those you see here in this room," Jordan's prospective employer said in German. "And there are a dozen or so *Stücke* in the other rooms."

Stücke in this context meant "things," "pieces," or even "parts."

It was a word the Nazis had sometimes used to refer to labor camp inmates. Jordan declined the job offer on the spot.

"I see you're one of my authors," he now said on the telephone. "We have an exciting list. I'd like to have lunch with you and tell you about it."

"Fine," said I. "But I'd like to keep my roles as Methuen author and *Times* book reviewer as far apart as possible."

"Good," laughed Jordan. "We'll have *two* lunches. Let's have the first one as soon as possible."

We made a date to meet at a midtown restaurant, and I brought along a notebook and pencil with which to record Jordan's reactions to the three chapters of my book I'd submitted.

"I haven't read your *thing*," he said as our appetizers arrived. "I've never cared for baseball. I suppose it's my European upbringing. The uniforms look silly to me. The ball-thrower—pitcher?—reminds me of a dog at a hydrant."

He then launched into an enthusiastic description of Methuen's forthcoming list of books.

But it didn't much matter because by that time I'd given up on Methuen. I'd long since decided to carry on regardless of whether I had a publisher. This proved to be a sensible attitude, because in the spring of the following year, I was informed by my agent that Methuen was no longer interested in publishing any projects except textbooks. Since my baseball book could in no way be considered a textbook, I was free of any obligation to the publisher, and the publisher was free of any obligation to me. Once again—and even more emphatically than before—I was on my own.

Yet I kept on writing my book and remembering my season in baseball. Inevitably, my feelings eventually grew nostalgic. Even to this day, I'll occasionally project some pleasant image onto the screen of my memory and let it play like a film until I drift off to sleep. Sometimes the image will be of the salmon bake on Seattle's Kitsap Peninsula during the All-Star game festivities, and I'll see the throng of people filing past those enormous inscrutable totem poles like happy children on a school picnic. Sometimes I'll watch batting practice at Fenway Park and hear the hollow echo of the fans and Reggie Jackson shouting playful insults back and forth at each other.

But more and more as time passes, the film of memory that unwinds shows a September evening at Yankee Stadium, when the Yanks play a meaningless night game with the Cleveland Indians. I've gone to the ballpark early to tie up various loose ends that the season has left hanging. I want to talk with batting coach Charlie Lau about his hitting theories and about his rumored disagreement with Ted Williams. I've tried to reach Williams at his winter home in Florida, and he has refused to return my calls, but still I want to hear Lau's side of the reported dispute. When I asked Lau the previous night for an interview, he told me to meet him in the Yankee dugout sometime between four and five the following evening. But when I get there a little after four, Lau is busy pitching batting practice to a couple of Yankee players, so I've wandered around for a while tending to various odds and ends.

I've run into Cliff Johnson. There was a story in the *Times* a few days before claiming that Yankee manager Billy Martin, in retaliation for Johnson's injuring Goose Gossage earlier in the season, ordered one of his pitchers to throw at Johnson's head and even rewarded him for doing so with a gift of a few hundred dollars. The story met with strenuous denials all around, naturally enough, but it has made Johnson an object of cautious curiosity this evening, and a few reporters who are bear-baiting him over by the Cleveland dugout have brought out the raucous side of big Cliff that I'd so missed seeing back at spring training.

HENRY HECHT OF THE *NEW YORK POST*: How much they paying you now?

JOHNSON: I ain't telling you a motherfucking thing, 'cause it's none of your business. It's more'n you're gettin'.

HECHT: Okay, congratulations! Lend me ten thousand. I'm broke.

JOHNSON: [To anyone within earshot.] Stay away from this little motherfucker. He's a truh-BULL-maker!

LEHMANN-HAUPT: Have things really improved for you in Cleveland?

JOHNSON: Well, I should think so. I'm having fun.

LEHMANN-HAUPT: Are you playing as much as you want?

JOHNSON: Yeah, every day. I'm having fun.

LEHMANN-HAUPT: [After a long pause during which Johnson's slightly Oriental features turn more and more hooded and menacing.] Ah, I thought maybe I *wouldn't* ask you about the, ah . . . incident.

JOHNSON: [Grinning wolfishly.] Well, then don't!

LEHMANN-HAUPT: Okay. [Laughing nervously.] That's all I wanted to know.

I've wandered back to the clubhouse and found Reggie Jackson alone at his locker, changing into his uniform to the sound of ballroom dance music pouring out of a large radio on a shelf in his cubicle.

LEHMANN-HAUPT: This is a little complicated, but please bear with me for a minute.

JACKSON: Sure.

LEHMANN-HAUPT: Do you remember how you came to the All-Star game in Seattle without your Yankee uniform?

JACKSON: Sure do.

LEHMANN-HAUPT: So you wore a Seattle Mariner uniform for the team photograph?

JACKSON: Yeah.

LEHMANN-HAUPT: Well, right after the All-Star game, I ran into Joe DiMaggio in Portland, Oregon, and he asked me what had happened at the game. So I told him about your forgetting your uniform and being so willing to have your picture taken in something other than a Yankee uniform, and he thought for a moment and then said something like this: "Y'know, it's a funny thing, but I was at an All-Star game a couple of years ago, and for some reason I was wearing a Seattle Mariner uniform. And I remember that Reggie Jackson was there. I wonder if he saw me in that uniform and remembered. I wonder if that's why he was willing to be photographed in a Mariner uniform."

JACKSON: He did?

LEHMANN-HAUPT: Was he right?

JACKSON: Well, I just don't remember what All-Star game he's talking about. I don't remember ever seeing him in a Mariner uniform. He might have been, but I don't remember.

LEHMANN-HAUPT: It's certainly a revealing story about DiMaggio. That he would think that you would . . .

JACKSON: Joe and I have . . . there's something that Joe feels for me.

LEHMANN-HAUPT: Really.

JACKSON: Ah, I've talked to him a hundred . . . Whenever he's somewhere he'll always seek me and say hello. He's invited me to play golf with him. He lives in the Bay area. He's always spent time and talked with me, and he doesn't do that with hardly anyone.

LEHMANN-HAUPT: I know.

JACKSON: He's a very, very private person.

LEHMANN-HAUPT: Yes, I was surprised by his openness.

JACKSON: Yuh, yuh. What he said about me: It was a great opportunity to take a shot at me, but he took it and projected something we have in common. That's showing friendship.

I've talked to George "Boomer" Scott, the big first baseman who has recently been traded from the Red Sox. Scott is standing with a bat behind the batting cage, timing his swing to Charlie Lau's pitches. I ask him if he followed major-league baseball as a child. Scott continued to swing as he talked.

SCOTT: Oh, yeah! Sure!

LEHMANN-HAUPT: Who was your team?

SCOTT: The Yankees and Giants.

LEHMANN-HAUPT: Were you from this area?

SCOTT: Nope, Mississippi. Got a chance to see them play a lot on television. National TV. Saturday game of the week. The Yankees and Giants. Never will forget it. Mickey Mantle. Yogi Berra. Elston Howard. Whitey Ford. Bobby Richardson. Tony Kubek. Clete Boyer.

LEHMANN-HAUPT: The early fifties.

SCOTT: Yup. The Giants! Willie Mays, Don Mueller, Bobby Thomson, Hank Thompson, Al Dark, Wes Westrum. They were my boys.

LEHMANN-HAUPT: Who was your hero? Did you have any particular person?

SCOTT: Willie Mays! Willie Mays! Say, Hey, Willie!

LEHMANN-HAUPT: Did you ever play games as a child in which you imagined you were . . .

SCOTT: Oh, sure! All the time! That was it! That was it! Shit, I used to throw rocks up—I used to go in the railroad track and play the Giants and Dodgers game, and Yankee-White Sox, Yankee-Giant, every ballclub—throw rocks up . . .

LEHMANN-HAUPT: You mean fungoing rocks?

SCOTT: [Chanting.] Yeah, get me a broomstick! [He holds the bat in his right hand and flips an imaginary object with his left hand.] Throw a rock up! Mickey Mantle! Swiiinnnng! Loooonnnng drive, waaaay back. [Chuckling.] I called that shit, yeah.

LEHMANN-HAUPT: How long would the broomstick last?

SCOTT: Half a day. Yep, you do all that shit.

LEHMANN-HAUPT: Have you ever, playing in the major leagues—while you were playing—remembered yourself doing that?

SCOTT: Oh, sure. Sure. I remember it now!

LEHMANN-HAUPT: But I mean actually during a game, for instance when you were batting.

SCOTT: Oh, sure, sure. Shit, when I came up here and played on an All-Star team and got a chance to see Mantle, Mays, Aaron, all those guys on the same team, I thought about it right there on the field. These guys that I used to go about as a kid imita-tin'—now I'm on the same ball diamond with 'em, at the same level with 'em.

LEHMANN-HAUPT: And how does it feel. I mean how does it feel at that moment when you're . . .

SCOTT: Oh, unbelievable!

But the best part of that memory-film begins with me sitting in the Yankee dugout, waiting for Charlie Lau. Often when I run it through my mind, I embroider it with fantasy. I'm looking out at the vast spaces of the stadium, feeling the unusual sense of peace that seems to hang in the blue air. The grass, still sunlit, hasn't yet taken on that painted look that the arclights will give it. The tiers of empty seats echo the "tocks" of the batted balls and lend the space an intimacy it will lose when the crowd begins to arrive. The sky, bordered by the grandstand, is a bottomless pool of afternoon blue.

I sit at the home-plate end of the Yankee dugout. I watch Charlie Lau, who is throwing batting-practice balls from the pitcher's mound, and I eavesdrop on Dom Scala, the chunky bullpen catcher, who is strapping on his shin guards and gossiping with a couple of stadium policemen about their recent tours of duty. Once again I'm reminded of the army, of a timeless organization where every man fits in like a bearing or a bolt. I feel part of it too now; I'm no longer an intruder. I sit in the dugout with the piece of a broken bat in my hand, the first souvenir I've dared to take from baseball, even though it's a splintered fragment. The players regard me with amusement when they see the object in my hand. "Ya didn't get much of that one," says Bobby Murcer in his Oklahoma twang. "You won't get a hit with that," says Yogi Berra.

Finally, Charlie Lau walks off the mound and nods his head at me to show he's ready for our interview. He walks to the far end of the dugout, where I meet him and sit next to him.

LEHMANN-HAUPT: Was there any general thing that you tried to do with the team this year?

LAU: What do you want me to say? We didn't do well.

LEHMANN-HAUPT: That can hardly be blamed on the batting coach.

LAU: Well there were some pluses, as well as some minuses. As far as overall philosophy, no. I stress preparatory stance and, of course, balance, although they're very closely related. But what can you do? Nettles got off to a good start and then . . .

LEHMANN-HAUPT: . . . got hurt!

LAU: . . . the hand that he needed he hurt. He played for the rest of the year like that, and of course he had a lot on his mind too. Negotiating a contract and so forth. But just the basic fundamentals was all I tried to do—watch the ball and hope they're gonna hit it.

LEHMANN-HAUPT: What about the business of, ah, hitting *down* on the pitch.

LAU: I really don't ever talk about that.

LEHMANN-HAUPT: It's not part of what you teach?

LAU: Not really. I think that what you do below the waist—if you transfer your weight properly—is what matters.

LEHMANN-HAUPT: Well, why am I under the impression that in. . . ? Um, I guess there was gossip that in Kansas City you were teaching them to hit down on the pitch and take advantage of that artificial surface.

LAU: Well, gossip is gossip.

LEHMANN-HAUPT: It's not true then?

LAU: I didn't talk about hitting down. I talk about line drives, but I don't talk about that. I talk about getting on top of the ball a little bit, but again it comes from what happens below the waist.

LEHMANN-HAUPT: I see. Did anyone ever tell you about Ted Williams—how he was carrying on at the Boston training camp, about. . . . Again, this is gossip. I didn't hear this from him. But some . . . one of the Boston writers said that Williams ap)parently was very exercised by your notion of swinging down on the ball, because, he said, since the pitcher is standing on a mound, and, you know, releasing the ball from above his head . . .

LAU: We spoke at a clinic together in Cherry Hills, New Jersey, this year.

LEHMANN-HAUPT: Before spring training?

LAU: Yes. But I didn't stay around to hear him. He said he came up to listen to me. I don't think we're all that different, from what I can gather. But I really don't care what he thinks . . .

LEHMANN-HAUPT: Well, I'm sure you don't. I was just curious. It made an interesting story—that a guy in another training camp would be that concerned about what another batting instructor was doing.

LAU: Well, I've never talked about hitting down. I might have started out that way five years ago, but, ah, there're a lot of things that he says that I don't agree with either. And if you want to pursue his ideas a little bit—in theory he might be right, but I've never seen anyone yet that could do it.

LEHMANN-HAUPT: "Do it"? You mean uppercut the ball?

LAU: Swing up at the ball, up.

LEHMANN-HAUPT: Right.

LAU: I think if you stand around the cage and ask any knowledgeable baseball man, he'll say, "Forget it, you can't do it!" In theory it sounds great, but he hasn't shown me yet anybody he's ever worked with that could do it.

LEHMANN-HAUPT: Hmm.

LAU: But enough about Ted Williams. What else do you want?

LEHMANN-HAUPT: In spring training, I noticed that you were getting the hitters to take little steps as they waited for the pitch.

LAU: Well, I think you saw George Scott just now?

LEHMANN-HAUPT: Yes. You had him doing it too.

LAU: What does a golfer do? You play golf?

LEHMANN-HAUPT: Yeah, a little.

LAU: If you try to hit the ball being still, can you?

LEHMANN-HAUPT: Being still? You mean me being still?

LAU: Yes, you.

LEHMANN-HAUPT: No, I don't think so.

LAU: I don't think you can. I think that a golfer has to do . . . I think they call it the "waggle" or "wiggle"?

LEHMANN-HAUPT: Yeah, "waggle," when you bend your wrists [doing it] like that?

LAU: Well, that's the forward press. There has to be something to get you going. We experiment with different people different ways. But it's the same thing; it's the same principle involved.

LEHMANN-HAUPT: Right. Willie Stargell, for instance, has the most elaborate routine. I mean, you'd think he'd be worn out by the time the pitch came.

LAU: But it works well for him.

LEHMANN-HAUPT: It works. Right.

LAU: The older you get, the more you have to do.

LEHMANN-HAUPT: You have to pump yourself up, in effect. Like a weight lifter almost. You said earlier that what you did below the waist mattered most.

Lau: Yes, balance.

Here, as I get closer to sleep, I like to let the conversation veer wherever it wants to.

Sometimes I say to Lau: "I've found—you know, driving a golf ball—that if you start moving your arms down first, after the backswing . . ."

"No," he answers, "never your arms first. Your hips . . ."

"No, no. That's my point. If you hold your hips back, building tension, and then release them suddenly so that they get ahead of your arms later, if you see what I mean."

"I don't."

"Well, it's hard to explain," I tell him. "But I swear I can drive a golf ball fifty yards farther that way. If I swing right, which isn't always."

"I don't . . ."

"Do you suppose it would work with hitting a baseball?"

"Show me."

I get up and assume a batting stance in front of the dugout. "I mean . . ."

"No, no," Lau protests. "I mean go ahead and do it."

"Do what?"

"Take a couple of cuts in the cage."

"You're kidding. You mean now? Here?"

"Why not?"

"In street clothes?"

Lau looks at his watch. "It's early yet. Go get a uniform from Pete Sheehy."

"Is that legal? Joe DiMaggio told me . . ."

"Who'll know? George isn't here. Billy won't care. Just don't sue us if you pull a muscle or step in front of a pitch."

Here I walk along the length of the dugout, then step down the stairs into the runway that leads into the clubhouse. Filled with trepidation, I debate turning right at the clubhouse door and simply leaving. But this is the moment of a lifetime. To take a few swings in Yankee Stadium.

Pete Sheehy, the equipment man, doesn't blink an eye when I ask him for a uniform and state my size. Handing me a uniform, a cap, and a pair of shoes, he directs me to a corner cubicle. A couple of the players in the clubhouse seem to be suppressing laughter as I shyly undress, hang my streetclothes in the locker, and begin to put on the pinstripes. At first I feel devoured by the uniform. The socks itch, the cleats feel too tight, the sleeves of the shirt seem to flap. But when I stand, I feel light and springy, as if the outfit could carry me.

When I mount the dugout steps again, Lau is over by the batting cage, talking with Goose Gossage, the big relief pitcher. I approach them, wondering if they are cooking up some practical joke. Lau gestures to a row of bats lying behind the cage and tells me to grab one that feels right. I pick one up. It is surprisingly light.

"Step in there and try to hit a few off the Goose, if you can," says Lau. "Then try to show me what you mean about that thing with your hips. Swing easy at first."

I walk around the front of the batting cage and approach the plate. I feel tiny. As I position myself in a right-handed stance I look out at the bleachers, which seem a mile or two away. A subway groans behind the huge center-field scoreboard. The late afternoon sun blazes in the windows of distant apartment buildings and gives them the look of blank-faced monsters with multiple eyes of fire.

Standing on the mound behind a low protective screen, Gossage seems to be waiting for some signal. I step away from the plate and take a couple of shaky half-swings. I think about Gossage. I remember a night a few weeks earlier when a small group of reporters was kibitzing with him and asking him about the other Yankee relief pitcher, Ron Davis, who has the mannerisms of a farmboy. "Is he simpleminded?" somebody asked Gossage. "No, he's a little naive," said Gossage thoughtfully. "He doesn't know some things." Then a mischievous glint came into his eyes. " 'Course he's simpleminded too." I wonder if Gossage will be mischievous now.

Stepping back to the plate, I nod to Gossage. He flips the ball with his right hand and goes into his familiar windup. I'm trembling all over. The ball comes in low, fast, but distinctly visible, not so much humming as whispering. I let it go by and watch it hit the back of the cage. It's not that much faster than some batting machines I've hit against at amusement parks. I'll be all right. I won't get killed.

"Don't be afraid to swing," somebody calls from behind me. Gossage winds and throws again, seeming to put a little more effort into the pitch. This time as the ball approaches I swing, grunting helplessly. To my surprise, I catch a piece of the ball and foul it off sharply into the netting overhead. Didn't feel bad at all. Saw the ball better. Somebody yells, "Hey, way to go, man."

I step back and take two more practice swings, a little harder now. Just meet it, I say to myself. I step up again. Gossage winds, throws; the ball breaks slightly away as it comes in. I wait until it is almost past me and then swing easily. I feel solid contact and look for the ball. It's looping out toward short right field. Somebody claps behind me.

"Not half bad," says Lau. "Now show me what you mean." I look for Lau at the side of the batting cage. When I see him among several other spectators, I pantomime a swing, exaggerating the movement of my hips. Lau frowns, pulling down the corners of his mouth. I notice over his shoulder that Billy Martin has come into the Yankee dugout and is pacing with his hands thrust into his back pockets like his mentor, Casey Stengel.

Gossage throws again. Hard. I corkscrew my back as I've just done for Lau, and hit the ball high and deep along the left-field foul line. The ball seems to float forever and drop just short of the seats. "Way to throw to him, Goose!" somebody yells. I sneak another look at the dugout and see that Martin is watching now. Gossage throws again, and this time I put some muscle in my swing. The crack of the bat feels sweet. The ball is rising on a line in the night sky. Lau is whistling. Martin is stepping onto the field. Somebody is even cheering.